Religion,
Education, and
the American
Experience

RELIGION AND AMERICAN CULTURE

Series Editors
David Edwin Harrell Jr.
Wayne Flynt
Edith L. Blumhofer

Religion, Education, and the American Experience

*Reflections
on Religion
and American
Public Life*

EDITED BY
Edith L. Blumhofer

Introduction by Martin E. Marty

THE UNIVERSITY OF ALABAMA PRESS
Tuscaloosa and London

Typeface: Galliard

∞

The paper on which this book is printed meets the minimum requirements of
American National Standard for Information Science–Permanence of Paper for
Printed Library Materials, ANSI Z39.48-1984.

Library of Congress Cataloging-in-Publication Data

Religion, education, and the American experience : reflections on religion and American
public life / edited by Edith L. Blumhofer ; introduction by Martin E. Marty.
        p.   cm. — (Religion and American culture)
Includes bibliographical references and index.
     ISBN 0-8173-1146-7 (cloth : alk. paper)
     1. Religion in the public schools—United States. 2. Universities and colleges—United
States—Religion. 3. Christian education—United States. I. Blumhofer, Edith Waldvogel.
II. Religion and American culture (Tuscaloosa, Ala.)
     LCIII .R46 2002
     379.2′8′0973—dc21

                                                                    2002002309

British Library Cataloguing-in-Publication Data available

Contents

Preface

In 1996 the Pew Charitable Trusts made a generous grant to the University of Chicago Divinity School to fund the Public Religion Project. For the next three years, Martin E. Marty directed the project's multifaceted explorations of religion's roles in American public life. The Public Religion Project completed its assignment in 1999, and some of its work has moved under the aegis of the Martin E. Marty Center at the University of Chicago Divinity School. The Public Religion Project commissioned the chapters that follow with the hope that they will help readers participate thoughtfully in engaging the critical issues at the intersection of religion and American public life.

Among the spheres of influence in which religion and public life meet in contentious, complex, and crucial ways is education. The Public Religion Project convened three conversations among experts in education, religion, and community life to consider what issues seem most urgent at the start of the new millennium.

Discontent with public education has prompted considerable public debate about the actual or potential role(s) of religion in resolving the social and moral concerns that often complicate instructional questions. Curricular matters present troublesome challenges, too. What about religion and science or the role of religion in explaining historical events? Efforts to explore "teaching about religion" in an increasingly pluralistic society call into question old patterns of talk about "separation of church and state." Critics complain about public educators who profess to be value neutral when they exclude religion, charging that they promote alternative religious outlooks. At the primary level, more and more parents opt out of the system, select curricula that mirror their own moral choices, and school their children at home.

If the debate about religion and education waxes eloquent at the primary level, it is no less animated on college campuses. The proliferation of religious studies departments in tax-supported colleges and universities during the past four decades is a sign of vitality. But how does the university treat religion? Or do religious forces in society understand higher education? How has pluralism altered the role of university chaplains?

Many private liberal arts colleges have their roots in the religious hopes of individuals and groups. Denominationally related colleges, for example, wrestle with the meaning and relevance of denominational identity in an increasingly mobile and secular society. New situations of realized pluralism complicate circumstances in many schools that once were anchored by religious particularism.

These and many other issues lend urgency to ongoing debates that impact the education of leadership for tomorrow. The chapters that follow delve into some of them and explore the contours that frame choices in this complex landscape (or—to borrow Martin Marty's label—schoolscape) of American public life.

Religion,
Education, and
the American
Experience

Introduction

Martin E. Marty

For three years, the Public Religion Project wrestled with issues that brought together concerns over religion, of course, and education. The staff and advisers chose that combination as one of the most urgent issues to consider in America at the turn of the millennium.

On at least three occasions, we gathered in conference and conversation experts who represented a variety of professions, disciplines, experiences, commitments, and interests in respect to the various levels (K–12, college, university, postdoctoral) of schooling that go on in the United States today.

They also represented a rich sampling of the religious diversity that marks national life. There were people who held pro and con positions in respect to tuition tax vouchers; home schoolers and those who have no use for home schooling; and representatives of many kinds of viewpoints dealing with both private and tax-supported public higher education.

Much of what we learned from those meetings, atop our own staff research, forms the basis of the book *Education, Religion, and the Common Good* (Jossey-Bass, 2000). In that work, I try to capture one of the main themes of our meetings: educator after educator, religious scholar after religious scholar, kept pressing on us the need to see the various levels of education "seamlessly," as it were. That is, if forces that Americans code-name "secularization," "modernization," "relativization," "pluralism," and "multiculturalism" represent problems and possibilities in private and public colleges and universities, they trickle down and take different forms in primary and secondary education, public and private.

Vice versa, the battles on the front lines in local school districts, parent-teacher associations, and curriculum and library committees—though they will often have their own code names such as "evolution versus creationism," "school prayer advocates versus secular humanists," and "sex education at school versus sex education at home and church"—are often reflections of higher education battles and places from which agendas for college and university leaders are drawn.

Although listening, recording, collating, and integrating what we learned from that process helped provide the basis for a systematic treatment, "taking religion and education whole," we also thought that something would be missing if we did not offer to the reading public some sense of what I would call the thickness, the richness, of the conversations. Another way to put it: in one of the two books we are publishing on education and religion, readers should become familiar with the way people on the front lines talk about the subject.

So we have invited back some of these frontline, in-the-trench leaders to involve themselves with their subject, not always worrying about whether everything they say will check out with poll takers, focus groups, survey researchers, or generalists. We think that the encounters made possible on these pages will serve as bids to readers to continue the conversations we have had—and to throw themselves personally into probes and controversies that can all too often sound remote and abstract.

The one chapter that reflects our interest in education "at all levels" is by Warren A. Nord, who happens to be as expert as anyone writing today on religion and education at those levels. He coordinates concerns of elementary and high school education with what goes on in teachers' colleges, universities with all their specialties, and faculty rooms or classrooms, where knowledge gets transmitted and opinions formed. So his is probably the widest front line with the deepest trenches. Read Nord and you will gain a perspective or a rationale from which to appraise other chapters in this book and this topic in general.

Nord speaks a good deal about how liberal arts education looks or should look when it has religion in view. But liberal arts includes social sciences and humanities, and the humanities signal many disciplines.

History, philosophy, and literature are no doubt the foremost of these. We choose literature for our sample, having been impressed by the way Roger Lundin deals with the many dimensions of literary studies in a time when words such as *postmodernism* and *deconstruction* color inquiries. How do religion questions survive and thrive in such contexts?

The second part of the book focuses on the liberal arts college and, in one case, the graduate university world insofar as they relate formally to religious institutions. Although—call them what you will—church-related colleges, colleges of the church, Catholic, or other confessionally related universities are a relatively small part of the higher education world and market, what goes on in them is revelatory of societal trends. What is everybody's job is nobody's job. These church-inspired, church-related campuses are the locales where in concentrated form one can deal with the questions that arise regarding authority, freedom, secularization, and confessional commitment.

In this trio, Robert Benne asks a question about the shape and trend of such institutions and of the whole higher educational venture when it is religiously founded, connected, or tinged. Benne often introduces himself as someone who was explicitly asked to teach at a church-related college that had drifted quite far from that relation. At some such schools, there are faculty who want to be "more secular than thou"; some are restless in respect to specific religious heritages; many are indifferent; some show casual interest; and there are now many more than a few years ago who would like to retrieve religious traditions, recast them in a pluralist society, and draw upon them. Benne is on the front line in that work and reports on six other schools that face some of the issues with which he deals, as must everyone who reads this book and cares about higher education and religion.

Speaking of being on the front lines, few citizens are more exposed to the counterforces on this subject than are college and university presidents. Mark U. Edwards Jr. recently presided at St. Olaf College, one of the six schools that Benne has studied. Edwards talks of commitments based in religion, ethnicity, and academic backgrounds and the effects of pluralism on them. What including his essay here means for us is this: readers get a glimpse over the shoulder or into the mind of someone who by position is strategic. Survey after survey informs us that the choice and perspective of the president tells much about the aspirations and attitudes of boards of trustees, alumni, and constituencies as they come into contact with the world of faculties and students. Edwards has devoted himself with uncommon background (a religious historian) and public commitment to the values of "college of the church" education and shows what that means.

The third prominent scholar who writes concerning church-related institutions is Charles Zech, who first narrows the subject by treating only one kind of school—Roman Catholic—and then broadens it by employing the coordinating tools available to social scientists. After presenting results of an extensive analysis of how today's Catholic educators deal with church and culture, Zech goes further. He offers ten suggestions about how to strengthen the religion-and-education bond. Readers who are not Catholic will not only learn from this what is going on but also can get hints about how to borrow from what someone else is doing and apply it.

Next, the University of Notre Dame's Robert Sullivan explores the contemporary state of American Catholic higher education by delving into its structural and historical past and by examining how it accommodates spiritual, social, and intellectual realities. His discussion of the underlying issues that are often ignored in current discussions about institutional Catholic identity raises questions relevant to other religious traditions, too.

The third part of the book is the most personal of all, but in all three instances in this section, the essayists open us up to larger worlds and issues. In the middle of the twentieth century, there were almost no departments of religious studies in tax-supported colleges and universities. At the turn of the twenty-first century, there are many hundreds.

Today many collegians take such departments for granted. They are part of university budgets and planning; they often include majors and minors; their graduates often go on into advanced study of religious subjects. James Moyer does not take them for granted. He takes us behind the scenes and shows, with names and dates and occasions, the step-by-step process through which such departments come into being and mature. Every school does it a bit differently, but this close-up is a valuable snapshot of one prospering program.

Campus chaplaincy, ministry to students, being dean of the chapel —all these programs, services, titles, and assignments suggest that higher education is not all book learning. In virtually all public and most private colleges and universities the teaching is not confessional or dogmatic—indeed it tends to be disinterested, and the teachers try to be fair-minded, given the pluralist makeup of even most church-related schools. Nonetheless, anyone who cares wholistically about schools, education, and culture knows that worship, devotion, practical activity, and fellowship are components of fulfilled religious activity also on campus.

In that context, Alison Boden of the University of Chicago gives an accounting of the attitudes toward religion and spirituality that one finds in higher education, where academic freedom is prized. It is hard to take anything for granted, including the forms of worship and the directions of prayer. And yet students need and welcome ministry and ministers who against all odds put together programs of listening and speaking, counseling and preaching, and gathering and enabling, as Boden well illustrates.

Dean Boden says something about how "spirituality" and "religion" meet and contend with each other these days. We asked President Edison O. Jackson of Medgar Evers College in the City University of New York system to speak out on the African American tradition and his own experience. The reader will note that he walks a narrow trail or steps across lines between a spirituality that seeks to be generic and resources for it that tend to be specific.

The fourth part consists of a thoughtful evaluation of a growing trend at the elementary and high school levels—home schooling. Although the topic may seem unrelated to the preceding chapters, it nonetheless raises issues that have begun to impact college campuses as home-schooled students arrive in ever greater numbers. James Carper and Brian Ray address the larger issues at an introductory level and explore the grassroots sources of newer voices in the continuing discussion in the new millennium.

We have often noted that whereas some inheritors and exemplars of the old mainstream Protestant, Catholic, and Jewish heritages have learned to restrain confessional commitment, others welcome the specifics of these lineages. Some African American, Hispanic American, and Native American public figures, entertainers, and celebrities, for instance, are not so inhibited. In Chicago, there is considerable nervousness about identifying specific faiths with assumptions about the broader public. Yet in summer, at the lakefront park that brings the city together for events, there are very acceptable and well-patronized "gospel," "soul," "spiritual," and often religion-infused "blues" festivals for everyone.

Can we learn from President Jackson's efforts to put his faith to work in ways that the pastor at the black church down the block might think is too restrained and the skeptic on the faculty thinks is too explicit? From our three-year experience, we drew the conclusion that immediately under the surface of all the generalizing and universalizing that must go on in a complex society, the individuals with responsibility are often motivated by very particular religious visions and work out their vocations mindful of their responsibility to their audiences and their own hearts and consciences.

Part I
Religion in Liberal Arts,
Religion in Literature

I
Liberal Education and Religious Studies

Warren A. Nord

It has been clear for some time now that the long-anticipated death of religion has failed to occur. The vast majority of Americans continue to believe in God, and even if much of this belief is nominal, much of it is sincere. Conservative churches continue to thrive at the same time that America has become home to a bustling mix of the world's religions. There is considerable evidence of a widespread (if intellectually amorphous) spirituality in our popular culture. Religious voices are prominent in our culture wars, in battles over abortion and homosexuality, social justice and family values, capital punishment, and, of course, education. Our intellectual culture appears to be at least somewhat more open to religion. For example, the old sharp line of demarcation between science and religion appears to be blurring; interdisciplinary discussions in cosmology, the life sciences, environmental studies, and the health sciences often include theologians. Postmodernism has undermined Enlightenment certainties—perhaps opening doors to religion in the process. Departments of religious studies have become relatively common in universities since the 1960s, and over the last decade a new national consensus has developed about the role of religion in public schools—one that legitimates an expanded role for the study of religion.

Yet, textbooks ignore religion (except in the context of distant history). The new national content standards for K–12 education ignore religion (except, again, in the context of studying history). Courses in religion are not even elective possibilities in most public schools. The majority of public universities still lack departments of religious studies, and even where they do exist religion courses are likely to be electives taken by a minority of students. I think it safe to say that *most* students manage to earn their high school diplomas, their undergraduate degrees, and their professional and graduate degrees without ever encountering a *live* religious idea.[1]

In other words, they are *illiberally* educated—for in a culture and a world where religion continues to be influential, where religious ways of thinking and living continue to be *live options*, it would seem that educators must take religion seriously.

I will argue that the idea of liberal education does commit us to *take religion seriously* in both schools and universities. This means that religious voices must be included in the curricular conversation, that they be allowed to *contend* with the secular alternatives, that the field of religious studies be established in both secondary schools and higher education, and that some significant study of religion be required of all students. (For good measure I will also sketch civic and constitutional arguments for taking religion seriously.)

Of course, a great deal hinges on how we define religious studies. I will argue that as it is often understood the field of religious studies in higher education fails to take religion as seriously as it should—and needs rethinking. I will also say something about the importance of creating religious studies as an area of specialization in public schools and about how religious studies should be defined in that somewhat different context.

Liberal Education

I begin with three overlapping aspects of liberal education that are not, I trust, particularly controversial.

First, a liberal education is a *broad* education. It is the opposite of a narrow, specialized, or merely vocational education, one that is fixated on the present or on a particular community or historical tradition.

A liberal education typically provides breadth by requiring students to learn both about history and contemporary cultures other than their own and by requiring them to take course work in a variety of subjects. Of course, a liberal education can only be *so* broad: educators must choose and define the historical contexts, cultures, subcultures, and subjects that will be incorporated into curricula, and the criteria for making these judgments will inevitably prove to be controversial.

Whatever one thinks of the truth or value of religion, however, it is uncontroversial that religion has been *influential* historically, and, as such, the relevance of religion to this aspect of a liberal education is also relatively uncontroversial. Even within public schools (where fears of controversy often run rampant) it is widely acknowledged that students must study religion at least in the course of studying history.

The relevance of religion to the study of contemporary cultures is often less obvious to educators, and, as I have already noted, religion is not a subject in the curricula of most public schools or even of most public universities; when religion courses are offered, it is as an elective at all public and most private schools and universities.

On reflection this might be thought surprising. After all, religion continues to be *important* (do I need to say this?), and so we get to the second aspect of liberal education I wish to mention: a liberal education should have *depth* as well as breadth. A good liberal education is neither shallow nor superficial but digs deep into the ways in which we make sense of and find meaning in the world. It explores how we should live our lives; it has a moral dimension.

No doubt religion is important, in part, because it has influenced events and cultures and, therefore, helps explain why the world is as it is. It is also important because for most people, now as in the past, religions have addressed their ultimate concerns and provided ways of thinking about those inescapable existential questions about suffering and death, love and guilt, justice and injustice—about how to make sense of the world and how to live our lives—that we must confront because we are human. Nor can we avoid them if we are to be educated. (Of course, this is often what most interests students.)

Third, because a liberal education is characterized by both breadth and depth it inevitably and properly nurtures *critical thinking* by providing perspective on one's own time, culture, and values. It initiates students into an ongoing conversation in which representatives of various communities and traditions *contend* with each other about how to make sense of the world and how to live their lives. It is, by its nature, comparative and critical. It is required if we are to live *an examined life*.

No doubt an education can be more or less liberal, depending on the range of voices that are allowed into the curricular conversation. Of course, as we listen to the voices in the *cultural marketplace* we will hear many religious dialects and languages; indeed, we will hear a good deal of arguing about subjects addressed in the curriculum, and often these disagreements go to matters of religion.

What might it mean, for example, to be liberally educated about abortion? Surely it involves more than understanding biology; it requires a "deeper" understanding of the moral and spiritual dimensions of abortion—which are, of course, controversial—as well. Whereas students can be indoctrinated to take a particular moral position on abortion, education requires that they learn something about *various* ways in which abortion is understood in different communities and traditions, liberal and conservative, secular and religious, and how each of those traditions respond to each other. An educated person knows the arguments and can critically sort through contending ways of making sense of the evidence.

Of course, we disagree, often on religious grounds, not just about particular issues such as abortion but about how to make sense of those domains of life and the world incorporated into the "subjects" of the curriculum—psychology, history, sexuality, economics, politics, and nature—and here is where the problem of liberal education becomes more difficult. Let me give just one example.[2]

There are a variety of ways of constructing economic institutions and of thinking about the economic domain of life. Scriptural texts in various religious traditions address economic questions relating to justice and morality, poverty and wealth, work and stewardship. There is also a vast twentieth-century literature in moral theology that deals with economic issues. What is common to this literature is the claim that the economic domain of life cannot be adequately understood apart from religious categories.

Of course, none of this is mentioned in economics textbooks. If we put end-to-end all the references to religion in the ten high school economics texts I have reviewed in the last few years, they would add up to two pages out of forty-four hundred altogether, and all of the references are to premodern times. I found only one reference to religion in the forty undergraduate economics textbooks used at my university in a recent semester. And there is but a single reference to religion—a passing reference in a section on taxation and nonprofit organizations—in the forty-seven pages of the new K–12 national content standards in economics. Moreover, the high school texts and the standards say little if anything about the problems of greatest concern within religious traditions—poverty, consumer culture, justice, the Third World, human dignity, and the meaningfulness of work, for example.

The problem is not just that the texts *ignore* religion, however. A part of the problem is what they *do* teach—*neoclassical economic theory*. According to the texts, economics is a science, people are essentially self-interested utility-maximizers, the economic realm is one of competition for scarce resources, values are personal preferences, and value judgments are matters of cost-benefit analysis. Of course, *no* religious tradition accepts *this* understanding of human nature, society, and values. That is, the texts and standards "de-moralize" and secularize economics.[3]

To be sure, they are not explicitly hostile to religion; they do not overtly attack religious traditions or moral theology. Nevertheless, in some ways ignoring religion is worse than explicit hostility because students remain unaware of the fact that there are tensions and conflicts between their religious traditions and what they are taught about economics.

In fact, the texts give students *no sense* that what they are learning might be religiously controversial, and the national economics standards make it a matter of principle that students be kept in the dark about alternatives to neoclassical theory. As the editors put it in their introduction, the standards were developed to convey a single conception of economics, the "majority paradigm" or "neoclassical model" of economic behavior. To include "strongly held minority views of economic processes," they continue, would only risk "confusing and frustrating teachers and students who are then left with the responsibility of sorting the qualifications and alternatives without a sufficient foundation to do so."[4]

The problem here is less a matter of particulars (of facts or hypotheses) than of basic theories, philosophical assumptions, and worldviews. We teach students to screen out moral and religious evidence, arguments, concerns, and interpretations as irrelevant. No matter how commonplace this might be among economists, it is deeply controversial in our culture (indeed, it is not universally accepted among economists). No doubt there are ways of reconciling neoclassical theory and various religious traditions, but they are controversial and cannot be assumed; in any case, they are not mentioned in the texts or in the standards.

Now, the problem with the economics texts and standards is but one aspect of the much larger problem that cuts across the curriculum because it is likely that in *every* subject students will be taught to think in secular ways that stand in some tension with religious alternatives.[5] Moreover, this is almost always done uncritically—without informing students of the potential tensions and conflicts.

Too often we naively think that we guarantee a liberal education by way of distribution requirements that ensure that students take a variety of *subjects*. The problem, of course, is that we do not teach subjects, which are open to conflicting interpretations, so much as we teach *disciplines*—particular, often controversial, ways of interpreting subjects. Students who are exposed only to fundamentalist Christian interpretations of history, biology, and sexuality in a Christian academy would not be liberally educated. What, in turn, should we think when students are exposed only to secular interpretations of history, biology, and sexuality?

In fact, most education fails to reflect anything of the intellectually lively conversations in our culture about religion and many of the subjects of the curriculum—cosmology, the environment, health and healing, sexuality, politics, morality—and economics. The *educational* marketplace of ideas is a tightly regulated marketplace. No doubt most students will learn a little about religion in studying history, but even there we teach them to think about religion (and history) in secular categories. Education nurtures a *secular mentality*.

Ninian Smart argued, rightly, that because the scientific worldview is in "living contact and conflict with traditionally religious belief-systems" they must be "treated together. If they are not, then we are taking steps to entrench some determinate viewpoint into our educational system, and genuine pluralism is in this way eroded."[6] Indeed, it can be plausibly argued that we *indoctrinate* students when we uncritically initiate them into one way of thinking and systematically ignore the alternatives, marginalizing them, making them seem irrational.[7] Of course, if students are to think critically about the secular ways of understanding the world that pervade the curriculum, they must understand something about the religious alternatives—and those alternatives must be allowed to *contend* with their secular counterparts.

The literary critic Gerald Graff has argued that the established curriculum is *separatist* "with each subject and course being an island with little regular connection to other subjects and courses." It is important, he argues, "to bring heretofore excluded cultures into the curriculum, but unless they are put in dialogue with traditional courses, students will continue to struggle with a disconnected curriculum."[8] Graff is not talking about religion here, but the principle at issue is the same. Most of my students have no idea that there may be tensions and conflicts between their religious beliefs and practices and what they learn in studying economics or psychology or the sciences. Graff's solution is to "teach the conflicts"—indeed, to use this as an organizing principle for a liberal education.[9]

Yet we do not teach the conflicts. We do not initiate students into a curricular conversation about how to make sense of the world or the "subjects" they study so much as we give them a sequence of monologues, each conducted in isolation from the others. Moreover, it is highly unlikely that they will hear any religious voices in the process. This is *illiberal* education. If students are to be liberally educated they must—in a culture and world like ours—learn a great deal about religion.

Of course, just as students should learn to think religiously (and, therefore, critically) about the subject matter of their typically secular courses, so they should learn something of how to think critically about religion using the methods, theories, and categories of the secular intellectual disciplines. Given what we know about the mind from psychology, given what we know about society from sociology, given what we know about culture from anthropology, given what we know about texts from literary criticism—what sense can we make of religious experience, institutions, traditions, and literature?

A Brief Detour: Justice and the Constitution

Although my major concern is to locate religious studies within the context of liberal education, I think it is important to recognize that at least within *public* schools and universities there are also arguments for taking religion seriously grounded in justice and the Constitution.

Consider an analogy. Until the last several decades textbooks and curricula routinely ignored women's history and minority literature. We are now (almost) all sensitive to the fact that this was not a benign neglect, but a form of discrimination, of educational disenfranchisement. Of course, the problem was not only that minority and women's history and literature were ignored; it was that distinctively male, white, and Western ways of thinking and acting, and patterns of culture, were taught, and uncritically at that.

There are, of course, good *educational* reasons for including multicultural voices in the curriculum, but there are also reasons of *justice* —particularly with regard to *public* education. As a *civic society* we ought to treat each other with a measure of respect, and this means that we must take each other—with our various ideas and ideals, histories and subcultures—seriously.

Education has gone a long way toward addressing various multicultural agendas. Unfortunately, the multicultural movement has virtually ignored religion.[10] Few subcultures are so disenfranchised now, however, as are religious subcultures; indeed, religious identities and traditions are often more important to people than their ethnic, racial, or gender identities and traditions.

It may come as a surprise to many, but we are also *constitutionally* required to include religious voices in public schools and universities. It is, of course, uncontroversial that it is constitutionally permissible to teach about religion, at least when done properly. No Supreme Court justice has ever held otherwise, but there is a stronger argument to be made.

The Court has been clear that public education must be *neutral* in matters of religion—in two senses. It must be neutral *among religions* (it cannot favor Protestants over Catholics, or Christians over Jews or Buddhists), and it must be neutral *between religion and nonreligion*. Schools and universities cannot promote religion; they cannot proselytize; they cannot conduct religious exercises. Of course, neutrality is a two-edged sword. Just as public education cannot favor religion over nonreligion, neither can it favor nonreligion over religion. As Justice Black put it in the Court's seminal 1947 *Everson* ruling, "State power is no more to be used so as to handicap religions than it is to favor them."[11] Similarly, in his majority opinion in *Abington v. Schempp* (1963), Justice Tom Clark wrote that schools cannot favor "those who believe in no religion over those who do believe."[12] Moreover, in a concurring opinion, Justice Goldberg warned that an "untutored devotion to the concept of neutrality" can lead to a "pervasive devotion to the secular and a passive, or even active, hostility to the religious."[13] Of course this is just what has happened. An "untutored" and naïve conception of neutrality has led to the prohibition of *explicit* hostility to religion, when the usual hostility has been philosophically rather more subtle—though no less substantial for that.

The purpose of the Establishment Clause should be to promote what the legal scholar Douglas Laycock has called "*substantive* neutrality." Such neutrality requires government "to minimize the extent to which it either encourages or discourages religious belief or disbelief, practice or nonpractice, observance or nonobservance." Religion "should proceed as unaffected by government as possible."[14] In regard to the curriculum, "government must be scrupulously even handed, treating the range of religious and nonreligious views as neutrally as possible."[15]

No doubt, as I have suggested, many of the particular claims made by scientists and secular scholars can be reconciled with much religion. It is at the level of philosophical presuppositions or worldviews that they are often in tension or conflict. Yet we teach students, uncritically, to *interpret* experiences and evidence in secular rather than religious categories. Because public schools and universities teach students ways of thinking about the world that stand in some tension (or even conflict) with religion, they must also teach students about religion in some depth.

The only way to be neutral when we disagree is *to be fair to the alternatives.* That is, given the Court's long-standing interpretation of the Establishment Clause, it is mandatory in public education to *require* the study of religion if students are required to study disciplines that cumulatively lead to a "pervasive devotion to the secular."[16] Of course, students must learn about a *variety* of religions; neutrality also means that public schools and universities cannot promote or privilege a particular religion over others.

The Need for Religious Studies as a Field of Study

I have mentioned that it is uncontroversial that students should learn something about religion in studying history, but, as we have seen, they also need to be initiated, as they mature, into the sometimes unsettling critical conversation about truth and reality that is essential to a liberal education. They must learn something about religious ways of thinking about *any* subject—economics, biology, or sexuality, for example—that is religiously contested, ideally in the course of studying it.

So, for example, an economics text should include a chapter in which social scientific ways of understanding economics are contrasted with various religious alternatives. Students should learn that the relationship of religion to economics is controversial, and that although they will study economics as most economists understand it, not everyone agrees. Indeed, *every* introductory text and course should provide students with historical and philosophical perspective on the subject at hand, mapping connections and tensions with other disciplines and domains of the culture—including religion. (Charles Haynes and I have tried to provide such a map in our book *Taking Religion Seriously across the Curriculum.*)

At best, however, this strategy yields a *minimal* fairness—and proves inadequate. Given the amount of material that must be crammed into history, biology, and economics texts, few pages will be given to religious voices. Of course, making sense of religious ways of thinking about these subjects requires sophistication (as well as time), and most teachers, whatever their level, are poorly prepared by *their* educations to take religion seriously, no matter how religious they are in their personal lives. Moreover, professional organizations often reject the inclusion of religion in *their* domain of the curriculum: the major science organizations have made it clear, for example, that there is no room for religious views of nature in science courses. Of course, the variety of religious traditions and the complexity of religious language, symbolism, practices, and theology render religion even more difficult for the typical religiously illiterate student than those secular disciplines on which we lavish all our time and resources.

In higher education, courses on religion are found in a variety of academic disciplines (the sociology of religion, the psychology of religion, the philosophy of religion, the anthropology of religion)—though the interest in religion in these disciplines is typically thin, and students will likely encounter little discussion of it apart from these specialized courses.[17]

In any case, religion is sufficiently *complex* that it cannot be caught in the methodological nets of any particular discipline. Moreover, like politics and economics and literature and psychology, religion is a sufficiently *important* domain of life to warrant a field of study devoted to it. In any case, religion will be taken seriously *only* if there are teachers competent to teach about it in all its complexity, and a *robust* fairness (or neutrality) is possible only if students *are required* to study religious as well as secular ways of making sense of the world in some depth.[18] This will happen only when religious studies is accepted as a field of study and students are required to take course work in it (an admittedly radical idea).[19]

Religious Studies and Higher Education

As a result of the increasing secularization and specialization of scholarship over the course of the nineteenth century, theology was gradually exiled from the undergraduate curriculum to seminaries and divinity schools, and by the end of that century it had largely disappeared from colleges and universities.[20] It was only after World War II that a movement developed for departments of religion, and it was only in the 1960s that they became commonplace (well, *relatively* commonplace: in 1993, 36 percent of public colleges and universities and 60 percent of private colleges and universities had programs, often with departmental majors, in religious studies).[21] This growth was in part due to the assurance provided by the Supreme Court's 1963 ruling in *Abington Township v. Schempp* that the *secular* study of religion was in fact constitutional.

At first, faculty in the new departments of religious studies were drawn, of necessity, from other disciplines—from history, sociology, philosophy, literary criticism, the ancient languages, Near Eastern and Oriental studies, and theology. With this kind of interdisciplinary background, scholars in religious studies have worried a good deal about whether it is actually a *discipline* with a more or less common methodology or intellectual approach—and the consensus is that it is not. As Walter Capps put it, "Religious studies is a multiform subject-field within which a variety of disciplines are employed to treat a multiplicity of issues, interests, and topics."[22] Something like environmental studies, scholarship in religious studies is united by its subject rather than by a discipline.

Still, for all of its diversity, I will risk a few generalizations.

Advocacy and Theology

According to the American Academy of Religion's 1991 self-study, *Religious and Theological Studies in American Higher Education,* "religious studies" is the name of the "scholarly *neutral* and *nonadvocative* study of multiple religious traditions."[23] Certainly the dominant view within the field is that the epistemological and methodological commitments of religious studies are those of secular scholarship. Religious studies is descriptive and explanatory; its purpose is not to proselytize or promote religion but to employ secular methods to understand religion.[24] As William Scott Green once put it, "Religion is the subject we study, not the way we study it."[25]

Of course a teacher might advocate religious positions without taking up theology, but the vast majority of scholars at public universities and many at private universities wish to draw a sharp distinction between the secular discipline of religious studies and theology—and exclude theology from religious studies. This is especially so among faculty in universities with graduate programs, and, according to the self-study, the "younger the scholar and the more recently out of graduate school, the more evident is the antipathy to 'theology.'"[26]

Even in traditionally *religious* colleges the conventional wisdom has become, according to James Tunstead Burtchaell, that there are "two quite distinct styles of religious instruction on the campuses: disinterested, non-normative studies, conducted in a regular academic department, and ministerial studies based on an assumption of shared commitment, in marginal divinity schools." Underlying this distinction is what Burtchaell characterizes as an "inflexible understanding" to the effect that "a rigorous academy would not harbor learned discourse about religion in its central precincts unless conducted with the systematic detachment of nonbelievers."[27]

Understanding Religion from the Outside

It is often assumed that in public universities teachers cannot advocate religious positions or do theology for constitutional reasons, but the opposition to advocacy and theology cuts much deeper. In his study of the field Walter Capps concluded that the "overall intent" of the field of religious studies has been to make "the subject of religion intelligible by utilizing analytical and interpretive methods that were sponsored and, thus, legitimated, by the Enlightenment. . . . Academic respectability followed since it could be demonstrated convincingly that religious studies, like other fields and disciplines that have their roots in the Enlightenment, is the methodological translation of the subject of religion into workable and certifiable means and instruments of intelligibility."[28] Religious neutrality and the adoption of methodologies drawn from the secular humanities and social sciences have been, in effect, the price of admission to the academy (albeit a price happily paid by most scholars in the field). Even so, there continues to be considerable suspicion of departments of religious studies on the part of university faculty and administrators who fret that they may be divinity schools in disguise (contributing to what Martin Marty has called a "more secular than thou" attitude on the part of many scholars in religious studies).[29]

Of course postmodernism has had its influence in religious studies —undermining some of the old Enlightenment convictions about objectivity. Still, the governing idea is that in attempting to render religion intelligible it is approached from *the outside,* using categories and methods drawn from the secular scholarship rather than from religious traditions.

Understanding Religion from the Inside

This does not mean that scholars do not appreciate the importance of taking religion seriously on its own terms, *from the inside* (as has been more characteristic of the humanities than the social sciences). Indeed, a 1990 report of the American Academy of Religion *(Liberal Learning and the Religion Major)* emphasizes the importance of "an empathetic study of the 'other.'" According to it, the "study of religion is both empathetic and critical." Nonetheless, if "criticism is uninformed by an empathetic understanding of the criticized, it chiefly serves to confirm the moral or cultural superiority of the critic. For that a liberal education is scarcely needed."[30] True.

That report goes on to argue that the people and texts studied in religious studies courses challenge our ways of thinking: "They talk back," as the report puts it. Indeed, we have much to learn from them because religious folk "have coped with intractable environments, severe climates, plagues, tyrants, powerful enemies and their own frailties, and they have sustained viable communities over long periods of time. They are experienced. They have wrestled with angels, they have danced over the void, they have been terrorized by demons, they have emerged from the earth and have journeyed to the spirit world, they have known powers that we can only name, they have encountered mysteries, they have confronted death. Their words are often shrewd, sometimes wise, even sublime. They challenge our own ways of life, they contradict our wisdom, they pose severe tests of self-examination. They teach us."[31]

Nevertheless, if students must be exposed to religious voices, those voices are typically to be found in texts; they are not the voices of their teachers, who are expected to refrain from agreeing with any of them (at least in their roles as teachers).

Pluralism

According to the same 1990 report, religious studies is "intrinsically multi-cultural, directed to more than one religious tradition." This emphasis further distinguishes religious studies from theology, reflects a growing sensitivity to the variety of ways in which people are religious, and grows out of a widespread conviction that "religion cannot be studied academically without comparative insight." According to the report, "The academic study of religion is not ethnocentric, much less Christocentric, or even theocentric. It is directed to the cultural specificities of each religious tradition under study. It brings no preconceived definition of generic 'religion' to its study, but interrogates the tradition itself to discover what is 'religious' in it, on its own terms."[32] We understand religion only by understanding religions.

With this emphasis on comparative studies and the differences between religious traditions has come an interest in non-Western ways of being religious, a "globalization" of religious studies, an expansion of biblical studies to include sacred scriptures more generally, and an interest in studying neglected and oppressed peoples—Third World and minority religions, oral traditions, and women's religion.

Liberal Education Again

I have argued that a good liberal education requires that religion be taken seriously; this, in turn, requires that religious voices be included in the curricular conversation, that they be allowed to contend with secular voices, and that they be studied in sufficient depth that students are able to make sense of them. Clearly, much course work in religious studies allows students to hear religious voices—to encounter primary source texts drawn from various religious traditions—and to study them in depth. The question is whether religious ways of thinking and living are allowed *to contend with* the secular alternatives. Are religious ways of thinking and living presented as live options in their intellectually, morally, philosophically, or spiritually most compelling forms for understanding the world here and now? Does course work allow discussion of the relative adequacy of religious and secular epistemological and methodological commitments—both in the study of religion itself and in the study of other domains of life? The likely problem is that because of its own secular epistemological and methodological commitments, religious studies is unlikely to challenge (at least in any direct way) the commitments and methodologies of the other disciplines in the academy that, cumulatively, marginalize religion from our intellectual life and that result in *illiberal* education.

In a recent article Kimberly Patton has suggested that the triumph "of the study of religion in the battle to be accepted as a legitimate scholarly discipline, shining somewhere in the firmament between the pole stars of the social sciences and the humanities, has taken its toll in how we tend to allow ourselves to teach religion." Too often, she suggests, one "encounters a deep seated allergy to the contemplation of ultimateness. It is embarrassing for us as teachers to be reminded that religious traditions actually make truth claims."[33]

John Dixon puts it this way: because "religious studies" makes *studies* rather than religion its primary focus students learn that "truth is in the systems of study" rather than in the religion that is studied—though he acknowledges that the "actual effect is far more muddled than that, simply because so much of the material we study is more powerful than the prejudices of the methods we apply to them, and many teachers are exceedingly respectful of the integrity of their subject."[34] Still, because there is a tendency for everything sacred to become grist for the mill of secular scholarship, students do not learn how to think religiously so much as they learn to think in secular ways about religion.

Consider an analogy. Political scientists often assume that the truth is to be found in the scientific method they employ rather than in the (normative) ideological, philosophical, and political beliefs and values of the politicians, voters, and writers they study—and, as a result, they do not teach students to think politically so much as to think scientifically about politics. Surely, however, what is most important in studying politics, at least from the perspective of a liberal education (and of many students), is sorting out whether Democrats or Republicans, capitalists or socialists, have the more reasonable position. What is justice? How should I live?

Arguably, the primary value of religious studies *as part of a liberal education* lies in its ability to enable students to think in an informed and critical way about the existential dimension of life—about ultimate concerns and religious truth claims. The secular methodological commitments of the field are likely to discourage teachers from *grappling* with these questions, however; indeed, they may be thought to be less than respectable. This is a profound problem, for a liberal education must help students think through these questions.

Of course, it is important to keep in mind that the mission of the field of religious studies goes well beyond that of providing liberal education to undergraduates. Research and advanced study may well focus on efforts to understand and explain religion using the methodologies of the humanities and social sciences. (No doubt I am drawing this distinction much too starkly, and more nuance is needed.) Moreover, the "second-order" secular study of religion can often enlighten our thinking about first-order religious claims.

Advocacy and Theology Again

It is surely possible to have students study religion "from the inside," explore questions of existential concern, and allow religious voices to contend with secular voices while the teacher remains neutral about the adequacy or rightness of religious claims. (Even here there may be a small measure of advocacy: that is, the teacher is not taking religion to be a mere cultural artifact to be explained but is conveying the idea that religious voices are legitimately part of an ongoing conversation about the truth.) Still, we might wonder whether teachers *must* remain neutral, detached, "objective."

George Marsden has noted, for example, how peculiar the emphasis on detachment and objectivity is; imagine, he suggests, asking blacks and feminists to conceal their personal commitments in courses in black studies and women's studies.[35] David Ray Griffin has argued that given other "professions of belief that are regularly made as a natural part of university teaching, it would be arbitrary to exclude in principle professions of belief in the existence and causal efficacy of a being who would in our tradition most naturally be called 'God.'"[36] No other discipline, not physics or philosophy or psychology, is required to bracket questions about the nature of ultimate reality; why must religious studies do so?

William F. May has pointed out that no "faculty in philosophy would be content simply to offer courses in the history of philosophy. Philosophers would deem it important for students to study with faculty members who themselves engage in philosophizing, that is, who wrestle with metaphysical, ethical, and epistemological issues."[37] Indeed, philosophers continue to wrestle with the existence of God (more now than a few decades ago). Why then should not scholars in religious studies argue about the existence of God and a host of other religious claims drawn from a *variety* of religious traditions?[38] Who is better prepared to take on this task?

Walter Capps argued that in their concern to avoid theology, scholars in religious studies assume too easily the role of outsiders, observing a fixed religious reality. Religions are, however, dynamic realities that are shaped and reshaped as understanding grows, and "in this respect, understanding plays both a constitutive as well as a descriptive and analytical role." Capps argued that scholars are extremely well placed for proposing religious insights of their own; they are "entitled to the full use of creative reflection" and have "every right to advance theories regarding the truth and falsity of particular truth claims." So, for example, scholars might tell us "how the religious spirit might be advanced" and "whether or not there are grounds for cooperation between the religions of the world, or even as to whether or not religion is a detriment or enhancement to the progress of civilizations."[39]

I agree. We might also wonder whether theologians should be part of this conversation.

In his 1992 presidential address to the American Academy of Religion, Robert Neville argued for including theology as a discipline *within* religious studies—so long, that is, as it is "publicly objective," for theologians "need to make themselves vulnerable to criticism from all sides and to sustain themselves through the process of correction."[40]

Theology is typically taken to be grounded in revelation or a faith-tradition and, as such, is not open to falsification or assessment by critical reason—and, consequently, no fit matter for the reasoned give and take of a curricular conversation.[41] Nonetheless, many theologians *are* willing to run the gauntlet of critical assessment. Gordon Kaufman defines *critical theology* as theology "that opens itself willingly to severe criticism from outside perspectives (as well as from within)" and "is formulated through the exercise of critical judgment with respect to all pertinent evidence and arguments."[42] Critical theology may be grounded historically and personally in a particular faith-community that makes claims about a historic revelation, but it takes seriously the task of reasoning about those foundational claims and is open to the possibility of falsifying evidence. In Griffin's terms, religious claims "are not assumed to be products of infallible revelation, but are treated as hypotheses to be tested" by "seeing whether they can lead to an interpretation of reality that is . . . more self-consistent, more adequate to all the relevant data of experience, and more illuminating of those data."[43]

Of course the whole idea of objectivity and critical reason has become problematic over the last several decades, and some advocates of theology point to the postmodernist contention that *all* worldviews are grounded in "faith-communities" so that, epistemologically, science, social science, and theology are in the same boat. Faith, Griffin argues, is "a necessary ingredient in the rational-empirical method, whatever the subject matter," modern science included; theology differs from other worldviews only "by being more self-conscious of the source of its faith-perspective."[44] Stephen Webb claims that postmodernism vitiates the old distinction between theology and religious studies: everyone models ways in which "the particularity of faith hangs together (or does not hang together) with various critical discourses." Indeed, "it can be said that every teacher of religion (and the provocation is intentional) is a theologian now."[45] Marsden has argued that if scholars are going to operate on the postmodern assumption that all judgments are "relative to communities" then we should "follow the implications of that premise as consistently as we can and not absolutize one or perhaps a few sets of opinions and exclude all others." Universities should foster a broad pluralism that allows "all sorts of Christian and other religiously based intellectual traditions back into the discussion."[46]

I would put it this way. All scholars are embedded in intellectual and cultural traditions—the most rigorously skeptical scientist or philosopher as well as the most dogmatic theologian. The question is whether we are going to live within these traditions uncritically *and convey them to our students uncritically* or be open to the full range of human experience and evidence in reasoning about them, risking falsification. Scientific, philosophical, and theological claims are no different in that they can each be accepted and taught dogmatically or they can be critically assessed. The key to rationality is not some particular method—scientific method, for example—but the willingness to think critically about one's most basic assumptions in light of the full range of human experience. Science can be just as dogmatic (in uncritically excluding moral, psychic, or religious experience as knowledge yielding) as some theology is.[47]

Of course, in holding that theology must be subject to critical review, I do not mean to hold it hostage to any narrowly scientific conception of criticism. Theological claims often acquire their meanings by being embedded in traditions, in ritual and religious practices, in dense thickets of religious symbolism, in ways of life. As Neville has pointed out, critical judgment often requires participation in a "community of practice and belief. For a theological claim to be publicly vulnerable does *not* mean that it must be reduced to what is easily grasped by an external observer."[48] Indeed, religious traditions can generate powerful intellectual and cultural critiques of Enlightenment rationalism, and if we are not wed to Enlightenment (or any narrowly naturalistic) definitions of knowledge we might even argue that on a truly objective assessment of the *full* range of evidence, there are good reasons for accepting and advocating a religious interpretation of the world.[49]

No doubt there is a huge political risk in admitting theology to departments of religious studies. There is, as I have noted, a widespread (often justified) concern among scholars in religious studies that their field is viewed with suspicion by colleagues and administrators precisely because it is confused with theology. Still, let us be clear about the principle at issue.

Academic Freedom

Scholars in religious studies, like their colleagues in other disciplines, are entitled to academic freedom. Indeed, the American Association of University Professors' *Declaration of Principles* (1915) singled out scholars who work in philosophy and religion—the domains of "ultimate realities and values"—as particularly in need of the protections of academic freedom. The *Declaration* notes that in interpreting "the general meaning and ends of human existence and its relation to the universe, we are still far from a comprehension of the final truths, and from a universal agreement among all sincere and earnest men." Here, as elsewhere, "the first condition of progress is complete and unlimited freedom to pursue inquiry and publish its results." Of course, "it is scarcely open to question that freedom of utterance is as important to the teacher as it is to the investigator." Indeed, the confidence of one's students "will be impaired if there is suspicion on the part of the student that the teacher is not expressing himself fully or frankly, or that college and university teachers in general are a repressed and intimidated class."[50]

No doubt the authors of the *Declaration* had in mind the protection of science from religion, but the principle surely cuts both ways. If a neo-Darwinian biologist can argue that evolution and ultimate reality are purposeless, surely a scholar in religious studies can argue that reality is purposeful; if a Freudian can argue that God is nothing more than the neurotic projection of our unconscious minds, surely a scholar in religious studies can argue that some religious experiences are veridical experiences of God; if a philosopher can argue that the existentialists had it right and that reality is absurd, surely a scholar of religious studies can argue that the religious thinkers have it right and that God gives meaning to reality. Only an unprincipled freedom would allow antireligious claims but not religious claims in the classroom. There should be no reason why scholars in religious studies should not be able to take positions on the ultimate questions of human existence as much as philosophers or cosmologists or psychologists.[51] (This is not to deny, of course, that there may be good pedagogical reasons for remaining neutral in many situations.)

Academic freedom has legal standing as well. The Supreme Court began to address questions of academic freedom only in the 1950s, largely as a consequence of legislative efforts to exclude communists from the academy. The landmark case was *Keyishian v. Board of Regents* (1966) in which the Court anchored academic freedom in the First Amendment. Writing for the Court, Justice Brennan held that "our nation is deeply committed to safeguarding academic freedom, which is of transcendent value to all of us and not merely to the teachers concerned. That freedom is therefore a special concern of the First Amendment, which does not tolerate laws that cast a pall of orthodoxy over the classroom. . . . The classroom is peculiarly the 'marketplace of ideas.' The Nation's future depends upon leaders trained through wide exposure to that robust exchange of ideas which discovers truth 'out of a multitude of tongues, [rather] than through any kind of authoritative selection.'"[52] Unfortunately, as legal scholar David Rabban has noted, "the Supreme Court's glorification of academic freedom as a 'special concern of the First Amendment' has produced hyperbolic rhetoric but only scant, and often ambiguous, analytic content. The Court has never explained systematically the theory behind its relatively recent incorporation of academic freedom into the first amendment."[53]

Moreover, the Supreme Court has never ruled in a case involving the academic freedom of a teacher to take sides *in a matter of religion* where the Establishment Clause might also come into play. Still, the principles seem clear. Because scholars have academic freedom they cannot be taken to speak for the state, to be agents of the state, and hence are not bound by the Establishment Clause, which is binding only on government. No doubt a department of religious studies cannot be a seminary in miniature; it cannot have as its purpose to promote any religious claims or religion generally. The university, as a state institution, cannot take sides. At the same time it can, and must, allow individual scholars in religious studies (as in all disciplines) to take sides on religiously contested questions.[54] Neutrality means that the state cannot tolerate a pall of secular any more than religious orthodoxy.

Of course, academic freedom does not provide a license for indoctrination. The AAUP *Declaration* states that the university teacher

"in giving instruction upon controversial matters, while he is under no obligation to hide his own opinion under a mountain of equivocal verbiage, should, if he is fit for his position, be a person of a fair and judicial mind; he should, in dealing with such subjects, set forth justly, without suppression or innuendo, the divergent opinions of other investigators; he should cause his students to become familiar with the best published expressions of the great historic types of doctrine upon the questions at issue; and he should, above all, remember that his business is not to provide his students with ready-made conclusions, but to train them to think for themselves, and to provide them access to those materials which they need if they are to think intelligently."[55]

Moreover, according to the AAUP's 1985 "Observations on Ideology," where "ways of finding out and assessing the truth are precisely what is under debate, good teaching requires exposing students to all major alternatives. A department ought to try to insure that different currently debated and important approaches to its subject are presented to its students fairly and objectively, so that students are able to make informed choices among them."[56] Academic freedom cannot trump liberal education.

Religious Studies in Public Schools

Because public schools are different kinds of institutions from (even public) universities, religious studies must be understood somewhat differently in the two contexts.

As in higher education, religion had largely disappeared from textbooks and the curriculum of public schools by the end of the nineteenth century. Since *Abington Township v. Schempp* (1963) made clear the constitutionality of "teaching about religion" (when done properly), there have been a smattering of religion courses (usually "The Bible as Literature" and world religions courses) here and there in public schools. For a variety of reasons, however—fears of controversy, lack of prepared teachers, constitutional concerns, and, most important, a failure to appreciate the educational relevance of religion—courses in religion have not become common. In 1988, however, a group of seventeen religious and educational organizations—the American Jewish Congress and the Islamic Society of North America, the National Association of Evangelicals and the National Council of Churches, the American Federation of Teachers, the National Education Association, the National School Boards Association, and the American Association of School Administrators among them—endorsed a statement of principles regarding religion and the public school curriculum that said the following: "Because religion plays significant roles in history and society, study about religion is essential to understanding both the nation and the world. Omission of facts about religion can give students the false impression that the religious life of humankind is insignificant or unimportant. Failure to understand even the basic symbols, practices, and concepts of the various religions makes much of history, literature, art, and contemporary life unintelligible."[57]

As a result of this and other "common ground" statements it need no longer be controversial to claim that the study of religion has a legitimate, even important, place in the public school curriculum. In practice, however, the study of religion has been relegated almost entirely to the study of history and almost always to fairly distant history at that. There has been no clarion cry for including religious voices elsewhere in the curriculum, much less for developing a new field of religious studies. Indeed, the idea of religion courses and a new field of religious studies will strike terror into the hearts of more than a few educators.

The thrust of my argument has been that there are powerful educational, political, and constitutional arguments for taking religion seriously in the curriculum, and the arguments apply to schools as much as to universities. The study of religion is not a matter of optional curricular enrichment but is essential to being an educated person.

Indeed, educators will be shortsighted if they find these proposals too controversial. It is important to remember that it is *also* controversial to leave religion *out* of the curriculum. It is in part because public schools do not take religion seriously that many religious parents have deserted them, and, if the Supreme Court upholds vouchers, as they may well do, the exodus will be much greater. In the long run, the *least* controversial position is the one that takes *everyone* seriously. If public schools are to survive our culture wars, they must be built on *common ground,* and there can be no common ground when religious voices are left out of the curricular conversation.[58]

Some educators will find it unrealistic to expect such reforms, but several decades ago textbooks and curricula said little about women and minority cultures. Several decades ago, few universities had departments of religious studies. Now multicultural education is commonplace, and many (if not most) universities have departments of religious studies. Things change.

If there is to be a new field of religious studies in K–12 education, however, it must look somewhat different from its counterpart in higher education.

Liberal Education

Of course the primary purpose of creating the field is to ensure that students acquire a good liberal education; it is not to promote advanced study or research. Course work in religious studies should provide students some sense of the role of religion in history and culture, some understanding of religious ways of thinking about fundamental existential questions, and some appreciation of the varieties of religion.

It should also initiate students into a curricular conversation in which religious voices are allowed to contend with secular voices over the meaning of different domains of life as they are reflected in the curriculum. As I have argued, to teach students about every "subject" in the curriculum in secular categories only is not constitutionally neutral, and it does not constitute a good liberal education. Students should learn something about several different religious ways of making sense of the major, religiously contested issues addressed in the curriculum: the origins of the world and the meaning of nature; politics and morality; economics and justice; sexuality and human nature. Students should learn enough about religion to enable them to understand, and participate in, our ongoing cultural discussion of these issues—and not (uncritically) accept the current conventional secular wisdom of the educational establishment. That is, the primary purpose in K–12 schooling is not to make religion the object of study (using the methodologies and theories of the humanities and social sciences); it is rather to include *religious* voices in the curricular conversation.

Neutrality and Academic Freedom

Because they do not possess full academic freedom, public school teachers, unlike public university teachers, must be understood to be agents of the state and, as such, must remain religiously neutral. They are employed to teach an official, governmentally approved curriculum—which must also be religiously neutral.

As we have seen, the AAUP principles of academic freedom were devised by, and for, *scholars*, and K–12 teachers are not (at least by virtue of their profession) scholars. Moreover, courts have upheld fairly extensive rights for state legislatures, state departments of education, and local school boards to control public education and limit academic freedom, though they have supplied no unambiguous guidelines and have often attempted to balance a measure of freedom with a measure of community control.[59] As Van Geel puts it in his study of school law, "The board retains its authority to control the basic curriculum, but at the same time the teacher is permitted, within limits, to bring to the students' attention alternative viewpoints and perspectives. This approach prohibits the board from simply requiring the teacher to read from a board-prepared script."[60] The school must be a marketplace of ideas, but teachers do not have the right to disregard the curriculum or teach as true whatever they choose.

With more mature students, teachers may be free to express (not preach) their own religious (or antireligious) views, at least if asked, but because public school students are less mature than university students they are more likely to confuse the teacher's advocacy of, or hostility to, religion with the official position of the school and the state—a particular problem for the courts. Of course what counts as neutral (or, as I prefer to put it, as robustly fair) is not easy to say but requires a good deal of sophistication and the ability to make complex contextual judgments.

Teacher Education

The 1991 AAR self-study notes agreement "across the spectrum" about "one point that requires the attention of the field in the future." The "vast majority of entering students have had no *academic* preparation for the higher study of religion." As a result, "many call for the field to concentrate its energies upon the introduction of the study of religion into secondary education."[61] Yet if many have called, few have done anything about it.

If students are to be better prepared, teachers must be better prepared. The vast majority of teachers are not prepared to teach about religion; many know little about religious traditions other than their own—if, indeed, they have one. If religion is to be taken seriously, major reforms in teacher education are necessary. Departments of religious studies must begin to take responsibility for educating teachers in collaboration with schools of education and for provoking discussions about the need for religious studies as a certifiable field in K–12 schools.

Of course *all* teachers (and school administrators) must acquire at least a rudimentary understanding in their education course work of the constitutional and educational frameworks that govern the role of religion in the curriculum. Unhappily, most teacher-educators have little understanding of them; religion is not taken seriously in most schools of education.

All teachers who deal with religiously contested matters should know something about the relationship of religion to their particular subjects and disciplines. Ideally, they should be required, as part of their certification, to take at least one course that relates religion to their subject ("Religion and Science," "Religion and American History," "Religion and Literature," and so on), but whether required or not, departments of religious studies should make such courses available as electives. Moreover, every teacher-training institution should offer an elective course for prospective teachers and administrators on religion and education (perhaps jointly planned and taught by faculty in the department of religious studies and school of education) that deals in some depth with the relationship of religion and education.

If there are to be religion *courses* in secondary schools, as there must be, then there must be teachers competent to teach them, and this means that religious studies must become a certifiable field, requiring at least an undergraduate minor. Considerable thought and collaboration among scholars in religious studies, schools of education, and state departments of education will be necessary. Because of constitutional constraints, the nastiness of our culture wars, and fears of controversy, religion, more than any teaching field, requires care in the development of the curriculum that prepares teachers.[62]

Conclusions

There may well be powerful religious reasons for taking religion seriously as part of a liberal education. I want to be clear, however, that the educational, civic, and constitutional arguments I have given for taking religion seriously are fully *secular* arguments. (Indeed, courts would properly reject religious arguments for including religion in the curriculum of public schools and universities.) K–12 public education is, with regard to religion, deeply illiberal, politically unjust, and unconstitutional. These are not small matters, and something of a revolution must be worked to right the situation. A part of what is required is the development of the field of religious studies in secondary education—and that will require considerable attention from the scholars in religious studies in universities.

The situation is somewhat better in higher education because of the existence of departments of religious studies (as well as occasional courses in other disciplines addressing religion). Still, in universities the vast majority of faculty are uninterested in religion (at least as scholars), most public universities still do not have departments of religious studies, and even when they do only a minority of students are likely to take courses in them. That is, higher education also fails to provide a truly liberal education for the majority of its students.

Of course a part of my argument has been directed at the field of religious studies itself. Acknowledging once again the rich diversity in the field and the many ways in which it *does* take religion seriously, I am still concerned that *too often* it fails to live up to the responsibilities imposed on it by the idea of a truly liberal education.

I end, then, where I began, by noting the irony that at a time of considerable religious vitality in our culture and intellectual life, we continue to exclude religious voices from a curricular conversation that is supposed to provide students with a liberal education. This should be recognized for what it is, something of a scandal.

Notes

1. See Warren A. Nord, *Religion and American Education: Rethinking a National Dilemma* (Chapel Hill: University of North Carolina Press, 1995), esp. chapter 4, and Warren A. Nord and Charles C. Haynes, *Taking Religion Seriously across the Curriculum* (Alexandria, Va.: ASCD, 1998), *passim*.

2. The following discussion of economics is abbreviated from a considerably longer discussion in Nord and Haynes, *Taking Religion Seriously*, 105–14.

3. Robert Wuthnow writes: "Asked if their religious beliefs had influ-

enced their choice of a career, most of the people I have interviewed in recent years—Christians and non-Christians alike—said no. Asked if they thought of their work as a calling, most said no. Asked if they understood the concept of stewardship, most said no. Asked how religion did influence their work lives or thoughts about money, most said the two were completely separate." Robert Wuthnow, *Christianity in the Twenty-first Century* (New York: Oxford University Press, 1993), 200.

4. National Council on Economic Education, *National Content Standards in Economics* (New York: NCEE, 1997), viii.

5. This claim is documented subject by subject across the secondary school curriculum in Nord and Haynes, *Taking Religion Seriously.*

6. Ninian Smart, *Religion and the Western Mind* (New York: Macmillan, 1987), 9.

7. I discuss the concept of indoctrination at much greater length in Nord, *Religion and American Education,* 160–91.

8. Gerald Graff, *Beyond the Culture Wars* (New York: Norton, 1992), 12–13.

9. Ibid., 12.

10. I discuss the relationship of religion to the multicultural movement and the "justice" argument for including religion in the curriculum at much greater length in Warren Nord, "Religion and Multiculturalism," in *The Politics of Multiculturalism and Bilingual Education,* ed. Carlos Ovando and Peter McLaren (New York: McGraw-Hill, 1999), 63–81.

11. *Everson v. Board of Education,* 330 US 1, 16 (1947).

12. *Abington Township v. Schempp,* 374 US 203, 225 (1963).

13. Ibid., 374 US 203, 306.

14. Douglas Laycock, "Formal, Substantive, and Disaggregated Neutrality toward Religion," *DePaul Law Review* 39 (1990): 1001–2.

15. Douglas Laycock, "Religious Liberty as Liberty," *Journal of Contemporary Legal Issues* 7 (fall 1996): 348.

16. I discuss the constitutional argument for including religion in the curriculum at much greater length in Nord, *Religion and American Education,* 241–49.

17. This should be, on reflection, at least a little surprising, as George Marsden has noted. "Keeping within our intellectual horizons a being who is great enough to create us and the universe, after all, ought to change our perspectives on quite a number of things. One might expect it to have a bearing on some of the most sharply debated issues in academia today. . . . Why, in a culture in which many academics profess to believe in God, do so few reflect on the academic implications of that belief?" George Marsden, *The Outrageous Idea of Christian Scholarship* (New York: Oxford University Press, 1997), 4.

18. For further discussion of "minimal" and "robust" fairness see Nord, *Religion and American Education,* chapter 7.

19. All undergraduate students should be required to take a semester-long course, and all high school students should be required to take one year-long course in religious studies. See Nord, *Religion and American Education,* chapters 6 and 7.

20. No doubt religious organizations, religious rhetoric and symbols, and chapel services survived around the periphery of some public universities well into the twentieth century, but religion had long since disappeared from the curriculum. For the story of the secularization of higher education see George Marsden, *The Soul of the American University* (New York: Oxford University Press, 1994), and Jon H. Roberts and James Turner, *The Sacred and the Secular University* (Princeton: Princeton University Press, 2000).

21. *Religious Studies News,* November 1993, 8.

22. Walter H. Capps, *Religious Studies: The Making of a Discipline* (Minneapolis: Fortress Press, 1995), 331.

23. Ray S. Hart, "Religious and Theological Studies in American Higher Education," *Journal of the American Academy of Religion* 59 (winter 1991): 716. My emphasis.

24. No doubt individual teachers of religious studies pursue a variety of agendas. A few, particularly in religiously affiliated colleges, retain an old-fashioned confessional approach, seeing it as their task to nurture students' understanding of, and commitment to, their religious traditions. Others see it as their task to "problematize" religion, to disabuse students of their religious naivete—even of their religious convictions, as George Marsden has suggested. Some may problematize *all* frameworks of thought—perhaps because they are committed to some variety of postmodernism or perhaps to encourage students to think for themselves. I suspect that more try to maintain some kind of "objectivity" or neutrality.

25. William Scott Green, "Something Strange, Yet Nothing New: Religion in the Secular Curriculum," *Soundings* 71 (summer–fall 1988): 274.

26. Hart, "Religious and Theological Studies," 732.

27. James Tunstead Burtchaell, "The Decline and Fall of the Christian College I," *First Things* (April 1991): 29.

28. Capps, *Religious Studies,* 345.

29. Martin Marty, "Half a Life in Religious Studies: Confessions of an 'Historical Historian'," in *The Craft of Religious Studies,* ed. Jon R. Stone (New York: St. Martin's Press, 1998), 153. Marty attributes this attitude primarily to the desire to escape the "old wounds" of childhood religion.

30. American Academy of Religion, *Liberal Learning and the Religion Major* (1990): 13.

31. Ibid., 15.

32. Ibid., 9–10.

33. Kimberly C. Patton, "'Stumbling Along between the Immensities': Reflections on Teaching in the Study of Religion," *Journal of the American Academy of Religion* 65 (winter 1997): 837–38.

34. John W. Dixon Jr., "What Should Religion Departments Teach?" *Theology Today* 46 (January 1990): 369–70.

35. George M. Marsden, "The Soul of the American University: An Historical Overview," in *The Secularization of the Academy*, ed. George M. Marsden and Bradley J. Longfield (New York: Oxford University Press, 1992), 36.

36. David Ray Griffin, "Professing Theology in the State University," in *Theology and the University: Essays in Honor of John B. Cobb, Jr.*, ed. David Ray Griffin and Joseph C. Hough Jr. (Albany: State University of New York Press, 1991), 10.

37. William F. May, "Why Theology and Religious Studies Need Each Other," *Journal of the American Academy of Religion* 52 (December 1984): 750.

38. Many scholars in religious studies would argue that making the existence of God the central religious claim privileges the Western religious traditions. See the very helpful essays in William J. Wainwright, ed., *God, Philosophy, and Academic Culture* (Atlanta: Scholars Press, 1996).

39. Walter Capps, "On Religious Studies, in Lieu of an Overview," *Journal of the American Academy of Religion* 42 (December 1974): 377, 374, 378.

40. Robert Cummings Neville, "Religious Studies and Theological Studies," *Journal of the American Academy of Religion* 61 (summer 1993): 191.

41. *Theology* is sometimes taken to be a peculiarly Christian word and, as such, suspect in a field that does not wish to privilege any particular religious tradition. The argument here is not that peculiarly Christian approaches to religion should be privileged but that religious studies should take seriously internal intellectual efforts to think through the fundamental beliefs and values of various traditions as they engage the surrounding culture.

42. Gordon D. Kaufman, "Critical Theology as a University Discipline," *Theology and the University*, 38.

43. Griffin, "Professing Theology in a State University," 7. Almost needless to say, the lines quickly blur here among critical theology, liberal theology, natural theology, and the philosophy of religion.

44. Ibid., 8.

45. Stephen H. Webb, "The Voice of Theology: Rethinking the Personal and the Objective in Christian Pedagogy," *Journal of the American Academy of Religion* 65 (winter 1997): 766–67.

46. Marsden, "Soul of the University," 38–39. Also see Marsden's *Outrageous Idea of Christian Scholarship*, 26–31.

47. See Nord, *Religion and American Education*, 179–87.

48. Neville, "Religious Studies and Theological Studies," 197.

49. See especially E. M. Adams, *Religion and Cultural Freedom* (Philadelphia: Temple University Press, 1993).

50. AAUP, *Declaration of Principles* (1915), reprinted in *Academic Freedom and Tenure: A Handbook of the American Association of University Professors* (Madison: University of Wisconsin Press, 1967), 164.

51. Of course, academic freedom is not meant to protect the claims of incompetent scholars. A historian who taught students that the Holocaust did not happen would almost surely be incompetent, and academic freedom was never meant to defend incompetence. Similarly, a scholar's defense of, or attack on, religion must be professionally competent if it is to be protected. Almost needless to say, such judgments are often controversial; the principle is not. See Nord, *Religion and American Education,* 265–69.

52. *Keyishian v. Board of Regents,* 385 US 589, 603 (1966).

53. David Rabban, "A Functional Analysis of 'Individual' and 'Institutional' Academic Freedom under the First Amendment," *Law and Contemporary Problems* 53 (summer 1990): 230.

54. Although the Supreme Court has never weighed academic freedom against the Establishment Clause there is one appellate court decision that clearly cuts against the grain of my position—an appallingly bad decision by the Eleventh Circuit Court in *Bishop v. Aronov,* 926 F2d 1066 (1991). Interestingly, the district court had gotten it right; see *Bishop v. Aronov* 732 F. Supp. 1562 (N.D. Ala 1990). I discuss this case at some length in Nord, *Religion and American Education,* 269–74.

55. AAUP, *Declaration of Principles,* 169.

56. AAUP, "Some Observations on Ideology, Competence, and Faculty Selection," *Academe* 72 (January–February 1986): 2a.

57. *Religion and the Public School Curriculum: Questions and Answers,* reprinted in Charles C. Haynes and Oliver Thomas, eds., *Finding Common Ground: A First Amendment Guide to Religion and Public Education,* rev. ed. (Nashville: Freedom Forum First Amendment Center at Vanderbilt University, 1994), chapter 6: 2–3.

58. It is religious conservatives, of course, who are most critical of public schooling—and most likely to leave. Still, my argument is that public schooling does not take *any* religion seriously; it marginalizes *all* religion—liberal as well as conservative, Catholic as well as Protestant, Jewish and Muslim and Buddhist as well as Christian.

59. In *Zykan v. Warsaw Community School Corporation,* 631 F2d 1300, 1305 (1980), the Seventh Circuit Court of Appeals noted that the breadth of the powers of local school boards "reflects the perception that at the secondary school level the need for education guidance predominates over many of the

rights and interests comprised by 'academic freedom.'" There are limits, however. In *Board of Education v. Pico*, 457 US 863, 864, 866 (1982), Justice Brennan acknowledged that the discretion of school boards "must be exercised in a manner that comports with the transcendent imperatives of the First Amendment," and he went on to quote from *Griswold v. Connecticut:* "The State may not, consistently with the spirit of the First Amendment, contract the spectrum of available knowledge." Also, in *Zykan*, 631 F2d 1300, the court held that local boards cannot impose a "pall or orthodoxy" on secondary school classrooms.

60. Tyll Van Geel, *The Courts and American Education Law* (Buffalo: Prometheus Books, 1987), 222.

61. Hart, "Religious and Theological Studies," 776.

62. Charles Haynes and I have addressed the nature of these reforms at some length in Nord and Haynes, *Taking Religion Seriously,* chapters 1–2 and *passim.*

2
Beyond the Boundaries: Literature, Religion, and Science

Roger Lundin

"Something there is that doesn't love a wall," intones the speaker in Robert Frost's "Mending Wall," a poem that reads like a charter for the interdisciplinary studies movement and that charts the course of twentieth-century literary studies in an uncanny fashion.

> Something there is that doesn't love a wall,
> That sends the frozen-ground-swell under it,
> And spills the upper boulders in the sun;
> And makes gaps even two can pass abreast.
> . . . The gaps I mean,
> No one has seen them made or heard them made,
> But at spring mending-time we find them there.[1]

"Mending Wall" is a poem about the need for creating boundaries and the need for breaking them, and what it says seems as true of the divisions between academic disciplines as it is of the old stone walls that to this day divide the landscapes of rural New England. For more than a century, American colleges and universities have parceled out the domains of knowledge into different fields of study, marked the lines between these fields with care, and trained specialists to tend their own narrow plots of land. Over the past century, numerous disciplines have been created or refined, and their success in developing and perpetuating their practices has been nothing short of remarkable.

For most of that period, the field of literary studies stood as a walled-in garden that yielded a host of unique but exotic growths. According to Terry Eagleton, the walling off of literature was made possible by a modern assumption "that there was an unchanging object known as 'art'" and "an isolatable experience called 'beauty' or the 'aesthetic.'" In the early modern period, when literature no longer found itself in the service of the church or the pay of wealthy patrons, it became plausible, even desirable, to cite the uselessness of literature as its most important attribute. An art with no worldly purpose might serve an otherworldly end. Stripped at last of its rhetorical and political functions, literature could consider itself impervious to the forces that overwhelmed all other human endeavors. It could present itself as a haven and rationalize its loss of a public role as a vital private gain. "Having lost his patron," Eagleton observes, "the writer discovered a substitute in the poetic." Literature was "extricated from the material practices, social relations and ideological meanings in which it is always caught up, and raised to the status of a solitary fetish."[2]

Yet the events of the twentieth century made it amply apparent that we could not protect literature, nor could it shelter us from the ravages of nature and vicissitudes of history. The experience of two world wars—with their record of mass destruction, genocide, and atomic weapons—nullified the many claims made in the nineteenth century on behalf of literature's salvific powers.[3] In perhaps the finest book on literature and modern warfare, *The Great War and Modern Memory,* Paul Fussell documents the devastating blow dealt to the British literary and cultural enterprise by the First World War. Nineteenth-century optimism could not account for twentieth-century terror. To find a vocabulary adequate to describe that terror, "it would take another war, and an even worse one, before such language would force itself up from below and propose itself for use."[4] Thus, however vigilantly literature's advocates patrolled the walls between their art and the world, the ground-swell of twentieth-century history broke through those walls and brought questions about the history and uses of literature back into the debate about its nature. "Something there is," it seems, "that doesn't love a wall."

As one who treasures his own field of English and the crops it yields, I understand the impulse to fence it off and protect its growth. Indeed, to a degree, I honor the boundaries, for I have no desire to teach literature as though it were indistinguishable from history or philosophy, nor do I believe it would be right or useful to do so. Yet it also no longer seems wise or feasible to treat literature as though it consists, in the words of one critical observer, of "a set of ciphers, an agenda of mysteries, a collection of secular scriptures" abiding inscrutably beyond history.[5] In light of the changes that have swept through contemporary intellectual life, should not religiously committed literary critics let the gaps in the disciplinary walls stand long enough to permit commerce between the fields and learn what the forces are that don't love those walls? If Christian scholars believe of Christ that "in him everything in heaven and on earth was created," do they not have a duty to care about the yield of other fields and the study of what it is that "holds all things together" (Col 1:16–17)?

History in the Heavens

As an example of a boundary-breaking discovery, there was in the mid-1990s a "frozen-ground-swell" that spilled up from beneath the barriers between disciplines. I refer to the remarkable story of the Hubble telescope, which in 1996 began beaming to earth photos of the heavens that were as stunning in their beauty as they were staggering in their implications. We awoke one morning to learn that the universe as we knew it had grown larger by a factor of five. In the pictures that came from the Hubble, astronomers found evidence of approximately forty billion galaxies never before known to have existed. At the beginning of this century, scientists were not sure that more than one galaxy existed. Now we had fifty billion of them on our hands.

In ways we cannot imagine, the knowledge we have gained from the Hubble telescope will influence study across the disciplines for years to come. It will change the way we read some poems, amplify our interpretation of the history of ideas, and deepen our understanding of the psychological dynamics of modern men and women. We can make assertions such as these with confidence because of what we know about the rise of science in the modern world. Since at least the sixteenth century, revolutions in cosmology have been intertwined with vast shifts in cultural and intellectual history. In the past several decades, Stephen Toulmin, Paul Feyerabend, Thomas Kuhn, and others have demonstrated for us the connections between scientific systems and cultural paradigms. Metaphors order the way we picture the heavens, and the pictures we have of those heavens shape the metaphors we use to write our poems and comprehend our lives.[6]

That such a close, reciprocal relationship exists between metaphor and science was also made evident in the recent renovation of the Hayden Planetarium in New York City. As Edward Rothstein explains, in the old exhibit at the planetarium, the earth had been at the center of things, and "there was no question about where one was or who one was in that artificial cosmos. One was a child of earth." At the heart of that exhibit, a large machine projected "on the ceiling images in which humanity could see a reflection of itself."[7] To Rothstein, the old exhibit consisted of too much metaphor and too little science. It allowed the mind to humanize the alien heavens, but it did not permit the universe itself to make a truthful imprint upon human consciousness.

Everything has changed, he says, with the renovation of the Hayden. If Copernicus and Galileo "showed that humanity is not at the center of the universe, here humanity is not even at the center of the planetarium." The exhibit's designers used various methods of "de-centering," creating a walkway in which each successive inch represents the passage of 3.6 million years. After a one-hundred-yard walk—a journey of thirteen billion years—a visitor at last arrives at the advent of human history, which is represented by the width of a single human hair. Relentlessly, the exhibit spurns allusions to mythology and all comforting human associations. "Instead of bringing the cosmos home, the home has been thrust, untethered into the cosmos."[8] As the designers of the new exhibit see it, they have humbled language and the human imagination, making them bend the knee before a vast and indifferent universe.

The remake of the Hayden Planetarium is but a brief episode in a centuries-long drama involving astronomy and the metaphorical imagination. This cosmological conflict has genuine relevance for literary study, because in good measure the modern scientific revolution prompted the building of the barriers that now separate the academic disciplines. For a student of literature, that is, an interdisciplinary study of the past uncovers the history of the construction of the walls that separate the disciplines in the present. Copernicanism and Newtonian physics transformed our understanding of humanity's place in the universe, and in doing so they shaped every area of cultural and academic life, including the study of literature.[9]

Although the Hubble discoveries will not have the impact of the Copernican revolution, they nevertheless point to religious issues at stake in contemporary literary study as well as to the complex relationship between literature and science. Evidence of their importance surfaced in a news story that appeared shortly after the first Hubble photos were published. "By showing the universe is bigger and more diverse than we ever thought, these discoveries, in effect, show that we are even less significant than we ever thought," wrote Peter Kendall, using images much like those to be employed several years later in accounts of the Hayden renovation. "But they somehow have exactly the opposite effect," he said of the photos. "They show just how clever we are, that if we noodle away at a problem long enough we can pry the lid off secrets we have no earthly right to know."[10]

When I first read it, that passage intrigued me because it echoed the brilliant introductory chapter to Karl Barth's study of Protestant theology in the nineteenth century. In accounting for the Enlightenment view of humanity's place in the universe, Barth focuses his attention upon the Copernican revolution. "Eighteenth century man," argues Barth, "was the man who could no longer remain ignorant of the significance of the fact that Copernicus and Galileo were right, that this vast and rich earth of his, the theatre of his deeds was not the centre of the universe, but a grain of dust amid countless others in the universe."[11]

Barth notes the sobering potential of the Copernican system, which evicts human beings from their home at the center of the universe and leaves them searching for a dwelling place in the empty heavens. Yet instead of having led to what Barth calls "an unprecedented and boundless humiliation of man," the Copernican revolution put man more fully "in the centre of all things, in a quite different sense, . . . for he was able to discover this revolutionary truth by his own resources and to think it abstractly." Paradoxically, the response to the displacement of the earth from the center of the universe "was those philosophical systems of rationalism, empiricism and scepticism which made men even more self-confident." Thus emboldened, eighteenth- and nineteenth-century men and women spun grand stories about their cosmic importance until, in Barth's words, "the geocentric picture of the universe was replaced as a matter of course by the anthro-pocentric."[12]

According to Barth, early modern science and its philosophical as-sumptions paved the way for an unprecedented celebration of the power of human thought. In the eighteenth century, Western men and women "began to be conscious . . . of a capacity for thinking which was responsible to no other authority than" themselves. In Barth's words, that century saw the rise of "the ideal of a science of history and of natural science, without presuppositions and possess-ing supreme intellectual dignity in virtue of this very absence of pre-suppositions."[13] The self envisioned here was as free of obligations as it was of presuppositions. Secure in its autonomous state, it was at liberty to explore its increasingly vast inner domains as well as the endless reaches of the universe arrayed against it.

Before the triumph of the Newtonian model of the universe, Walter Ong points out, it had been plausible to think of "praise" and "honor" as qualities that not only resided in subjects but also belonged to ob-jects. Where we see praise as something we give to an object or person beyond us, for the pre-Newtonian English speaker it was also a quality that inhered in the objects that humans praised. "For the sixteenth-and seventeenth-century mind, the value in the object and the praise elicited by the object tend to be viewed as one whole," writes Ong.[14]

The understanding of the world that made this possible vanished over the course of the seventeenth century, Ong claims, and a daunt-ing new world came into being. In this world, loquacious subjects stand apart and contemplate the silent objects they face. This mod-ern world is one in which the auditory images long central to Judeo-Christian understandings of the truth give way to the dominant visual metaphors of modernity. In other words, we no longer think so much of hearing the word of God but of holding a worldview. The modern understanding of science brings with it what Ong calls a "hypertrophy of the visual imagination," which "crowds spatial models, and noth-ing but spatial models, into the universe of the mind." And in the end, that hypertrophy is the sign of that "evolution in human thought processes which is simultaneously producing the Newtonian revolu-tion, with its stress on visually controlled observation and mathemat-ics" and the silent universe we have come to take for granted.[15] As Barth had seen the geocentric picture giving way to the anthropocentric view, so does Ong's account of the "nonrhetorical universe" point to the fact that the universe's silence would eventually prompt the poet to try to fill the void.

A silent universe gives stark evidence of what George Steiner has called "the retreat from the word." Steiner argues that in addition to spawning rationalism, empiricism, and scepticism, the Copernican and Newtonian revolutions also established the outlines for the modern academic disciplines. Modern intellectual and cultural history represents a "retreat from the word" that began in the seventeenth century and has continued to this day. Until the seventeenth century, "mathematical thought . . . was anchored to the material conditions of experience. These, in turn, were ordered and ruled by language." Both the classic and the Christian visions of the world sought to contain the world within the boundaries of a language that was in turn embodied within the Godhead through the person of Christ. "In the beginning was the Word," the Gospel of John proclaims, bearing witness to the *Logos* that undergirds, sustains, and orders creation. For this reason, both the classical and Christian traditions "bear solemn witness to the belief that all truth and realness—with the exception of a small, queer margin at the very top—can be housed inside the walls of language."[16]

Yet from the seventeenth century on, "mathematics ceases to be a dependent notation. . . . It becomes a fantastically rich, complex and dynamic language. *And the history of that language is one of progressive untranslatibility.*" Beginning with Newton, "this extension of mathematics over great areas of thought and action . . . broke western consciousness into what C. P. Snow calls 'the two cultures,'" one based broadly in the humanities and the other in the sciences. The rift between these two cultures gave rise to the disciplinary domains in which contemporary Christian scholars live and move and have their being. A chasm yawns between what Steiner calls "the languages of words and of mathematics," and that chasm "grows constantly wider" in the modern world.[17]

It was this chasm to which Hans Jonas referred when he drew parallels between contemporary naturalism and ancient gnosticism. In modern thinking about science and the self, the isolation of the human presence within nature "constitutes the utter loneliness of man in the sum of things." As embodied creatures, human beings share in the "mechanical determination" of the natural world, but they no longer believe themselves to be part of an ultimate "meaning of nature." As a consequence, Jonas writes, "that by which man is superior to all nature, his unique distinction, mind, no longer results in a higher integration of his being into the totality of being, but on the contrary marks the unbridgeable gulf between himself and the rest of existence."[18]

This gulf has set the boundaries and defined the territories of modern intellectual life. On one side of the chasm stand the humanities; firmly planted on the other side are the hard sciences; and in between, straining and straddling the gap are the social sciences, not sure whether they should use the language of poetry or that of mathematics. Since the eighteenth century, the study of literature has consisted of seemingly tireless efforts to define literature over against science, mathematics, and the alienated world they have produced. For the first century of that argument, the nineteenth century, literature appeared to have the upper hand in the dispute. Where science starved the human spirit, literature fed it; where science undermined moral values, literature shored them up; and where science emptied the self of emotions, literature poured them back into it.

M. H. Abrams has shown that in pitting literature against science, the romantic tradition was also transforming long-standing definitions of the art. From the time of Aristotle to the eighteenth century, the Western literary tradition had consistently defined literature as a mimetic activity, that is, an effort to *re-present* reality. The meaning of mimesis may have varied from period to period, as poets and critics argued over whether art was primarily meant to represent actual objects and events or whether its goal should be to embody an imagined ideal or possibility. Yet whatever their differences, for two millennia, theorists of literature held, in the main, that the fundamental purpose of art was to hold a mirror up to nature.

This mimetic consensus began to break down in the eighteenth century as it gave way to an expressive theory of art. In this process of change, methodological naturalism played a vital role. What purpose can there be in mirroring nature, and representing reality, if the thing to be imitated is but a lifeless cog in a vast machine? If values no longer inhere in objects but emanate from subjects, should poetry not express the needs of the subject rather than mirror the form of the object? For Abrams, the key eighteenth-century shift involved the replacement of the imagery of the poem as mirror for "that of the poem as heterocosm, 'a second nature,' created by the poet in an act analogous to God's creation of the world." By the middle of the twentieth century, the understanding of the poem as "heterocosm" had issued in the New Critical belief that poetry is "utterly diverse from scientific statement and scientific truth" because it is a "self-contained universe of discourse, of which we cannot demand that it be true to nature, but only, that it be true to itself."[19]

At the outset of modern literary studies, it was the English poet Samuel Taylor Coleridge who gave the romantic doctrine of poetry its most compelling formulation in his *Biographia Literaria*. In the well-known chapter 14 of that work, Coleridge maps the distinctions between poetry and other forms of knowledge, including scientific knowledge. In science, the immediate object of concern is the communication of "truths absolute and demonstrable," while in history the goal is the presentation of the truths represented by "facts experienced and recorded." Pleasure may be a derivative product of the search for truth in these fields, but it is not the immediate end. Poetry, however, pursues pleasure deliberately; it is that species of composition "which is opposed to works of science, by proposing for its *immediate* object pleasure, not truth; and from all other species" by virtue of the fact that it proposes "to itself such delight from the *whole*, as is compatible with a distinct gratification from each component part."[20]

The *Logos* philosophy of the classical world and the Christian tradition had conceived of the relationship of the part to the whole as a matter that encompassed the entirety of the created order. Here, however, Coleridge speaks of it primarily, though not exclusively, as a question pertaining to an individual work of art. If the natural world is a stormy place of decay and death, poetry may at least offer a shelter for the homeless human spirit. Coleridge took considerable consolation from this view, as did his contemporary, John Keats. Trained in medicine and afflicted by tuberculosis, Keats knew well the mutability of life and longed for the immortality of art. His "Ode to a Nightingale" contrasts the deathless song of the "immortal Bird" with the mortal world of human consciousness, "Where but to think is to be full of sorrow / And leaden-eyed despairs." And the only solace for sorrow is to be found within the sanctuary of art, wrote Keats in "Endymion":

A thing of beauty is a joy for ever:
Its loveliness increases; it will never
Pass into nothingness; but still will keep
A bower quiet for us, and a sleep
Full of sweet dreams, and health, and quiet
breathing.[21]

In the nineteenth century, the argument for poetry frequently employed the claim that it could uncover the spirit coursing through nature or the moral order undergirding it. According to Coleridge, William Wordsworth, and Ralph Waldo Emerson, among others, poetry could peer into the heart of things and find the spirit abiding there. What poetry discovered in nature brought comfort to the human soul, because it appeared to sustain the spiritual ideals of the Christian faith without requiring assent to its doctrines. "It is not words only that are emblematic; it is things which are emblematic," Emerson claimed in *Nature*. "Every natural fact is a symbol of some spiritual fact. Every appearance in nature corresponds to some state of the mind."[22]

Yet this romantic vision of spirit and nature could not survive the challenges that were to be posed to it in the final decades of the nineteenth century. In America, it gave way before a congeries of forces, including rapid industrialization and urbanization, the rise of evolutionary theory, and the trauma of the Civil War. Up until the war, Alfred Kazin has observed, the Bible remained an essential, indisputable personal resource for most Americans; after the war, Americans could no longer invoke God's purpose in supporting a particular political course. "Everything so long festering in the American heart over the need to believe that God does intervene in history—everything that was to be threatened after the war by the idea of nature as a self-operating mechanism—now flamed out with all the passion of war itself," Kazin claims.[23]

In the decades after the Civil War, the idealism cultivated by the romantic poets gradually gave way to the pragmatism promoted by the philosophers of naturalism. Over the same period, the academic study of literature in America was born, developed, and flourished, and the connection between these two developments was hardly incidental. For the broad sweep of the secularizing transformation of the American university in the century after the Civil War, George Marsden has written a comprehensive history, and for the discipline of English, Gerald Graff has offered the most thorough account. Graff notes that "strictly speaking, there were no 'academic literary studies' in America or anywhere else until language and literature departments were formed in the last quarter of the nineteenth century."[24] The teaching of literature in the vernacular had been undertaken sporadically on American campuses before the Civil War, but only in the decade after that conflict did such instruction become a widespread practice. As it was becoming established, that teaching of literature generally patterned itself after the dominant philosophic and scientific modes of discourse and inquiry. Like other sectors of the university, English departments at the end of the nineteenth century were stocked with academic professionals who believed themselves to be above conventional morality and beyond ideology, as they engaged in a disinterested search for truth.

For the academic professionals undertaking this disinterested search, methodological naturalism provided the necessary philosophical foundation for their activities.[25] Nothing had shaped the emerging naturalist consensus more completely than the publication of Darwin's *The Origin of Species* in 1859. In a 1909 tribute, John Dewey said that the appearance of that work "marked an epoch." With the theory of natural selection, Darwin overturned "conceptions that had reigned in the philosophy of nature and knowledge for two thousand years."[26] Dewey pictured Darwin as a liberator who had freed nature from a sense of indebtedness and obligation to any power beyond itself.

In doing so, Darwin also released intellectual reflection from its obsession with the idea of design. To account for the order they discovered in nature, and to prove the existence of the God in whom they believed, early modern Christian apologists had relied upon the argument from design, but Darwin seemed to do away with it. Where the Greeks and Christians had focused upon the idea of the *telos*, the end or purposeful order of life, Darwin shifted our attention to the *arche*, the genesis of life and the origin from which all order emerged in the struggle for survival.[27] After Darwin, to understand something meant not to trace it forward to its destined end but to track it back to its biological or chemical origin.

What Dewey presents as a happy revolution at the end of the nineteenth century others have portrayed as a melancholy evolution extending over the whole of modernity. This is Max Weber's "disenchantment of the world" and Charles Taylor's "loss of the ontic logos," which are their names for a process of diminishment that had been unfolding for centuries but which seemed to accelerate in the latter half of the nineteenth century.[28] In the final decades of that century, the "unprecedented boundless humiliation" long implicit in the Copernican revolution became at last explicit to writers such as Emily Dickinson, Herman Melville, Mark Twain, and Stephen Crane.

Yet although American poets and novelists registered a sense of cosmic homelessness in the last decades of the nineteenth century, few American philosophers seemed metaphysically displaced at the time.[29] At the precise point at which scientific and cultural forces began to press American novelists and poets to search for spiritual solace in a forbidding universe, the forces of professionalization were calling most American philosophers away from their metaphysical and spiritual concerns. In the history of the American college, philosophy had been allied with theology and a broadly defined conception of the moral sciences. Bruce Kuklick notes, however, that "as philosophy became a profession, its nature and the character of the men it attracted changed." The power of disciplinary exclusion was at work in philosophy, that is, as well it was in English studies. In the decades after the Civil War the amateur philosophers, the generalists with broad metaphysical, ethical, and political concerns, were all but banished from the profession. The professionals who replaced them abandoned "concerns outside the discipline," and their attention was "narrowed to a domain of more arcane interests" than those pursued by the amateur metaphysicians of the past.[30]

A distinct exception to this trend was William James. A man driven by mediating impulses, James worked tirelessly to effect a compromise between science and religion by means of his pragmatic understanding of truth. For James, religion "was true insofar as it worked and gave value to existence."[31] For James, the effects of belief were more important that its objects. With his creative pragmatic compromise, James believed that he had discovered a means of reconciling scientific knowledge with spiritual need. Yet no matter how hard he tried to conjure belief and take shelter within it, James found it hard to trust in a comfort of his own invention. He repeatedly betrayed in his writings an anxious sense of orphaned abandonment.

That anxiety is evident in key places in the lectures that became *Pragmatism*. Here, James outlines the differences between pragmatism, the pluriform view of truth that he champions, and rationalism, his term of opprobrium for the conviction that the truth is single and unified. "The alternative between pragmatism and rationalism is no longer a question in the theory of knowledge, it concerns the structure of the universe itself." Whereas the rationalist—for rationalist, read Christian theist, romantic idealist, or Common Sense moral realist—believes that "the mutable in experience must be founded on immutability," the pragmatist lives comfortably with the fact that "truth grows up inside of all the finite experiences. They lean on each other, but the whole of them, if such a whole there be, leans on nothing. All 'homes' are in finite experience; finite experience as such is homeless. Nothing outside of the flux secures the issue of it."[32] Wherever James managed to move the human psyche to house it comfortably in the universe, that universe remained for him a cold, lonely place, a thoroughly disenchanted realm.

With his strenuous efforts to reconcile science and religion, William James was a forerunner of a number of twentieth-century literary critics who were willing to appropriate the methods of science and trade upon its authority, even as they worked to develop aesthetic alternatives to the world that science had rendered. As a case in point, Gail McDonald argues that the two most prominent American modernist poets and critics, T. S. Eliot and Ezra Pound, deliberately sought the sanction of science while promoting poetry as its spiritual antagonist. Pound and Eliot wanted their audiences to believe that poetry and criticism were precisely like science in that they too "required long study and preparation" and made discoveries that were universal and objective and not "merely of local or personal significance."[33] Yet at the same time, like other modernist poets, they expected their art to heal the wounds that science had opened.

McDonald notes that in defending poetry with claims about its scientific rigor, Eliot and Pound echoed arguments that American educators had been making for several decades. For example, almost half a century before Pound and Eliot came upon the scene, the president of the University of Minnesota, William Watts Folwell, challenged his arts faculty to develop scientific methods for their intuitive disciplines: "What we demand then is, not rules, but principles; not mere tricks of art and sleight of hand, but science; science which explains and authenticates art; which makes men masters in their work, and not mere imitators and operatives."[34] In a similar fashion, in the wake of Pound and Eliot, Cleanth Brooks called for poetry and criticism to be as rigorous as science in their methods yet as comforting as religion in their message. In the classic text of the New Criticism, *Modern Poetry and the Tradition,* Brooks describes science as an "abstract" but undeniably "powerful" form of knowledge. Science does its necessary work well and tells its necessary story convincingly. Yet while the knowledge imparted by science is partial, poetry offers a comprehensive way of knowing. Poetry's description of reality includes "not only those elements which make the knowledge 'useful,' but other 'useless' elements as well." For Brooks, "science is power-knowledge" that may help to heat our homes, transport our food, and print our books, but it also "may contribute to hubris; whereas poetry (as an element of religion or merely as poetry), . . . constantly reminds man that the thing described lies outside man's control, and thus rebukes hubris."[35]

In identifying the "useless" as the definitive "extra" that belongs to poetry, Brooks looks back to Kant and Coleridge and forward to the dominant mode of defending poetry in the mid-twentieth century. Modernism promoted literature as a protest against the steely coldness of a diminished world and sought neither to re-present the world nor to change it, for poetry could say nothing to a world in crisis and do nothing for one beyond repair.[36] Instead, it offered aesthetic distance as a saving grace. To be brought into the ironic, paradoxical, and undecidable realm of literary experience was to be swept out of the world of dull facts and clashing beliefs and into a realm of poise, beauty, and calm. Keats had given this aesthetic stance a telling name in an 1817 letter to his brothers. He told them that he wanted to identify the quality that "a Man of Achievement especially in Literature" possessed: "I mean Negative Capability, that is when man is capable of being in uncertainties, Mysteries, doubts, without any irritable reaching after fact & reason."[37] Or as Oscar Wilde famously put the matter, at the end of the nineteenth century, in his "Preface" to *The Picture of Dorian Gray:*

> We can forgive a man for making a useful thing as long as he does not admire it. The only excuse for making a useless thing is that one admires it intensely.
> All art is quite useless.[38]

In this scheme of things, to be saved is to hover in a state of suspended judgment, holding everything in abeyance, deciding nothing, but leaving all to irony and uncertainty. This veneration of irony enabled those who held no strong theological commitments to approach the reading of literature with a feeling akin to religious awe. "More than anything else," Lionel Trilling wrote, "our literature is concerned with salvation. No literature has ever been so intensely spiritual as ours. . . . Certainly it has the special intensity of concern with the spiritual life which Hegel noted when he spoke of the great modern phenomenon of the secularization of spirituality."[39]

Theory and the Pyrrhic Victory

Trilling wrote his celebrated essay in 1961, and by the end of that decade, American literary studies would be changed dramatically. Tzvetan Todorov identifies the transformation as having taken place in that most volatile of years, 1968. "Until roughly 1968," he claims, "most American critics seemed preoccupied by one key question: 'What does the text mean?'" When confronted with a difficult text, those American critics "shared the conviction that their most important task was to discover as exactly as possible what the text meant." They may have disagreed about the best way of finding that meaning, but they remained of one mind about the need to discover it. Some called for criticism to pay close attention to history, others to the psychology of the author, and still others to the stylistic features of the text. Yet according to Todorov, after 1968, their question, "What does the text mean?" was rendered moot in American criticism by decon-struction's response—"Nothing at all"—and pragmatism's answer—"Anything whatsoever."[40]

Although Todorov's narrative oversimplifies the complex historical record, it does point to a genuine shift in theorizing about literature over the final decades of the twentieth century. Thomas Kuhn's *The Structure of Scientific Revolutions* made prominent and popular the idea that major developments in scientific thought were paradigm shifts, that is, changes in those fundamental metaphors that shape our or-ganization of knowledge. For Kuhn, scientific revolutions were as much shifts in world pictures as they were about the empirical discov-ery of new information. Kuhn acknowledged the central role that data and observation play in scientific theorizing, but many inspired by his argument took a looser view of the question. They granted to para-digms an all but complete determining power, and in the wake of Kuhn, it soon became commonplace to argue that in scientific discov-ery and understanding, the framework was all.

Nietzsche, of course, had prepared the way for this view of science with his animated admonitions against "lying in the dust before [the] petty facts" of nature. By arguing, in effect, that all knowledge is a matter of interpretation and that all interpretations are lies we tell to get what we want, he anticipated the modern rendering of science as a form of fiction. Yet it remains an open question whether Nietzsche's critique of knowledge and his depiction of science as a fictive dis-course would have had resonance in the Western world were it not for the political and cultural upheavals of the 1960s. The moral and po-litical revolution of that decade fed the dramatic epistemological skep-ticism that seemed to undercut, at last, the dominance of science.

For many in the discipline of literature who had been long inured to its twilight struggle against science, this newfound skepticism proved liberating. It meant that literature no longer needed to carve out an isolated space and stand in lonely opposition to science. Instead, it could now consider itself the epistemological equal of science and its moral superior. It could claim that literary study, and particularly the burgeoning field of literary theory, had the power to alter our perceptions of the world and, hence, the power to transform that world.

In 1980, Richard Rorty offered a lucid and forceful brief on behalf of literature in its struggle with science. He did so in "Nineteenth-Century Idealism and Twentieth-Century Textualism," an essay in which he argues that literature has replaced philosophy as the central discipline of our day, just as philosophy had usurped the authority of science at the beginning of the modern age. The idealists of his title argued a century ago that "nothing exists but ideas," and now, he notes, "there are people who write as if there were nothing but texts." Both the idealism of the nineteenth century and the textualism of the current day "adopt an antagonistic position to natural science," and both insist that we never can compare human thought or language with a natural reality free of human associations. In Rorty's version of modern intellectual history, science is merely a vocabulary that has proved useful for the exploitation of physical reality; it has been "handy in predicting and controlling nature." Though useful as a tool, science can offer us no privileged insights into the nature of reality, no clues as to the meaning or importance of nature and human experience. The idealists and textualists agree that "scientific knowledge is not what really matters. Both insist there is a point of view other than, and somehow higher than, that of science."[41]

After centuries of having struggled with a sense of its own inferiority, art now suddenly finds itself trumping science. According to the idealists, it does so by giving us privileged access to the spiritual dimensions of our being, whereas for the textualists it is irony that makes for art's superiority, for "the ironic modernist's awareness that he is responding to texts rather than to things, puts him one up on the scientist." The scientist is naïve in thinking of his activities as episodes in the saga of a search for the truth, whereas the literary person is savvy enough to realize that all that any of us can do—whether we are scientists, poets, politicians, or preachers—is to engage in the art of "putting together ideas, or constructing new texts."[42]

Originally, of course, the division between science and the arts was meant to secure for science pride of place as the privileged form of knowledge. The Newtonian revolution had established the explanatory supremacy of the physical sciences, and Enlightenment philosophy had provided theoretical confirmation for what scientific practice had already established. Rorty explains the Enlightenment justification of science by describing the distinction that Immanuel Kant made between the determinate and the reflective judgments. The determinate judgment has the task of establishing the incontrovertible knowledge that belongs to rational reflection and scientific observation; it "ticks off instances of concepts by invoking common, public criteria" and thereby lends additional credence to what science has already discovered or affirmed. On the other hand, the reflective judgment operates "without rules, . . . searching for concepts under which to group particulars."[43] The determinate judgment provides us with our hard knowledge, whereas the reflective judgment offers us the attractive images of life that our hearts desire and our spirits crave. As knowledge, the conclusions of the determinate judgment are for Kant superior to the creations of the reflective judgment. Yet at the same time, he grants that we cannot live without the comforts that the reflective judgment labors to produce. However illusory they might be, its consolations are therapeutic and necessary.

In fact, the arts have achieved such stunning successes as forms of therapy that they have displaced science as the commanding paradigm of our day. According to Rorty, it was romanticism that first inverted the value "Kant assigned to the determinate and reflective judgment." For the romantic poets and philosophers, it was the reflective judgment—"the activity of operating without rules, of searching for concepts under which to group particulars"—that was the most important. Twentieth-century textualism has built upon the romantic revolution; it now "wants to place literature in the center," he writes, "and to treat both science and philosophy as, at best, literary genres." As genres, they are flexible and adaptable and can be changed at will or on a whim by creative genius. "It is one feature of what I shall call 'literature' that one can achieve success by introducing a quite new genre of poem or novel or critical essay without argument."[44] It is a distinguishing mark of works of art that they do not conform to pre-existing rules, but create instead the very standards by which they will be judged, the vocabulary by means of which they will be assessed. The arts are not disputatious but irenic. They seek not to convince their opponents but to consume them.

Such an irenic quality was, we have seen, one of the traits of poetry that the romantic age found most endearing. The romantics sought to define poetry not as a rhetorical art of struggle and persuasion but as an expressive activity whose main focus became "the poet's natural genius, creative imagination, and emotional spontaneity."[45] "With ro-

manticism, the old agonistic poetic had been replaced by a new doctrine of creativity," notes Walter Ong. "The poet is irenic, or at least
neutral, uncommitted, free of dialogic struggle with an audience,
since for the 'creative' romantic imagination, the poem is no longer
a riposte but a simple product, an 'object' rather than an exchange."[46]
What centuries of argument and dispute had failed to do, poetry and
nature would now accomplish simply and without contention:

> One impulse from a vernal wood
> May teach you more of man;
> Of moral evil and of good,
> Than all the sages can.[47]

The goal of the formalist poem, it might be said, is to present a
transforming alternative to reality and not to argue about the possible
terms of the change. Yet where the New Critics opposed the order in
a single work to the disorder of history, Rorty follows the lead of the
structuralists and certain poststructuralists in speaking of the power
of language to ground and found an entire world. If all knowledge
is a form of literary activity, then history itself may be reinvented in
a manner analogous to the way a novel rearranges the world or a poem
calls a new reality into being, through acts of verbal fiat.

Rorty defines romanticism as the movement that first posited that
what matters most in life is not "the propositions we believe but what
vocabulary we use." By his definition, both the idealists of the nineteenth century and the textualists of the twentieth deserve to be called
romantics. Philosophy in the nineteenth century tried to account for
everything and to give it all a home in the haven of ideas, which was,
in turn, housed in the mind of God. Almost at the very moment they
had finished building that house, however, the wrecking crew of Darwin, Marx, and Freud began to dismantle it piece by piece, until by
the end of the twentieth century there was nothing left but rubble in
the ruins. Thus, "by the end of the [nineteenth] century the word
'philosophy' had become what it remains today—merely the name,
like the words 'classics' and 'psychology,' for an academic department
where memories of youthful hope are cherished, and wistful yearning
for recapturing past glories survive."[48]

Although metaphysical idealism did not survive the nineteenth century, it did leave behind a legacy, which was "the ability of the literary culture to stand apart from science, to assert its spiritual superiority to science." Kant had unwittingly made literary culture possible by relativizing the vocabulary of science. By showing "that everything can be changed by talking in new terms," Hegel consciously abetted the growth of that culture. And in the end, according to Rorty, it was William James and Nietzsche who "gave up the notion of truth as a correspondence to reality" and thereby made the eventual triumph of literary culture inevitable. They taught us that all intellectual activity had to do with the therapeutic use of linguistic tools rather than with a search for a truth beyond words. "Instead of saying that the discovery of vocabularies could bring hidden secrets to light, they said that new ways of speaking could help us get what we want," as Rorty puts it. They were "pragmatists" who discovered the true potential of romanticism by stripping it of its epistemological anxieties and metaphysical pretensions. James, Nietzsche, and company abandoned the "notion of discovering the truth which is common to theology and science."[49]

Instead of the fixity of truth, these postromantic figures embraced the flexibility of texts. There are, in Rorty's reading of the case, "weak" textualists and "strong" ones. The weak textualists are the modernist admirers of science—such as the New Critical formalists—who did their best to "imitate science," seeking a "method of criticism" and agreement once they had "cracked the code" of language. They sought the "comforts of consensus" and found in irony and archetype unifying forces capable of attracting worshippers of the verbal icon. The Nietzschean "strong" textualists, on the other hand, have no desire to worship the word but merely wish to use it. About texts, they ask themselves the same questions "which the engineer or the physicist asks himself about a puzzling physical object: how shall I describe this in order to get it to do what I want?"[50] Having forsaken the search for truth and its "privileged vocabulary," the strong textualists think of reading and writing as means of therapy and control. They help us to bring our desires into line with reality, both by training us to imagine comforting alternatives to reality as well as by equipping us with tools to fashion what we will out of that reality.

With the Nietzschean turn that came to literary studies in the 1960s and 1970s, we come full circle with the relationship of literature to science. Having been on the defensive since the seventeenth century, literature seemed to turn the tables with the Nietzschean move. If every facet of life—from the development of adolescent self-understanding to the charting of the heavens—has become a matter of textuality, then literature will be seen to have routed science. As Rorty puts the matter in the opening sentence of one of his recent books, romanticism may be defined as the discovery of "the idea that truth was made rather than found."[51] If that is the case, the developments of the last several decades would seem, at first glance, to represent a triumph of romanticism so complete that Wordsworth, Coleridge, and company could never have imagined it. As a simple case in point, consider a partial list of recent scholarly books whose titles take the form of either "The Social Construction of X" or "Constructing X." In the past two decades, we have had books on the "Construction" of: brotherhood, danger, emotions, facts, gender, homosexual culture, illness, knowledge, nature, quarks, serial homicide, urban schooling, and vital statistics, among others.[52] This is a world in which everything appears made, and nothing remains to be found.

One can say with confidence that this is not what Coleridge and Wordsworth had in mind with their romantic revolution. They opposed science not in order to eliminate it but to supplement the story it told. Theirs was an agonistic struggle with science, one in which both parties to the dispute were defined in part by the opponent against which they struggled. To Wordsworth and Coleridge, the truth of science was one thing, the truth of poetry and religion another. Nonetheless, neither was adequate to comprehend the whole. With postmodern pragmatism's definition of literature as the art of constructing the self and fabricating the truth, and with its reduction of religion to a form of therapy, the romantic poets would undoubtedly have taken issue. To them such a triumph of literature over science would appear to be a Pyrrhic victory indeed.

Literature versus Science: A Poetic and Theological Response

To imagine a constructive response to the problems this historical narrative has examined, I turn my attention in closing to the work of four poets from the past two centuries—Emily Dickinson,

W. H. Auden, Richard Wilbur, and Czeslaw Milosz. These are four strikingly different writers who span two centuries and continents; what they share in common, in addition to remarkable verbal abilities, are a keen interest in science, a passionate commitment to religious reflection, and an abiding concern for the language and thought of the Christian traditions. Their varied works contain a wealth of resources for thinking constructively about the complex relationship among literature, science, and Christian belief.

Each of these writers has understood that the relationship of literature to science, like that of religion to science, ought to be one of appreciative tension and not dismissive hostility. Dickinson, Milosz, and Auden, in particular, consider it futile to attempt to secure religious faith, human identity, and the poetic enterprise in isolation from the realities of scientific knowledge. Dickinson, for example, had come to maturity in the decade before *The Origin of Species,* so her early scientific judgments were shaped by the eighteenth-century theological argument from design rather than the naturalistic consensus of the late nineteenth century. At the Amherst Academy, she had been the student of Edward Hitchcock, the president of Amherst College and one of the leading geologists of his day. Hitchcock sought to reconcile geology and the Christian faith by drawing analogies between passages of scripture and the processes of nature. His *Religious Lectures on Peculiar Phenomena in the Four Seasons,* for example, argued for the theological supremacy of spring, the season in which new forms come to life each year and in which the Christian church celebrates the resurrection of Jesus Christ. Nature confirms the revelation of scripture, Hitchcock held, and the message of both was one of comfort and assurance. Young Emily Dickinson learned this lesson well, as she told a friend later in life: "When Flowers annually died and I was a child, I used to read Dr Hitchcock's Book on the Flowers of North America. This comforted their Absence—assuring me they lived."[53]

In her maturity, however, Dickinson faced a starkly different natural world, and though she found it to be a disenchanting sight, she did not flinch from the message that nature brought her. She considered it fruitless, for example, to deny the power of time and decay. In a witty but sober play on the "Ode on a Grecian Urn," Dickinson takes Keats's immortal "Truth" and "Beauty" and places them in a tomb.

The one who died for truth and the one who died for beauty declare themselves as "One – / We Brethren, are":

And so, as Kinsmen, met a Night –
We talked between the Rooms –
Until the Moss had reached our lips –
And covered up – Our names –[54]

As we have seen, for Keats, Coleridge, and other romantic poets, the aesthetic realm was to be a place apart from the push and pull and relentless decay of ordinary life. A thing of beauty was to be a "joy forever," as Keats put it, and poetry was to supply the enduring sanctuary that God's providence no longer afforded. Like everything else in the created world, even truth and beauty, the supposedly unassailable realities at the heart of the aesthetic realm, are mortal. There is no disciplinary wall that can keep out this intruder death.[55]

In this poem and elsewhere Dickinson registers an intensely felt, ultimately religious response to the dramatic scientific changes in her day. When she was born in 1830, the argument from design was securely in place on a six-thousand-year-old year; by the time that she began to write poetry in earnest, Darwin had published *The Origin of Species,* and the earth had grown suddenly older. With Copernicus and Galileo, it was space that had expanded so dramatically; now in Dickinson's lifetime, with Charles Lyell and Darwin, time now seemed stretched to the point of infinity. In one of her most perfect poems, Dickinson sets the brevity of human life within the ever-expanding span of this new scientific time:

Safe in their Alabaster Chambers –
Untouched by Morning
And untouched by noon –
Sleep the meek members of the Resurrection –
Rafter of Satin – and Roof of Stone –

Grand go the Years,
In the Crescent above them –
Worlds scoop their Arcs –
And Firmaments – row –

Diadems – drop –
And Doges – surrender –
Soundless as dots,
On a Disc of Snow –[56]

Here the heavens move with a sickening slowness, death claims its human victims relentlessly, and the whole of the human drama unfolds silently against a backdrop that overwhelms and annihilates human aspirations. The poem does not deny the resurrection, but it places that doctrine within a fresh and agonizingly elaborated context. This poem, like many others in the Dickinson canon, makes little effort to shrink from the emotional and spiritual implications of new scientific discoveries. Dickinson occasionally wrote poems pressing a romantic case for the immutability of art, but more often than not her work confronted unflinchingly the spiritual consequences of new scientific knowledge.

In responding to nineteenth-century science in this manner, Dickinson made important points of connection with historic Christian orthodoxy. She did so by reasserting, in an age of sentimentalized Christian eschatology, a sobering version of an Augustinian anthropology. German theologian Helmut Thielicke writes that the human self "stands at the place where [two geometrical lines] intersect." One is the intelligible world of human relationships, and the other is "the line of the cosmos." On this latter line, the human self appears as "an infinitely insignificant quantity." In contrast to the galaxies and billion of light years of space, the human individual "is an almost unimaginable trifle."[57] To be human is to walk between heaven and earth, longing for eternity but facing mortality. "What is man that thou shouldst remember him," the Psalmist asks. "Thou hast made him little less than a god" and little more than the creatures of the earth. To the degree that they drove Emily Dickinson to apprehend humankind's precarious position within creation, nineteenth-century scientific developments brought her closer to an Augustinian understanding of the human condition. In like manner, to the extent that they expose our cosmic vulnerability, the pictures from the Hubble telescope and the exhibits at the Hayden Planetarium may encourage contemporary Christian theorists of literature to wrestle with the substance of science rather than flirt with its methods.

Like Dickinson, their forebear from the previous century, W. H. Auden and Czeslaw Milosz found themselves confronting a baffling array of scientific discoveries and technological breakthroughs. Though troubled by many of those developments, both Auden and Milosz rejected the idea of poetry as a safe haven in a disenchanted world, and they spurned the aesthetic penchant for nostalgia. In their different ways, both Auden and Milosz considered the question of ethics—"How ought I to respond to what is?"—to take precedence over the question of aesthetics—"How might I imagine a world more fair than this?"[58]

In a poem titled "The More Loving One," for example, Auden faces the silent emptiness of the astronomical heavens and expresses not a sense of regret but one of responsibility:

Looking up at the stars, I know quite well
That, for all they care, I can go to hell,
But on earth indifference is the least
We have to dread from man or beast.

How should we like it were stars to burn
With a passion for us we could not return?
If equal affection cannot be,
Let the more loving one be me.

Admirer as I think I am
Of stars that do not give a damn,
I cannot, now I see them, say
I missed one terribly all day.

Were all stars to disappear or die,
I should learn to look at an empty sky
And feel its total dark sublime,
Though this might take me a little time.[59]

In this poem Auden recasts the debate about poetry in a disenchanted world, treating it as an ethical problem rather than an aesthetic one. Given the silence of the heavens, who am I to be and what am I to do in response? If I encounter an apparent blankness on the face of the created order, do I respond in anger or despair? Or do I resolve, "If equal affection cannot be," to "Let the more loving one be me?" Auden wittily acknowledges that for all the yearning we have for a vanished enchanted world—that grand Ptolemaic universe in which the heavenly spheres never stop singing—would we genuinely want the stars to love us with an all-consuming passion? And what if the stars were to disappear entirely? Even if this came to pass, we would adjust. We could get used to a "total dark" and find it to be "sublime, / Though this might take me a little time." For coming to terms with a disenchanted universe, the resources of language and the resiliency of the human spirit were sufficient for Auden.[60]

Milosz shares Auden's chastened view of poetry and its responsibilities. He survived the Nazi occupation of Poland, witnessed the events of the Holocaust at close range in Warsaw, and then endured years of Soviet occupation after the Second World War. Marked by a particularly strong sense of historical memory and personal regret, his poetry presents a modest view of itself as a craft. At the war's close, for instance, Milosz wrote "Dedication" and addressed it to "You whom I could not save." In the poem, he offers the multitudinous nameless dead "this simple speech as I would be ashamed of another." He promises that he will not seek to enchant them: "I swear, there is in me no wizardry of words" and then asks,

What is poetry which does not save
Nations or people?
A connivance with official lies,
A song of drunkards whose throats will be cut in a moment,
Readings for sophomore girls.[61]

In calling his a conniving, carousing, and sophomoric craft, Milosz means not to imply that a more lofty view might enable poetry to achieve a more noble set of political and cultural ends. Instead, he is acknowledging the limits of language and the waywardness of the human heart.

Yet to say this about the limits of poetry is not to despair about its nature or scope. In a 1975 poem, Milosz depicts a poet walking in the hills overlooking San Francisco. Assailed by his "companion, the spirit of desolation," he confronts the specter of his own utter insignificance:

Had I died long ago nothing would have changed.
The same stars, cities, and countries
Would have been seen with other eyes.
The world and its labors would go on as they do.

In a voice that hovers between profanity and devotion, the speaker of the poem commands the spirit of desolation to leave him, "for Christ's sake." After all, God's tasks are not the poet's: "It's not up to me to judge the calling of men. / And my merits, if any, I won't know anyway."[62]

The romantic tradition had celebrated the vatic power and role of the poet. It "glorified the lyric as the highest mode of poetry" and "declared its independence from local settings" and from "the service of specific audiences and social occasions." Stripped of its civil dimensions, "the quest [of poetry] became the allegory of inner discontent," and as a result, "the price art paid for its autonomy was its desperate isolation."[63] Like Auden, Milosz inherited this vatic legacy from romanticism and the modernist tradition, and he too struggled to move beyond the limits of that tradition. For Milosz, the poet is neither prophet nor seer: "I am no more than a secretary of the invisible thing / That is dictated to me and a few others," one of his poetic speakers explains. Such "secretaries" walk the earth "without much comprehension," understanding but little of all the wonders and mysteries they encounter. Their job is a simple one, that of taking dictation, "Beginning a phrase in the middle / Or ending it with a comma." They neither know the meaning of the fragments they record nor fathom fully the greater story in which they tell and play only a small part: "And how it all looks when completed / Is not up to us to inquire, we won't read it anyway."[64]

Here and elsewhere Milosz sounds a theme that has a distinct Christian resonance. His image of the poet as a secretary who transcribes without comprehension plays off the Pauline understanding of the incomplete nature of knowledge and the eschatological dimensions of the truth. "My knowledge now is partial," St. Paul writes to the

Corinthians. "Then it will be whole, like God's knowledge of me" (1 Cor 13:13). Milosz makes a similar point at the beginning of "From the Rising of the Sun," a long poem dating from the early 1970s. But he does so in a typical manner, not with an assertion but a question: "When will that shore appear from which at last we see / How all this came to pass and for what reason?"[65] In the poetry of Milosz, an "intuition persistently recurs—or is it rather a hope?—that he will attain the full truth when either his own life ends or humanity ceases to exist."[66]

For Milosz, such lofty thoughts ironically come from a mind self-confessedly clouded and confused. Few modern poets have been as ruthlessly self-critical as he has proved to be. He writes about tragic and exalted themes but does so in a state of consistent self-deprecation and self-doubt. Others may see him as a "strong, shrewd man," Milosz explains; "I am inclined to consider myself, rather, as a tangle of reflexes, a drunken child in the fog."[67]

This image of the child surfaces frequently in Milosz's work, and in this case also a biblical analogue seems pertinent. Addressing his audience as "God's children," the writer of 1 John assures them that their final identity is assured but hidden in Christ: "What we shall be has not been disclosed, but we know that when it is disclosed, we shall be like him, because we shall see him as he is" (1 John 3:2). What children do better than anything else is to play and to observe, and these are activities that Milosz the poet understands and celebrates. Wrenching poetry from the redemptive framework of the past two centuries, he reclaims for it a more modest set of powers and duties, those of noticing, recording, and delighting. "I liked the bellows operated by rope," Milosz writes of his memory of "A Blacksmith Shop." From childhood, he has fetched the sensory memory of that shop, where he stands in the doorway and does what he, a poet, is destined to do: "I stare and stare. It seems I was called for this: / To glorify things just because they are."[68] And in "glorifying things," Milosz has sought to remember that it is the glory of those things, and not the wonder of his poetic power, that matters most:

> Desiring greatness,
> Able to recognize greatness wherever it is,
> And yet not quite, only in part, clairvoyant,

I knew what was left for smaller men like me:
A feast of brief hopes, a rally of the proud,
A tournament of hunchbacks, literature.[69]

For Milosz's younger contemporary, the American poet Richard Wilbur, humility of this kind is most certainly in order, when one considers just what this poetic "tournament of hunchbacks" can accomplish. One of the most technically accomplished poets of the last half-century, Wilbur is also a writer of significant theological substance. A meticulous observer of the natural world, he seems to share little of the spiritual anxiety that assailed so many of his poetic forebears in the modernist tradition. When an interviewer in 1977 referred to the poet William Meredith's assessment—that Wilbur "obviously believes that the universe is decent, in the lovely, derivative sense of that word"—Wilbur responded simply. "Well, yes," he affirmed. "To put it simply, I feel that the universe is full of glorious energy, that the energy tends to take pattern and shape, and that the ultimate character of things is comely and good. . . . I don't take disorder or meaninglessness to be the basic character of things."[70]

Assumptions of this kind put Wilbur at odds with the oppositional thinking that has guided the modern academic study of literature. The naturalistic picture of the world simply does not have a hold on Wilbur's poetic attention or spiritual affections. Nor has methodological naturalism insinuated its way into his thinking about the nature or purposes of poetry. He has steadfastly resisted theories of poetry that speak of its power to create order or impart meaning where neither already exists. "When you discover order and goodness in the world," he explains, "it is not something you [as a poet] are imposing —it is something which is likely really to be there, whatever crumminess and evil and disorder there may also be."[71]

Where postromantic poetics has placed a stress on creativity and invention, Wilbur focuses instead on themes of discovery and response. A poetry of response takes seriously that to which it is responding, whether it be the past, the natural world, or the suffering of others. In an extraordinary recent poem about poetry and truth, Wilbur ponders our response to that world which comes to us as a gift that we find rather than as an alternative that we make. The poem is called "Lying," and its opening lines describe a seemingly harmless untruth: "To claim, at a dead party, to have spotted a grackle, / When in fact you haven't of late, can do no harm." To say that you have seen this unremarkable bird will neither damage "your reputation for saying things of interest," nor rupture "the delicate web of human trust." Later, however, "you may enjoy a chill of severance, hearing / Above your head the shrug of unreal wings."[72]

Why do we lie, then? Wilbur provided his own answer to this question in an essay written several years after the initial publication of "Lying." In this account, he speaks winsomely of his friendship in the late 1940s with André de Bouchet, who was to become one of France's leading poets. The two became close friends while studying at Amherst and Harvard. They were, Wilbur writes, "quite besotted with poetry, writing it constantly, continually theorizing about it." Though they were both politically earnest thinkers, they found themselves strangely attracted to a theory of poetry that ignored the political dimension altogether; they longed to write a "poetry which should be pure, disrelated, autotelic." Bouchet once remarked to Wilbur that it would be an act of genuine creativity to announce that one had seen a squirrel in front of Harvard's Fogg Museum, when indeed one had seen no such thing. By doing so, "one would thus harmlessly and disinterestedly introduce into the minds of one's friends a squirrel which had never existed."[73]

This, Wilbur explains, was the source of the grackle that appears in the opening lines of "Lying." It occurred to him that a poem about "truth and poetry" could begin with a "piddling and ludicrous instance of fraudulent 'creation,' and then proceed to take its implications seriously." The idea fascinated Wilbur because of the inherent power of poetry to "charge and heighten the world in language." With its incantatory powers, language constantly leaves the poet "prone to the illusion that he can make or unmake the world, or create an alternative reality." The temptation to think this way is strong, particularly in an age in which science seems to have stripped the world of mystery and enchantment. Nonetheless, Wilbur concludes, the dream of remaking the world is just that, a dream, and "in proportion as he is touched by that illusion he [the poet] confesses a timidity about doing what he can do—interact with the given world, see and feel and order it newly."[74]

Thus, no matter how powerfully we dream of creating things out

of nothing and redeeming the world through the enchanting power
of the lie, the truth remains:

> In the strict sense, of course,
> We invent nothing, merely bearing witness
> To what each morning brings again to light:
> Gold crosses, cornices, astonishment
> Of panes, the turbine-vent which natural law
> Spins on the grill-end of the diner's roof,
> Then grass and grackles . . .
> All these things
> Are there before us; there before we look
> Or fail to look.[75]

And that fact, that "all these things / Are there before us,"

> is what galled the arch-negator, sprung
> From Hell to probe with intellectual sight
> The cells and heavens of a given world
> Which he could take as but another prison.[76]

Satan, the "arch-negator," had long been considered a heroic figure
by the romantic poets, because he spurned the limits of creation and
turned to the joyful pretense of creating by destroying. The archetypal
figure here is the Satan of Milton's *Paradise Lost,* who "is certainly
more aesthetically satisfying than Milton's God, and Hell is livelier
than Heaven."[77] Wilbur says that he knew "from the beginning" that
Satan would appear in "Lying," because "the illusory aesthetic"—
of fictional squirrels and imaginary grackles—"is ultimately Satanic."
Satan seeks to establish himself as a rival to God, "but he can make
nothing, and is capable at most of parodies, impostures, and temporary destructions."[78] The original gnostic, this arch-negator can find
in the "given world" nothing but "another prison."[79]

At the close of a century that has seen both unspeakable horrors
and extraordinary discoveries, there is great appeal in a view of literature that sees its task as that of "bearing witness / To what each
morning brings again to light." There is a winsome virtue in literature
that sees itself as a form of testimony and bears witness to all that we

find before us as well as all that we as humans have made of what we have found. At the same time, there is much to be said for an understanding of criticism that sees the critic as a reader who is, in George Steiner's phrase, a "servant to the text." Though there is "nothing occult" in this approach to reading, Steiner acknowledges that "there is in its motivation and pursuit a contract with the transcendent. In the final analysis, the reader has subscribed to a contract of implicit presence. He must 'enact as if' the letter is the vessel, however opaque, however fragmented, of the spirit."[80]

The challenge for Christian literary criticism at the start of the twenty-first century is to pay close, devoted attention to the texts it studies as well as to the larger world those texts disclose. It cannot afford to shirk the knowledge that science opens before us, nor can it ignore the sorrowful complexities of historical life. Such a literary criticism needs to take delight in playful, creative human powers, but it ought never to dismiss the distinction between the imagined and the actual. Assuming the finitude of human life, even the finitude of the vast, overwhelming cosmos, it ought nonetheless to engage in the making and interpreting of literature as a noble form of child's play. Knowing that "it's not up to [us] to judge the calling of men" and recognizing that "how it all looks when completed / Is not up to us to inquire," such a criticism can accept the limits of the art and play in the light of hope. Poetry, after all, does not have to raise the dead. That is God's responsibility.

Of all these poets, perhaps Auden put this matter best in a work he wrote not long after his return to the Anglican faith of his childhood. At the conclusion of *The Sea and the Mirror*, a long poem on Shakespeare's *The Tempest*, Auden's narrator, Caliban, tells the audience that it is only when the severity of our condition has been exposed that we can hope for deliverance. When we "at last see ourselves as we are, neither cosy nor playful, but swaying out on the ultimate wind-whipped cornice that overhangs the unabiding void," we find that "there is nothing to say." Having no speech to offer, and possessing no power to fill the void, we can only wait to hear, for the "first time in our lives," the "real Word which is our only raison d'etre." Nothing has changed for us. Our world remains the disenchanted scene of "the massacres, the whippings, the lies, the twaddle" that "are still present, more obviously than ever."[81]

The only change is that "now it is not in spite of them but with them that we are blessed by that Wholly Other Life from which we are separated by an essential emphatic gulf." Through the workings of grace, we may recognize that it is "just here, among the ruins and the bones, that we may rejoice in the perfected Work which is not ours."

> Its great coherences stand out through our secular blur in all their overwhelmingly righteous obligation; its voice speaks through our muffling banks of artificial flowers and unflinchingly delivers its authentic molar pardon; its spaces greet us with all their grand old prospect of wonder and width; the working charm is the full bloom of the unbothered state; the sounded note is the restored relation.[82]

The "restored relation" of which Auden writes here is, of course, our relationship with God. Still, the note of hope that he sounds is pertinent to our understanding of literature as well. While humbled by the terrifying history in which it has been complicit and chastened by the sobering realities that science has uncovered, a contemporary Christian understanding of literature has good reason to rejoice in its "restored relation" to these and other disciplines. As Dickinson, Milosz, Auden, and Wilbur have shown, such relationships can serve as a source for poetry of great beauty and spiritual power. And for literary criticism and theory, they may lead the way to countless exciting discoveries of the boundless power of poetry and fiction to point to wonders in this world as well as in the world to come.

Notes

1. Robert Frost, *Collected Poems, Prose and Plays,* ed. Richard Poirer and Mark Richardson (New York: Library of America), 1995, 39.
2. Terry Eagleton, *Literary Theory: An Introduction* (Minneapolis: University of Minnesota Press), 1983, 21. It is revealing to see how thoroughly spatial and ahistorical were the modernist definitions of literature. T. S. Eliot described literary tradition as though it were a timeless body rather than a living, developing form: "The historical sense involves a perception, not only of the pastness of the past, but of its presence; the historical sense compels a man to write not merely with his own generation in his bones, but with a feeling that the whole of the literature of Europe from Homer and within it

the whole of the literature of his own country has a simultaneous existence and composes a simultaneous order. This historical sense, which is a sense of the timeless as well as of the temporal and of the timeless and of the temporal altogether, is what makes a writer traditional." See T. S. Eliot, *The Sacred Wood: Essays on Poetry and Criticism* (London: Methuen, 1920), 49.

3. George Steiner offers a particularly troubling argument, for he discerns not only the corrosive force of history at work on literature; in the twentieth century, he claims, we can also witness the dangerous power of literature over human agents. "We have little proof that a tradition of literary studies in fact makes a man more humane. What is worse—a certain body of evidence points the other way. When barbarism came to twentieth century Europe, the arts faculties in more than one university offered very little moral resistance, and this is not a trivial or local accident. In a disturbing number of cases the literary imagination gave servile or ecstatic welcome to political bestiality. . . . Knowledge of Goethe, a delight in the poetry of Rilke, seemed no bar to personal and institutional sadism." Literature may not humanize us, as the Victorians had taught us to believe; in fact, "it is at least conceivable that the focusing of consciousness on a written text, which is the substance of our training and pursuit, diminishes the sharpness and readiness of our actual moral response. . . . The death in the novel may move us more potently than the death in the next room. Thus there may be a covert, betraying link between the cultivation of aesthetic response and the potential of personal inhumanity. What then are we doing when we study and teach literature?" See George Steiner, *A Reader* (New York: Oxford University Press, 1984), 61.

4. Paul Fussell, *The Great War and Modern Memory* (Oxford: Oxford University Press), 1975, 174.

5. David Hollinger, *In the American Province: Studies in the History and Historiography of Ideas* (Baltimore: Johns Hopkins University Press), 1985, 81.

6. This observation has, of course, been made countless times in the past century. Nietzsche's perspectivism is in many ways the ultimate source of such later pathbreaking works as Heidegger's *Being and Time,* Gadamer's *Truth and Method,* and *The Symbolism of Evil* by Ricoeur. In the conclusion of *The Symbolism of Evil,* Ricoeur puts the matter this way: "'The symbol gives rise to the thought.' . . . There is no philosophy without presuppositions. A meditation on symbols starts from speech that has already taken place, and in which everything has already been said in some fashion." See Paul Ricoeur, *The Symbolism of Evil,* trans. Emerson Buchanan (Boston: Beacon, 1967), 348. There certainly are vast differences between Ricoeur's self-consciously Christian presuppositionalism and Nietzsche's post-Christian perspectivism. Nonetheless, what the two views share in common is a conviction that it is not possible for thought to begin from a position of Cartesian purity and clarity.

7. Edward Rothstein, "Cut Loose in the Cosmos, Mites of Dust without a Home," *New York Times,* February 19, 2000, A17.

8. Ibid.

9. James Turner provides a clear and succinct account of how science led the way in disciplinary matters: "Disciplinary specialization grew from the physical sciences. Their much-admired practitioners, as the nineteenth century moved toward the twentieth, increasingly communicated with each other in arcane dialects, more and more mathematized or otherwise formalized, more and more inaccessible to outsiders. In this practice lay the origin of 'disciplines,' conceiving of knowledge as segmented into unconnected pieces. The humanities could—and after 1900 increasingly did—behave in disciplinary ways." See Jon H. Roberts and James Turner, *The Sacred and the Secular University* (Princeton: Princeton University Press, 2000), 97.

10. Peter Kendall, "Discoveries in Deep Space: Infinity," *Chicago Tribune,* January 21, 1996, E1.

11. Karl Barth, *Protestant Thought: From Rousseau to Ritschl,* trans. Brian Cozens (New York: Simon and Schuster), 1969, 15.

12. Ibid., 15, 16.

13. Ibid., 16.

14. Walter Ong, *Ramus, Method, and the Decay of Dialogue* (Cambridge: Harvard University Press, 1983), 318.

15. Ibid. One of the ways that Martin Heidegger defines modernity is to call it the source of the idea of the world picture. "The world picture does not change from an earlier medieval one into a modern one, but rather the fact that the world becomes picture at all is what distinguishes the essence of the modern age. For the Middle Ages, in contrast, that which is, is the *ens creatum,* that which is created by the personal Creator-God as the highest cause. Here, to be in being means to belong within a specific rank of the order of what has been created—a rank appointed from the beginning—and as thus caused, to correspond to the cause of creation *(analogia entis).* But never does the Being of that which is consist here in the fact that it is brought before man as the objective, in the fact that it is placed in the realm of man's knowing and of his having disposal, and that it is in being only in this way." See Martin Heidegger, *The Question Concerning Technology and Other Essays,* trans. William Lovitt (New York: Harper Torchbooks, 1977), 130.

16. George Steiner, *Language and Silence: Essays on Language, Literature and the Inhuman* (New York: Atheneum), 1970, 14.

17. Ibid., 16–17.

18. Hans Jonas, *The Gnostic Religion,* 2d ed. (Boston: Beacon, 1963), 322–23.

19. M. H. Abrams, *The Mirror and the Lamp: Romantic Theory and the Critical Tradition* (New York: Oxford University Press, 1953), 272.

20. Samuel Taylor Coleridge, *Biographia Literaria*, ed. James Engell and W. Jackson Bate (Princeton: Princeton University Press, 1983), 2: 12–13.

21. John Keats, *Selected Poems and Letters*, ed. Douglas Bush (Boston: Houghton Mifflin, 1959), 39.

22. Ralph Waldo Emerson, *Essays and Lectures*, ed. Joel Porte (New York: Library of America, 1983), 20.

23. Alfred Kazin, *God and the American Writer* (New York: Alfred A. Knopf, 1997), 132.

24. Gerald Graff, *Professing Literature: An Institutional History* (Chicago: University of Chicago Press, 1987), 1.

25. For the modern naturalist consensus, see, among many other studies, Reinhold Niebuhr, *The Nature and Destiny of Man*, vol. 1, *Human Nature* (New York: Scribner's, 1941), 18–22; Charles Taylor, *Sources of the Self: The Making of the Modern Identity* (Cambridge: Harvard University Press, 1989), 337–51; and Steven C. Rockefeller, *John Dewey: Religious Faith and Democratic Humanism* (New York: Columbia University Press, 1991), 453–55.

One of the most compelling accounts of the aesthetic and spiritual impact of naturalism—upon a particular kind of temperament, to be sure—is contained in Henry Adams's famous account of "The Dynamo and the Virgin": "Historians undertake to arrange sequences,—called stories, or histories,—assuming in silence a relation of cause and effect. These assumptions, hidden in the depths of dusty libraries, have been astounding, but commonly unconscious and childlike; so much so, that if any captious critic were to drag them to light, historians would probably reply, with one voice, that they had never supposed themselves required to know what they were talking about. . . . [Adams] insisted on a relation of sequence, and if he could not reach it by one method, he would try as many methods as science knew. Satisfied that sequence of men led to nothing and that the sequence of their society could lead no further, while the mere sequence of time was artificial, and the sequence of thought was chaos, he turned at last to the sequence of force; and thus it happened that, after ten years' pursuit, he found himself lying in the Gallery of Machines at the Great Exposition of 1900, with his historical neck broken by the sudden irruption of force totally new." Henry Adams, *Novels Mont St. Michel, The Education*, ed. Ernest Samuels and Jane N. Samuels (New York: Library of America, 1983), 1068–69.

26. John Dewey, *The Influence of Darwin on Philosophy and Other Essays* (Amherst, N.Y.: Prometheus Books, 1997), 1.

27. Ibid., 9.

28. Max Weber, *The Protestant Ethic and the Spirit of Capitalism*, trans. Talcott Parsons (New York: Scribner's, 1958), 221–22; Taylor, *Sources of the Self*, 186–92.

29. In nineteenth-century literature, a sense of deep loss and abandon-
ment surfaces frequently. In many instances, it is represented by the figure of
the orphan, a powerful symbol of those states. See my "Interpreting Orphans:
Hermeneutics in the Cartesian Tradition," in Roger Lundin, Anthony C.
Thiselton, and Clarence Walhout, *The Promise of Hermeneutics* (Grand Rapids,
Mich.: Wm. B. Eerdmans, 1999), 1–64.

30. Bruce Kuklick, *The Rise of American Philosophy: Cambridge, Massachusetts, 1860–1930* (New Haven: Yale University Press, 1977), xxii.

31. Ibid., 293.

32. William James, *Writings 1902–1910,* ed. Bruce Kuklick (New York:
Library of America, 1987), 601.

33. Gail McDonald, *Learning to be Modern: Pound, Eliot, and the American University* (Oxford: Clarendon Press, 1993), 76.

34. Burton Bledstein, *The Culture of Professionalism: The Middle Class and
the Development of Higher Education in America* (New York: W. W. Norton,
1976), 285.

35. Cleanth Brooks, *Modern Poetry and the Tradition* (Chapel Hill: University of North Carolina Press, 1939), 91. In defending poetry against science in this passage, Brooks makes a direct connection of poetry to religion,
and it is intriguing to see how the development of university departments
of religion followed in many respects the pattern already set by English departments. In his recent study of the history of religious studies in the university, D. G. Hart tells of a 1930 conference at which the University of Chicago chaplain, Charles W. Gilkey, sought to defend the teaching of religion.
In doing so, Gilkey sounds like Pound, Eliot, and Brooks lauding poetry:
"Though science broke 'human experience up into specialized fields' and contributed to intellectual 'narrowness,' religion, like philosophy and art, 'sweeps
the whole horizon, faces its ultimate questions, seeks its deepest meanings.'
But religion trumped philosophy and art, in Gilkey's estimation, by calling
'men with an insistent imperative back into the valley of everyday living, there
to toil and to contend for the fuller realization in human life of the values
"showed in the mount." '" D. G. Hart, *The University Gets Religion: Religious
Studies in American Higher Education* (Baltimore: Johns Hopkins University
Press, 1999), 95.

36. David Hollinger sets modernism's pursuit of pleasure, and its rejection
of the didactic and rhetorical, in useful context: "If 'modernism' was not a
'world-view' for the critics of the mid-century decades, it was certainly a set
of suspicions about human beings and their world, a collection of senses that
could be explored the most safely if kept out of propositional form, and outside the realm of prosaic argument. It was a function of the scripture of
modernism to create and maintain for the exploration of these suspicions a

privileged foundation: a base free from the obligation to specify and to take a stand upon the political, moral, and metaphysical implications of those suspicions." See Hollinger, *In the American Province*, 85.

Of the many different forms that the relationship between stark naturalism and aesthetic modernism took, one of the most intriguing emerges in the memoirs of veterans of World War I and World War II. Paul Fussell's account of his own World War II experience illustrates the close connection between stringent naturalism and aestheticism: "The boredom, misery, and pain aside, what better preparation than a war for a lifetime devoted to the study of people and the language they're enmeshed in? The intensity of my new opposition to meaninglessness and vagueness, and ultimately dissolution, was perhaps one source of my later passionate concern with 'form' in art and expression." Of the host of veterans who went on to become distinguished teachers of literature, Fussell writes, "[They were] aiming at the teaching of English literature to a generation unbrutalized by war. We all hoped, secretly, if not openly, that our efforts would help restore subtlety, civility, and decency after their wartime disappearance. This seemed almost a religious act, demanding from its devotees their complete emotional and spiritual commitment. The world was now to be saved from its folly, brutality, and coarseness of conscience by the techniques of close reading and disciplined explication." See Paul Fussell, *Doing Battle: The Making of a Skeptic* (Boston: Little, Brown, 1996), 184–85. See also Alvin Kernan, *Crossing the Line: A Bluejacket's World War II Odyssey* (Annapolis: Bluejacket Books, 1997), 146–49.

37. Keats, *Selected Poems and Letters*, 261.

38. Oscar Wilde, *The Picture of Dorian Gray*, ed. Donald L. Lawler (New York: W. W. Norton, 1988), 4.

39. Lionel Trilling, *Beyond Culture* (Oxford: Oxford University Press, 1980), 8.

40. Tzvetan Todorov, *Literature and Its Theorists: A Personal View of Twentieth-Century Criticism*, trans. Catherine Porter (Ithaca, N.Y.: Cornell University Press, 1987), 40.

41. Richard Rorty, *Consequences of Pragmatism* (Minneapolis: University of Minnesota Press, 1982), 139.

42. Ibid., 140.

43. Ibid., 142–43.

44. Ibid., 142–43, 141, 142.

45. Abrams, *Mirror and the Lamp*, 21.

46. Walter Ong, "From Rhetorical Culture to New Criticism: The Poem as a Closed Field," in *The Possibilities of Order: Cleanth Brooks and His Work*, ed. Lewis P. Simpson (Baton Rouge: Louisiana State University Press, 1976), 160–61.

47. William Wordsworth, *William Wordsworth*, ed. Stephen Gill (Oxford: Oxford University Press, 1984), 131.

48. Rorty, *Consequences,* 142, 147.

49. Ibid., 149, 150, 151.

50. Ibid., 153.

51. Richard Rorty, *Contingency, Irony, and Solidarity* (Cambridge: Cambridge University Press, 1989), 3.

52. Ian Hacking, *The Social Construction of What?* (Cambridge: Harvard University Press, 1999), 1–2.

53. Emily Dickinson, *The Letters of Emily Dickinson,* ed. Thomas Johnson and Theodora Ward (Cambridge: Belknap Press of Harvard University Press, 1958), 2: 573.

54. Emily Dickinson, *The Complete Poems of Emily Dickinson,* ed. R. W. Franklin. (Cambridge: Harvard University Press, 1999), no. 448.

55. Walter Jackson Bate's biography of Keats offers a careful, balanced reading of the famous final lines of the "Ode on a Grecian Urn," discussion of which "already fills a small book of critical essays." See Walter Jackson Bate, *John Keats* (Cambridge: Belknap Press of Harvard University Press, 1963), 516. The message of the urn does indeed promise a surrogate form of religious comfort; "aloof from the brevity and sharp claims of human life," the urn can offer the unchanging order of aesthetic form. But it, the urn, is in the end, a "cold pastoral," and its comfort is sobering and chilling indeed. Bate, *John Keats,* 518–19. Emily Dickinson's sharp reminder of the mortality of art is neatly echoed in one of C. S. Lewis's most powerful sermons, "The Weight of Glory." In embracing aesthetic and cultural activity as a means of redemption, the contemporary world seriously misplaces its trust. "There are no ordinary people. You have never talked to a mere mortal. Nations, cultures, arts, civilization— these are mortal, and their life is to ours as the life of a gnat." C. S. Lewis, *The Weight of Glory and Other Addresses* (Grand Rapids, Mich.: Wm. B. Eerdmans, 1965), 15. Lewis's point is that because of the doctrine of the resurrection of the body, it is immortals with whom we deal every day of our lives, "immortals whom we joke with, work with, marry, snub, and exploit— immortal horrors or everlasting splendors." Lewis, *Weight,* 15. That is not to say, of course, that Emily Dickinson shared the convictions of C. S. Lewis concerning the resurrection of the body. She was too uncertain in her beliefs to have that said of her. Nevertheless, in her frank acknowledgment of the radical mortality of all human efforts, she undercut a good deal of the aesthetic sentimentalism of her day.

56. Dickinson, *Complete Poems,* no. 124.

57. Helmut Thielicke, *Nihilism: Its Origin and Nature with a Christian Answer,* trans. John W. Doberstein (New York: Schocken, 1969), 106–7.

58. That is not to say that either Auden or Milosz disparaged the work of imaginative longing. Both wrote powerfully of the desire of the human

heart to find an enduring realm in which to hope and rest. In the best critical study of Milosz yet published in English, Aleksander Fiut speaks of Milosz's lifelong attempt to interpret the Book of the world: "The Book that the poet tirelessly attempts to decipher is a representation, a repetition in words of the entire universe. It is a text that discloses the method for its own reading only to the initiated. It is a prefiguration of the world that like a parchment scroll God will roll up at the end of human history. Only then will the chasm between the subject and the objective, the sign and the signified, be bridged." Aleksander Fiut, *The Eternal Moment: The Poetry of Czeslaw Milosz*, trans. Theodosia S. Robertson (Berkeley: University of California Press, 1990), 195.

59. W. H. Auden, *Collected Poems*, ed. Edward Mendelson (New York: Random House, 1976), 445.

60. Edward Mendelson has written intelligently on the religious complexity of Auden's later poetry. He correctly notes that in the years immediately after his return to the Anglican faith of his childhood, Auden focused on a Barthian and Kierkegaardian "dialectic of human freedom and absolute commandment." In his later writings, however, the human distance from the absolute grew greater, and human freedom became even more powerful and capable of doing harm. At some length, Mendelson discusses "Friday's Child," Auden's tribute to the martyred Dietrich Bonhoeffer. Auden wrote this poem under the considerable influence of Owen Barfield's recently published *Saving the Appearances*, a 1957 work that argued forcefully in favor of a "participatory" understanding of knowledge that might overcome the subject-object distinctions that modern philosophy and science had brought to the fore: "Barfield proposed a new (yet also ancient) understanding based on imaginative 'participation' between observer and observed, a participation culminating in the 'final participation' of full religious faith, when all the idols of detached observation are swept away." See Edward Mendelson, *Later Auden* (New York: Farrar, Straus and Giroux, 1990), 428.

In "Friday's Child," Auden concludes that

Since the analogies are rot
Our senses based belief upon,
We have no means of learning what
Is really going on.

The argument from design leads us nowhere, in other words, but neither is the crucifixion a sure and certain source of knowledge concerning the nature and will of God:

Meanwhile, a silence on the cross,
As dead as we shall ever be,

Speaks of some total gain or loss
And you and I are free

To guess from the insulted face
Just what Appearances He saves
By suffering in a public place
A death reserved for slaves. (*Collected Poems*, 509–10)

In his questioning of the argument from design, as well as in his uncertainties about faith, Auden was guided by the conviction that poetry and religion could not protect themselves by trying, as the New Critics and structuralists had done, to make matters of the spirit as methodically rigorous as those of science: "Any defense of the poetic and personal realms must fail, Auden believed, if it adopts the methods of its adversaries. Most modern literature and thought had done precisely that: had insisted on plainspoken realism in art and on scientific detachment in ethics, or had withdrawn into opiate symbolism in art and existential drama in ethics" (Mendelson, *Later Auden*, 429).

61. Czeslaw Milosz, *Collected Poems, 1931–1987* (New York: Ecco Press, 1988), 78.

62. Ibid., 324.

63. Edward Mendelson, *Early Auden* (Cambridge: Harvard University Press, 1983), xvi–xvii.

64. Milosz, *Collected Poems*, 325.

65. Ibid., 253.

66. Fiut, *Eternal Moment*, 194.

67. Czeslaw Milosz, *Milosz's ABC's* (New York: Farrar, Straus and Giroux, 2001), 137.

68. Czeslaw Milosz, *Provinces: Poems 1987–1991* (New York: Ecco Press, 1991), 1.

69. Milosz, *Collected Poems*, 451. For Milosz, the relationship of poetry and religious belief to science is an exceptionally complex matter. He has taken the Copernican and Darwinian revolutions to heart and speaks of them with a genuine sense of poetic and spiritual loss: "The adversaries of the theory of evolution, invoking its conflict with the Bible, appraised the danger correctly, for the imagination, once visited by the images of the evolutionary chain, is lost to certain varieties of religious belief. Copernicus' discovery deprived the Earth of its central place in the universe, but the discovery of man's animal origins was no less a shock. Not only because the very singularity of being human was brought into question, but also because the attack was aimed indirectly at the meaning of human death. Nature in its incredible prodigality, producing the billions of creatures necessary to maintain the species, is absolutely indifferent to the fate of the individual. Once integrated into Nature,

man also changes into a statistical cipher and becomes expendable. This erosion touches every human being's perception of life in terms of salvation and damnation." Czeslaw Milosz, *The Witness of Poetry* (Cambridge: Harvard University Press, 1983), 43. Milosz is much like Dickinson in that scientific knowledge pushes him to the brink of unbelief but not over it.

70. Richard Wilbur, *Conversations with Richard Wilbur*, ed. William Butts (Jackson: University Press of Mississippi, 1990), 190–91.

71. Ibid., 190.

72. Richard Wilbur, *New and Collected Poems* (New York: Harcourt Brace Jovanovich, 1988), 9.

73. Richard Wilbur, *The Catbird's Song: Prose Pieces, 1963–1995* (New York: Harcourt Brace and Company, 1997), 138.

74. Ibid., 139.

75. Wilbur, *New and Collected Poems*, 9.

76. Ibid., 10.

77. Harold Bloom, *The Visionary Company: A Reading of English Romantic Poetry*, rev. ed. (Ithaca, N.Y.: Cornell University Press, 1971), 68.

78. Wilbur, *Catbird's Song*, 140.

79. It is again Hans Jonas who has drawn the compelling connections between ancient gnosticism and modern naturalism. He deftly compares second-century Valentinian gnosticism with Heidegerrian existentialism. The former argues that "what makes us free is the knowledge of who we were, what we have become; where we were, wherein we have been thrown; whereto we speed, wherefrom we are redeemed; what is birth and what rebirth." Jonas, *Gnostic Religion*, 334. In Jonas's words, this early Gnostic formula reminds us "of Heidegger's Geworfenheit, 'having been thrown,' which to him is a fundamental character of the Dasein, of the self-experience of existence. The term, as far as I can see, is originally Gnostic. . . . Life has been thrown into the world, light into darkness, the soul into the body. It expresses the original violence done to me in making me be where I am and what I am, the passivity of my choiceless emergence into an existing world which I did not make and whose law is not mine." Jonas, *Gnostic Religion*, 334–35.

80. Steiner, *A Reader*, 95.

81. Auden, *Collected Poems*, 340.

82. Ibid.

Part II
Religious Education

3
The Dying of the Light
or the Glimmering of the Dawn?
Robert Benne

James Burtchaell, in his magisterial work, *The Dying of the Light: The Disengagement of Colleges and Universities from Their Christian Churches,* makes this biting observation about Presbyterian colleges that have jettisoned their Presbyterian heritage: "Colleges that for fifty years have refused to disclose to their patronal presbyteries how many Presbyterians they enroll are faithfully reporting to the federal government how many students of Samoan extraction they enroll."[1]

Whereas the colleges seem eager to be accountable to the government's emphasis on diversity, they are less than interested in being accountable to the church by reporting the number of the only kind of persons—Presbyterians—who could in any meaningful sense make the college a "Presbyterian" college. This phenomenon is symptomatic of what Burtchaell calls "dying of the light." The church's tradition that brought forth and shaped the college no longer has any public relevance for it. It simply does not matter anymore how many persons of that tradition teach at or attend or lead the college. This in turn means that the vision (the particular Christian intellectual tradition) and ethos (way of life) borne by persons of that tradition also fall by the wayside along with the persons. All three—the persons and the vision and ethos they carry—are no longer publicly relevant to the life of the college or university.

In his huge book Burtchaell tells the sad stories of the secularization of sixteen (out of seventeen) schools from eight religious traditions. His book is the capstone of a number of books that have documented that same secularization process. *The Secularization of the Academy* edited by George Marsden and Bradley Longfield; *Exiles from Eden* by Mark Schwehn; *The Soul of the American University: From Protestant Establishment to Established Unbelief* by George Marsden; *Faith and Knowledge: Mainline Protestantism and American Higher Education* by Douglas Sloan; and *Contending With Modernity: Catholic Higher Education in the Twentieth Century* by Philip Gleason have all contributed their part in filling out the secularization thesis. A goodly number of other studies could be listed.

By and large, I believe, the secularization thesis is accurate. The vast majority of Protestant and Catholic colleges and universities have experienced the waning relevance of their sponsoring religious heritage. Reality must be faced, if not lamented. In some church-related institutions there are no longer persons who care about a meaningful relation to their sponsoring heritage. In others there are persons who care about that relation but who find themselves isolated and powerless in their "own" institutions.

Nevertheless, there are also a significant number of Christian institutions of higher learning where the public relevance of the sponsoring heritage is robustly maintained. There are even more where there is a weaker yet meaningful connection between the school and the parent religious tradition.

In other words, the secularization thesis does not tell the whole story in at least two ways. First, there are schools that have maintained their religious identity and mission in the face of great secularization pressures, some of them rather fully while others only partially. Second, the secularization process is not inexorable. The "fully Christian" colleges are not fated to succumb to secularization nor need the partially secularized complete the process. Indeed, I will show why and how the "fully Christian" have maintained and hopefully will continue to maintain their robust Christian character. In the larger book-length project I am completing, I will also show how the partially secularized can take important steps to reconnect with their sponsoring religious heritages.

In this chapter I intend to take up two tasks: (1) summarize briefly the effects of secularization on the bulk of church-related colleges as well as the underlying factors in that secularization process, and (2) examine why and how a number of high-quality colleges and universities have maintained a strong relation to their sponsoring religious traditions.

The Darkening Trends

What is lost in the secularization process is the public relevance of the Christian religious heritage in terms of vision, ethos, and the persons who bear that ethos and vision. The qualities of a particular heritage, as well as the persons who bear them, no longer are deemed important to the educational process. Yet why should they be publicly relevant? That is the key question. Those who support or do not resist secularization of the schools might rightfully ask: Why should a religious heritage be relevant to the ongoing enterprise of higher education. Should not religion remain distinct from the educational enterprise? Are they not two different things?

Those who resist secularization respond: On the contrary, faith and learning ought to be engaged, if not integrated. Why? The reason is because of the nature of religion if it is taken seriously. Religion, as Paul Griffiths has argued in his *Religious Reading: The Place of Reading in the Practice of Religion,* is an account of reality that is comprehensive, unsurpassable, and central.[2] That account is believed and lived by persons who participate in that living tradition. As a belief system it is articulated in a vision, and as an ethos it is expressed in a way of life.

As already mentioned, a religious account taken seriously by its adherents is envisioned and lived as comprehensive, unsurpassable, and central. It is comprehensive because its vision encompasses all of reality. It provides the umbrella of meaning under which all facets of life are gathered and interpreted. It does not leave the understanding of our world to completely secular sources. Although Christianity's comprehensive account does not profess to have all the relevant data and knowledge about life in this world, it does claim to offer a paradigm in which that data and knowledge are organized, interpreted, and critiqued. In other words, if religion is taken seriously its comprehensive account must be given intellectual relevance in the central educational tasks of the college or university. Furthermore, the Christian account is unsurpassable—it cannot be replaced by a better account without giving up the Christian account itself. Its essential core of meanings and values persists through time; it claims to be the vehicle of ultimate truth.

That truth has to be taken seriously in the educational enterprise if it is truly ultimate.

Finally, Christianity's account is central—it addresses all the essential questions of life. It conveys a Christian view of the origin and destiny of the world, of nature and history, of human nature and its predicament, of human salvation, and of our conduct of life.

The preceding description makes the Christian tradition sound completely intellectual. It is far from that. Any living religious tradition bears an ethos that is lived, not only thought. The Christian religious account is embodied in a way of life. Elements in that way of life include the practices of worship, music, celebrations of holidays and seasons, hospitality, and marking of rites of passage—including death, particular ways of relating to and caring for persons, and specific habits of mind and heart. Furthermore, a religious ethos embodies a pattern of moral action. Service to others is certainly part of that pattern. For many religious traditions, the idea of vocation is central —all humans are called by God to exercise their gifts in service to others through specific kinds of roles. Important to that pattern of moral action are guidelines and rules about how we should live together—rules governing issues of integrity, marriage and sexual life, dress, demeanor, and other matters of moral life.

Those who believe in a robust notion of Christian higher education believe that, like its vision, the ethos of a specific tradition should have important effects on the way of life of the college that it sponsors. Although the college is not the church, core convictions about human flourishing and how we should live in the world should have some discernible effect on the school's life. If not, the claims of comprehensiveness, unsurpassability, and centrality are neglected or contradicted. On the contrary, those claims ought to be crucially involved in answering these questions: What are we educating our students toward? What way of life do we hold to be normative?

It should be obvious by this time that a specific religious vision and ethos cannot be publicly relevant in a college or university without persons who carry them. If a religious tradition is to make its vision and ethos effective in the school it sponsors, it needs a critical mass of persons who bear the DNA of that tradition. It needs them as board members, administrative leaders, faculty, staff, and students. It is perhaps possible for those who are not participants in the tradition to know it, respect it, and even further it, but it seems unlikely that they can embody it in a way that committed participants can.

The upshot of the many important studies I have mentioned above is that the Christian tradition as vision, ethos, and persons has gradually lost significance in the majority of colleges and universities related to the various specific traditions. That is, the claims involved in Christianity's account of life in our world have been marginalized in those schools. Using the three components of a living tradition as an organizing schema, I will briefly summarize the ways in which they have waned in importance in the great majority of church-related colleges and universities. For reasons that will become evident, however, I will take them in reverse order.

Persons

The most dramatic and noticeable feature of the vast majority of church-related colleges and universities is that fewer and fewer persons of the parent heritage occupy the student body, administration, faculty, and boards of the schools.[3] At their founding, colleges and universities were often characterized by boards, administration, and faculty unanimously from the sponsoring church. That was less the case with students because most schools needed to recruit students beyond their own denomination for economic reasons.

Nonetheless, as time and secularization have progressed, that unanimity has moved through majority then minority then token status. In many secularized colleges and universities, statistics about religious membership are assiduously avoided. Could there be any clearer evidence of the waning importance of the religious tradition's relevance? How, indeed, could one have a Lutheran school without Lutherans except by adapting the conviction that religious belief and participation are irrelevant to the life of the school?

Perhaps one could argue that as schools mature they are more interested in maintaining their identity as Christian schools, not as denominational schools. Such an argument has great merit because in many ways Christianity's religious account of the world is shared by most Christians and need not be borne solely by communicants of a particular tradition. Nevertheless, there is still the problem of the school's relation to its tradition. A church relation without the mediation of that church tradition by active links of persons within the school is not very compelling. There can be no mediation of the tradition's vision and ethos without at least a critical mass of members from that tradition. Moreover, the secularized schools witness to the loss of relevance of their sponsoring tradition by not caring for that critical mass. Certainly if they do not even keep track of how many of their communion are involved in their educational enterprise, it is highly unlikely that they will intentionally recruit board members, administrators, faculty, and students from that communion. Religious identity has become insignificant for them.

Ethos

As we asserted earlier, worship is one of the key elements of religious ethos.[4] The early church-related colleges had frequent chapel services that the whole community was required to attend. Chapels were often imposing buildings given central location. The time for the services they offered was kept clear of other distractions so that everyone could go. They were "public" chapels. For most church-related colleges and universities the story has been one of gradual retreat. First was the dispensation from required chapel. Then came an alteration of the chapel content from religious to more secular. Then there were fewer chapel periods during the week. Then chapel services occurred at "unprotected" times for those who might care to attend. Then chapel was for special events only. Then, for many schools, there were no chapel services at all.

A similar fate awaited baccalaureate services and public prayer before class or for college events. The same became true for religious organizations on campus, though, interestingly enough, as mainstream denominational organizations waned or died off, interdenominational evangelical groups such as InterVarsity have come in to fill the vacuum.

As secularization continued, the sense of being part of an ongoing communal history diminished. Fewer and fewer "remembered Joseph," and, even more sad, few cared if they did or did not. Instead of being in a continuing common enterprise characterized by many covenantal elements, members of the school saw themselves as individuals with their own academic purposes joined to the school by a more contractual calculus. Such attitudes undercut the school's sense of tradition and community. Persons with such attitudes were less likely to affirm and enjoy common worship, to see themselves as sons and daughters of a living tradition, to commit themselves to a common life with students and staff in which there were mutual affections and obligations, and, above all, to cherish the religious elements in the tradition, which more and more came to look like arbitrary demands that were bothersome, if not oppressive.

Without a substantive sense of tradition and community, secularizing colleges became less willing to assume the role of in loco parentis.[5] The loss of tradition was accompanied by a loss of confidence in its values and of the faculty's willingness to be models for a particular way of life and, above all, to enforce the rules that delimit a moral pattern of life. Part of that loss was the growing reluctance to promote a Christian sexual ethic.[6] This reluctance spilled over into matters of manners and dress. Students—and to some extent, faculty—were set free from the guiding patterns of a Christian tradition.

Meanwhile, a whole new profession—called "student affairs" or "student life"—emerged to fill the vacuum left by the departure of in loco parentis. Trained in secular graduate schools, the student affairs officials often adopted a utilitarian morality that we could call the "public health ethic." This approach tried to limit the gross effects of student behavior and bend it to more constructive ends. It did this by showing the bad effects on the students themselves precipitated by their bad behavior. One important positive element in this transition, however, was the introduction of "service" as an important value and activity of the school. Yet even in this effort the school rarely drew upon Christian rhetoric in its task of inspiring student behavior. Explicit Christian ideals became more and more out of place as secularization proceeded.

So, we have both person and ethos, two elements defining the character of a school's life and mission. In the life of Christian colleges and universities up to World War II and into the 1950s these two elements carried the bulk of the DNA of the institution. In fact, for those colleges who were unable to articulate a theological vision of what they were all about, ethos and persons carried the day. Unfortunately, because they had little definition of their identity and mission, they had few criteria to select the kind of faculty and leadership that would sustain their tradition. When the great expansion of the late 1950s and 1960s came, they simply hired on the basis of nonreligious criteria. Soon the critical mass of persons disappeared and with them the ethos they bore.

Vision

We argued above that the Christian faith as a living tradition is an account of life that is comprehensive, unsurpassable, and central. Theology gives an articulated account of that faith. It, too, aims at comprehensiveness, unsurpassability, and centrality. One would think, then, that theology would be amply employed by Christian colleges and universities to articulate their identity and mission, to stipulate the relation of revelation and reason in their particular tradition, to gather a theology department in which its members would gladly carry that vision on behalf of the school, to help construct a coherent liberal arts curriculum, to elaborate a public justification of the school's ethos, and, very important, to provide a Christian intellectual tradition with which the whole school in its many departments could engage.

Sad to say, however, it was precisely here that the vast majority of Christian colleges and universities were weakest. They either lacked the theological resources or the willingness to use them, so they most often relied on ethos and the persons who carried it. True enough, the schools often had mission statements that trumpeted their Christian character. Nonetheless, these statements were rarely theologically sophisticated, and as time went by their character was gradually diluted from specifically Christian claims to broader American ideals and then finally to general "values" talk.[7]

The dilution of Christian substance in the mission statements was symptomatic of something far more serious, the secularization of the internal intellectual life of the school. As secular disciplines developed they became more autonomous and demarcated. They claimed their own methodologies, their own discourse, and their own set of special truths. They trucked no interference from religion, which to them seemed arbitrary and irrational. In the face of this powerful development, most religious schools of the Protestant and Catholic mainstream simply retreated. Instead of proposing a robust engagement of these fields by Christian perspectives, the field was given over to them, mainly because there were few adequate Christian intellectual resources to carry that engagement off. In short, there was little theological vision of an articulate sort.

Thus, the most serious part of secularization rumbled on almost unimpeded. Fields of learning developed independent of and sometimes hostile toward the Christian account of reality. Students in Christian schools were in many cases taught perspectives that clashed with the Christian worldview. In addition, there were few willing to insist that such perspectives be scrutinized by the Christian account from which the school originally sprang. Such a challenge, of course, would have been mutual. The secular disciplines would have engaged the Christian account. Nonetheless, such a dialogue would have been just the thing for young Christian students making their way in higher education. It would have enabled them to live their lives more wholly.

There were simply not enough persons with theological sophistication to bring off such an engagement. Moreover, because the college had not defined its religious identity and mission clearly, more and more administrators, faculty, and staff were recruited with little understanding of or appreciation for such an engagement. In due time the engagement of secular and Christian accounts was interpreted by the secularizing college as unintelligible at best and subversive at worst. The heart of the college's enterprise, its intellectual activity, was liberated from religious "interference."

The vast majority of Protestant and Catholic foundations have manifested these darkening trends. Some have succumbed to them completely, others only partially, and a few strongly resisted them. It is important at this point to note, however, that secularization did not mean death for most of these schools caught in its forces. Many redefined themselves around other purposes than their traditional ones and maintained an ambivalent relation to their parent heritage. A number got involved in an array of professional and pre-professional programs, some very successfully. Quite a few became excellent liberal arts colleges of a secular sort, and a larger number became generic, moderately successful liberal arts colleges with only a trace of their tradition detectable. A sizeable number continued to adapt to market conditions for the sake of survival, which left them with little sense of internal direction. The country is dotted with the sorts of colleges that once were connected to their religious tradition but now are going it on their own, so to speak.

What were the underlying factors in this powerful secularization process? The answer to that question would itself take a chapter, if not a book. Still, let us delve into a number of factors that made the process so pervasive and powerful. There were external challenges faced by all colleges. One was the demand of a competitive educational market. Many church-related colleges had to recruit students from many religious traditions in order to survive. This is one reason for the almost unanimous flight from "sectarian" identifications. The schools dampened their specific denominational identities and then often proceeded to do the same with their Christian identities. Then they continued to worry about survival or "market share" and became cautious about putting their religious identities up front. Increasingly, as the notion of "consumer sovereignty" has strengthened, schools have become even more reluctant to promote their Christian character. They do not want to deter anyone from enrolling. Ironically, of course, this has meant that the school's identity has become more generic, and it has to struggle for other ways to become distinct. Unfortunately, other colleges and universities are in the same boat, and the struggle for students revolves around finding some competitive edge that becomes more illusive and ephemeral all the time.

A second external challenge has been even more powerful. The emergence of the great secular research universities has meant that faculty destined for church-related schools have been trained in what has been called the "Enlightenment paradigm," that is, that all trustworthy knowledge is the result of universal scientific rationality. In this view traditional religion was parochial and irrational. Knowledge and morality derived from it were not credible. Religious and religiously based moral beliefs best be kept private, isolated on Sundays and in the intimacy of the heart. They have little relevance for genuine intellectual and ethical inquiry. Sad to say, this view often permeates large numbers of faculty even in church-related colleges. Talking about the relevance of the Christian intellectual tradition makes them exceedingly nervous, even if they are Christian, because for them there is no Christian intellectual tradition that can respectably engage secular learning. The force of this attitude drove many leaders and faculties of church-related colleges into full retreat. They accepted the Enlightenment paradigm and hired people who were the best that they could get regardless of their religious convictions or viewpoints. After all, if Christianity had no credible intellectual substance, why should religious conviction be relevant in the hiring process?

Although postmodernism has broken the hegemony of the Enlightenment paradigm, it has ambiguous meanings for church-related colleges and universities. In secular schools postmodernism has sometimes opened doors for Christian perspectives. After all, if women and African Americans and gays and Marxists can speak from their perspectives, why shouldn't Christians? In Christian secularizing institutions, however, the Christian viewpoint often becomes the target of the postmodernists. Like the Enlightenment paradigm in the secular schools, the Christian worldview in the Christian school is interpreted as hegemonic, totalizing, and oppressive. It is the view that must be "de-centered."

These two external challenges have been formidable. Part of their power is that they have become internalized in the church-related colleges and universities themselves. Leadership becomes enthralled by market thinking, even when it does not have to be. Faculties become captive to the Enlightenment and postmodern viewpoints and refuse to recognize the claims of the Christian intellectual tradition. The external "enemy" becomes us. Nonetheless, the secularization of the schools is not simply the result of external forces. There were plenty of internal weaknesses to go around.

One of them, oddly enough, was the schools' accommodation to the generally Christian American culture that surrounded them. The normative culture of pre-1960s America seemed to undergird the general Christian tasks the colleges and universities assumed. America's graduate schools turned out persons who fit the needs of almost all schools, including the Christian ones. All the schools had to do was select goodly numbers from their own tradition. Persons and ethos carried the day. Although secularization of learning had been proceeding apace in the research universities for more than a generation, there still seemed to be no yawning chasm between what the Christian colleges needed and what those universities provided. Besides, many of the faculty owned only master's degrees in their fields and were generalists who easily accommodated to the vague Christian ethos of the school. Thus, one could maintain "our" college or university by virtue of the fact that a large percentage of the population of the school were our kind of people, even as the surrounding culture propped up the school with its friendly set of meanings and values. The school did not really have to define itself sharply and hire carefully. The tradition seemed to be guaranteed by inertia.

Another serious internal problem was that many Christian colleges and universities were shaped by American pietism, which put a premium on the religion of the warm heart and the internal virtue of the solid character. Pietism downplayed the intellectual dimension of the Christian life so that when the Enlightenment challenge came along, it was all too willing to give up ground in intellectual matters to secular learning.[8] If such a response was more or less atheological, a number of other theological responses were inadequate. "Two-kingdoms" or "two-spheres" theological orientations separated intellectual life from religious, implicitly capitulating to the Enlightenment idea that religion had little credible intellectual content. "First-person" theologies argued that all genuine quests for the truth were ontologically grounded in God; therefore, secular learning need not be subject to critique or dialogue from a religious point of view. Liberal theology tended to project increasingly general and vague theological affirmations, in effect giving up the real substance of the educational enterprise to the intellectual currents of the day.

Yet finally, the partial, and sometimes complete, disengagement of massive numbers of mainstream Protestant and, for that matter, Catholic colleges and universities, was a function of a waning confidence in the Christian account of reality—its comprehensiveness, unsurpassability, and centrality. That is, at bottom this matter was a crisis of faith or at least confidence in the intellectual potency of faith. Deep down, educational leaders and faculties no longer believed the faith was comprehensive, unsurpassable, and central. Other sources of inspiration and knowledge had eclipsed the Christian account. Other ways of life had replaced the Christian ethos. Secularization was a natural step "forward."

Beacons of Light

Although most church-related schools are noticeably secularized, some colleges have kept a strong relation to their sponsoring religious heritage. They have not only resisted the secularization process but also maintained and increased their quality as measured by the major norms of excellence formulated by secular agencies. In a book-length study to be completed in the near future, I will carefully examine six of them, though there are many more that could be the subjects of my inquiry. The six I will focus on are Wheaton College, Calvin College, St. Olaf College, Valparaiso University, Baylor University, and the University of Notre Dame. They have both quality and soul.

One of the reasons I have selected these six is that they are acknowledged as quality schools.[9] Even in the eyes of secular ranking agencies that could not care less about their fidelity to their religious heritage, these schools appear as excellent schools. Commitment to the public relevance of their religious heritage has clearly not harmed them.

With due regard for limitations of space, let us proceed to examine why and how these quality colleges and universities have maintained their character as Christian schools. As above, we might discuss them under the rubrics of people, ethos, and vision. Before we get to the "hows," however, let us attend to the "why."

Contrary to the colleges and universities that succumbed markedly to secularizing pressures, the ones I have selected have never lost confidence that their religious heritage as people, vision, and ethos is publicly relevant to the educational enterprise. Indeed, they hold fast to the conviction that an adequate education can be offered only by attending to the comprehensive, unsurpassable, and central character of the religious account to which they are pledged as colleges and universities of the church. So, a short answer to the "why" question is simply this: these schools have had confidence that the religious account that sponsored them was publicly relevant; they have had clarity about how it was relevant; and they have had the courage to follow through on their convictions.

Now to the "hows." Put simply, the aforementioned schools have ensured that there were enough persons in crucial positions to bear their tradition's ethos and vision and thereby to shape their school's identity and mission.

Persons

Wheaton and Calvin Colleges have taken the clearest and boldest steps toward ensuring that sufficient numbers of their tradition are in charge of the educational process at their schools. They insist that everyone on their board, administration, and faculty is a full participant in the religious heritage that sponsors the college. We could call them *orthodox believers' colleges*. In Wheaton's case, every adult member of the college's community—including the staff—must commit to the Wheaton College Statement of Faith. In addition, they commit to a Statement of Responsibility that obligates them to high behavioral standards, including the avoidance of tobacco and alcoholic beverages. Students are not required to sign the Statement of Belief, though they must commit to the Statement of Responsibility. Interestingly enough, Wheaton's robust relation to Christian tradition is not to a concrete church but rather to the evangelical tradition that is expressed in many churches. Thus, nearly 100 percent of board members, administrators, faculty, and students are evangelical Christians. Indeed, because Wheaton has been such a national beacon of evangelicalism, bright evangelical students from around the country apply to Wheaton in more than ample supply. Wheaton is deeply nourished by the evangelical stream of religious life in America.

In Calvin's case, every board member, administrator, and tenured faculty member must be a member of the Christian Reformed Church or of the small number of churches that are in confessional fellowship with it. Administrators and faculty must also pledge to send their children to private Christian schools. (Earlier the requirement was to send them to Christian Reformed Schools, but this has been somewhat relaxed.) Partly because of the large network of these Christian Reformed Schools operated by the Christian Reformed congregations, Calvin is provided an ample supply of young people from the school's sponsoring tradition. Some 54 percent of the student body are Christian Reformed young people. Increasingly, however, evangelical students who admire the Christian character and intellectual rigor of the college have been attracted to Calvin. They make up fully 46 percent of the remainder of the student body.

The other four schools, which we could designate the *Christian presence* schools, are not quite as stringent in their personnel requirements. Notre Dame, for instance, struggles with the tension of achieving topflight research university status and at the same time of remaining Catholic. Its board has a heavy predominance of Catholic members, its president is a member of its sponsoring order, the Congregation of the Holy Cross, its faculty is roughly 40 percent Catholic, and its student body is right at 85 percent Catholic. In addition, it has many mechanisms for increasing the number of Catholic persons on the faculty. It proliferates centers and institutes that deal with Catholic themes and issues. Its provost awards faculty positions in departments that can show that those positions will enhance the Catholic character of the university.

Baylor has long had a requirement that its administrators and faculty be practicing Christians or Jews, and its board is 100 percent Baptist. Its student body is nourished by the large Baptist community in Texas. Increasingly, its president and provost insist that all new faculty hires must be practicing Christians or Jews who support the engagement of faith and learning. Furthermore, 50 percent of new faculty hires are to be Baptist. For a large university of thirteen thousand, Baylor is unusually committed to achieving a critical mass of administrators and faculty from the Baptist tradition.

The Lutheran schools—St. Olaf and Valparaiso—both have strong majorities of Lutherans on their boards, their top administration is Lutheran, and they maintain around a 40 to 50 percent Lutheran faculty. St. Olaf's student body is roughly 50 percent Lutheran, whereas Valparaiso's is about 40 percent, with, however, another 25 percent being Catholic. Although new hires at St. Olaf are now scrutinized by the dean for their support of the mission of the college, a fairly large cohort of faculty was recruited in the 1980s without serious attention to that support. Valparaiso has perhaps the least systematic policy of the six schools we are examining for maintaining a critical mass from its tradition, though it draws upon a strong and public

Lutheran identity. For example, its honors college, Christ College, has a faculty led by theologically literate Lutherans and enjoys a student body that is 70 percent Lutheran.

All six colleges I have examined tend their religious identity by insisting that persons from their tradition inhabit important positions in their schools, and all are nourished by students from their respective faith communities. They are all aware that one cannot have a Christian school without a critical mass of persons from their specific religious tradition.

Ethos

We can begin our discussion of ethos by considering the role of chapel in these schools. All six of them find a crucial role for public worship in their respective lives. Wheaton, again, is perhaps the most insistent of the six. Chapel, which is given a "protected" time in a very large nave, is required three times a week for all students. The chapel holds right at twenty-four hundred, which gives room for all the students and a good contingent of faculty. Chapel is also broadcast and telecast on campus. At least one service is purely worship, and the two others feature college or guest speakers on religious themes. Calvin has well-attended but voluntary services five times a week under the direction of one of the most articulate and respected theologians of the Christian Reformed tradition. Its Friday hymn-sing is the most popular of the weekday services, and its Sunday evening student-led service draws up to nine hundred students. Both colleges have extensive networks of Bible and theological study in the dorms.

Notre Dame is well known for the religious quality of its dorm life, led by rectors for each of its twenty-seven dorms. The rectors are normally priests or nuns who reside in the dorms and organize their religious life. Attendance at one weekly mass is strongly encouraged, and about 85 percent of the students attend. The priests and nuns are also present for counseling and spiritual direction of the students. In addition, there is a large and beautiful basilica on campus that offers mass at least twice a day. Baylor is the only school among the six that does not have a centrally located, large chapel. It does have chapel twice a week, however. Students must attend a certain number of times over the course of their years at Baylor. The chapel periods are a mix of worship and lectures on many themes. Baylor also possesses a widespread network of student religious organizations and Bible study groups.

St. Olaf and Valparaiso are justly known for their high-quality chapel worship. Both have voluntary chapel services five times a week, as well as major services on Sunday. Both have chapel at "protected" times. There are also evening and early morning services. Both schools have staff ministries and employ luxuriant student gifts for choral and instrumental music. Both employ full-time organists. Student attendance varies from one hundred to three hundred for ordinary weekday services but burgeons for special events and holidays. Few faculty go to chapel daily, but many attend at least once a week. Both schools vary their worship through the week and provide at least weekly occasions for the Eucharist. Services are well planned and take place in imposing buildings. Valparaiso's Chapel of the Resurrection is unsurpassed in size and grandeur as well as in stunning art work and architecture.

A good share of the religious heritage of St. Olaf and Valparaiso is carried by extensive programs in music and the arts. St. Olaf offers majors in four areas of the fine arts. It possesses a fine arts FM station comparable to those in the great cities. Its top choir is nationally known, and its other choirs and music programs elicit participation by 40 percent of the student body. Religious teaching and devotion often accompany practice and performance in the many music programs. The directors are also religious teachers. Much the same can be said for Valparaiso. Its music programs are flourishing and draw many gifted students who want to join the enterprise. Full-scale concerts are held in its magnificent chapel. Its drama department features teams of students who put on religious dramas in local congregations in the region. Valparaiso sustains an art museum on campus as well as an influential journal of the arts and politics, the *Cresset*. In both schools, music and the arts are genuine vehicles of Christian meaning and creativity.

In five of the six schools Christian symbols and art abound. Baylor, true to its less liturgical and artistic Baptist tradition, is the odd man out. The others, however, make it clear that one is attending college or university in "Christian space."

All are committed to Christian service to the world and have extensive mechanisms for students and faculty to become involved in mission and/or service projects. Moreover, all are willing to use public Christian rhetoric to motivate and justify service to others.

Wheaton is the most vigorous in taking up in loco parentis responsibilities. Although the rather detailed Statement of Responsibility includes a number of "thou shalt nots," it contains far more injunctions to live actively and positively as Christian persons in community. Faculty are expected to be spiritual guides and exemplars. It is not unusual to see students and faculty praying together in informal circumstances. Calvin, although not quite as detailed in its expectations, is organizing its curriculum to foster not only Christian intellectual virtues in its students but also moral ones. Faculty are expected to minister to the whole person, not just the intellectual part.

As mentioned earlier, Notre Dame places much of its student formation under the direction of clergy rectors in its dorms. Baylor relies on the Baptist fervor of its student Christian groups. St. Olaf and Valparaiso utilize their worship, music, and arts for student formation as well as informal dorm groups. St. Olaf attempts to inculcate a sense of vocation or calling in all its students, mostly through faculty example. Valparaiso has a strong formation process in place in its honors college, Christ College. Nonetheless, none of these schools attempts to instill a behavioral rule as carefully or closely as either Wheaton or Calvin.

In terms of general atmosphere, Wheaton certainly exemplifies an evangelical piety. Students and faculty are straightforward in their Christian identity and convictions and are willing to challenge both other students and faculty to live with integrity. There seems to be very little rebellion or alienation among the students. They knowingly came to a Christian college and are willing and eager to abide by its ideals. Calvin emphasizes Christian intellectuality more than Wheaton and prizes that above all in its faculty and students. Its students are imbued with a strong sense that they are to be transformers of the world about them.

Notre Dame is a national symbol of Catholic higher education. It is filled with a heady dose of Catholic pride in being a first-rate academic institution, in its religious heritage, and in its aura of affluence and achievement, not least in football.

St. Olaf and Valparaiso are both struggling fairly successfully in maintaining a Lutheran humanism without the roots they once had in strong ethnic traditions. A flavor of those traditions is still present, but Lutheran atmosphere is now more likely borne by the rich mixture of Christianity, music, and the arts, especially as they converge in the chapel programs of the schools.

There are many other dimensions of Christian ethos expressed and transmitted in these schools, but the above will have to suffice. The main point made thus far is that the way of life of the sponsoring religious tradition has a recognizable effect on the day-to-day life of the college or university. These are identifiably Christian schools.

Vision

These schools employ a specific theological vision for defining and shaping their identity and mission. Contrary to their secularized or secularizing compatriots, they possess several important characteristics: the ability to articulate a clear, theologically defined vision; the confidence that that vision is adequate to the task of shaping the life of the school; and the courage to follow through in insisting that it be relevant for all the facets of the life of the school, especially its academic sphere. Interestingly enough, the recent attention given to the secularization processes that have deracinated many other church-related schools has served to sharpen their vision. They do not want to go down the path of secularization, and they realize that a primary means of staying on track is to employ a clear theological vision.

Calvin College is the most remarkable in this regard. It has perhaps been the most stable and robust beacon of theological clarity, confidence, and courage. Long before other Christian colleges had developed a theology for relating faith to learning, Calvin was exercising one that was carefully thought out. A good deal of this has to do with the insistence that all members of the ongoing academic community subscribe to the Reformed theology of the Christian Reformed Church. This unanimity of vision at a very basic level has given Calvin a firm foundation from which to proceed. Nevertheless, Calvin does not stop there. Its basic Reformed theological orientation is supplemented by a further theological/philosophical consensus, the Kuiperian view of how faith and learning should be related. Calvin subscribes to a particular kind of Reformed epistemology. The assumption behind it is that the Christian worldview constructed by the Bible and Reformed theology is indeed comprehensive, unsurpassable, and central. Secular fields of learning are scrutinized for their implicit worldview, critiqued, and in principle brought into harmony with the Christian worldview. In theory there should be no final contradiction in worldviews. Secular ones must ultimately be transformed toward the Christian.

This Calvin vision is thoroughly embedded in the college's personnel. Even the board is educated in this vision and is capable of holding administrators and faculty accountable to it. Calvin's president and provost are grounded in this vision and make sure permanent faculty hires consent to it. The mission statement of the college explicitly reflects it, as does the curriculum. The whole effort of the college is guided toward the integration of faith and learning for all its participants so that they might enter the world as whole Christians who will serve and transform the world. It is no accident that many Calvin graduates become professors in other church-related colleges and universities where they contribute strongly to the cause of Christian higher education.

Calvin's theological vision has been an example and beacon to many Christians and Christian colleges. Its theologians and philosophers have articulated the vision of integration not only for Calvin itself but also for many others who lacked such clarity, confidence, and courage.

Wheaton, though an *orthodox believer's school* like Calvin, proceeds a bit differently. Having established an evangelical statement of belief to which all permanent members of the academic community subscribe, Wheaton then manifests a number of philosophies of education. Some are of the "add on" variety in which the Christian freight of the college is transmitted by its ethos, not its academic enterprise. Recently, however, it seems that the Reformed approach exemplified so strongly at Calvin is gaining ground at Wheaton. Faith and learning are to be integrated along Reformed lines. Wheaton is clear about its mission and says so forthrightly in its mission statement. It socializes its new faculty into the Reformed faith/learning model that is increasingly dominating Wheaton's approach.

Wheaton's vision parallels that of Billy Graham, who has been so closely associated with the college. Moving over the decades from the anti-intellectual, dispensationalist, premillennialist, sectarian, and fundamentalist features that marked the early Graham, Wheaton, like Graham, has become far more appreciative of the intellectual quest, more classically Protestant, more ecumenical, and more open to biblical criticism. In other words, Wheaton has moved from fundamentalism to moderate evangelicalism. Its vision reflects this vibrant and growing part of the larger evangelical movement. Its faculty expresses the emergent evangelical confidence that evangelicals and their institutions can contribute with Christian integrity to the life of the mind.

Wheaton's theological vision is embedded deeply in its board, which is made up completely of evangelicals but at the same time reflects a number of currents within evangelicalism. The president and provost both have sophisticated theological understandings of the college's identity and mission. They can and do articulate them while they employ them in the selection of faculty. Wheaton insists that all faculty share in the vision, not just tolerate or support it.

Baylor also aspires in many ways to be an *orthodox believer's university*. As stated earlier, for many years it has required that faculty be observant Christians and Jews. Still, like many church-related institutions, there was little attention given to whether that observance had any effect on the academic life of the institution. For the most part the believing was assumed to have an effect on ethos, which was all the university expected.

The last decade, however, has witnessed a strong effort to connect the Christian intellectual tradition and secular learning. Inspired by the Reformed vision of Calvin College, the president, provost, and deans are attempting to make that vision Baylor's own. They are doing it by taking great care in recruiting faculty, by doing faith and learning seminars for new faculty, and by encouraging the integration of faith and learning in all departments of the university, including its graduate departments. At the same time, Baylor is trying to lift its quality as a research institution. Currently in the top one hundred national universities, it aspires to be in the top fifty. To the architects of Baylor's vision there seems to be no great conflict between its Christian character and excellence. They contend that ample numbers of Christian intellectuals and scholars are out there. Nevertheless, if there were a conflict between the two goals, it seems clear that the Baptist, Christian character of the university would be assigned the highest priority.

Notre Dame is intentionally a *Christian presence* university, not an *orthodox believer's.* A good deal of this orientation has to do with its Catholic theological vision of the intellectual quest. It also has to do with Notre Dame's goal of making it into the top rung of research universities. Catholic theology insists that all genuine quests for truth are legitimate and will lead in principle toward Truth itself. Participants in the quest do not have to be Catholic or even Christian. Moreover, pluralism of viewpoint is deemed helpful in the quest for truth; therefore pluralism is built into the selection of faculty. There is a Catholic confidence that reason and experience are finally not in conflict with revealed truth. Reason and experience are not viewed in the Catholic vision as completely fallen as they are in the classical Reformed view. All quests should in principle lead toward a unified and coherent Truth, for which the university as a Catholic university stands.

Such a theological vision allows the university to recruit the best available faculty in its quest to be a topflight research university. This approach, though, risks the danger of recruiting a portion of the faculty who do not care about the university's Catholic character or about the specific Catholic way of relating faith and learning. Nonetheless, this danger is counterbalanced by an administration that has many levers to pull in maintaining the Catholic character of the academic enterprise and by very large theology and philosophy departments that carry the Catholic vision of "faith seeking understanding." Furthermore, as noted earlier, the university has spawned many centers and institutes that deal with Catholic themes or embody Catholic social teachings.

Currently it is clear that the president, the provost, who is a Wheaton College graduate, and the trustees of the university have a theological vision for Notre Dame's identity and mission as a Catholic university. What is not clear is whether that vision will be embedded for the future in the faculty that actually bears the intellectual life of the university.

St. Olaf and Valparaiso share many features with regard to vision. Both have been closely related to their Lutheran heritage in terms of persons, ethos, and theological vision. Their theological visions inform mission statements in which the school's Christian grounding is forthrightly articulated. As Lutheran schools, their vision of Christian higher education is a dialectical one. Less skeptical of autonomous reason than their Reformed compatriots and perhaps more skeptical than their Catholic colleagues, they assign a tentative autonomy to reason. With fewer expectations of transforming learning by faith (Reformed) or of the converging of faith and reason (Catholic), they attempt to foster a dialogue—perhaps an uneasy one—between faith and reason. This uneasiness is illustrated by the continuous discussion that ensues at both schools about the nature of the school as a Lutheran college or university. Both are currently observing anniversaries in which this ongoing reflection is at a high pitch.

This dialectical model is a difficult one to maintain because it assumes that most members of the faculty have enough knowledge of and respect for the Christian intellectual tradition to engage in dialogue with it. Both Valparaiso and St. Olaf have had histories of strong Christian intellectuals modeling such a dialogue. Such exemplars are still present in sufficient numbers to keep the dialogue going. Nevertheless, as in the case of Notre Dame, there is less care given to selecting new faculty who will enthusiastically participate in this dialogue than that exercised by Wheaton, Calvin, and Baylor. Furthermore, like Notre Dame, programs for educating new faculty into the theological vision of the school are not as systematic as at the other three schools. Finally, like Notre Dame, there is a real risk of losing the critical mass of persons needed to carry forward the animating vision of the school.

Conclusion

In this chapter I have tried to show what the secularization process has meant for the majority of mainstream Protestant and Catholic colleges and universities. I have also tried to show that a goodly number of church-related schools—represented by the six colleges and universities I have examined and visited—have not succumbed to that process. They have kept their religious traditions publicly relevant to the life of their school in terms of persons, ethos, and vision. They are examples of a "robust" relation to their sponsoring heritages, though it is clear that they maintain their robust relation in different ways and with varying degrees of success.

Such schools exhibit the kind of character and soul that adds a rich diversity to American higher education. They contribute variety to a homogenizing educational world in which matters of substantive meaning and morality are kept at arm's length. Indeed, there are many secular reasons for rejoicing that such schools continue to thrive. Nonetheless, the main reason for such rejoicing lies elsewhere. It lies in the fact that these schools take seriously Christianity's public relevance for the whole educational enterprise. They proceed with the conviction that the Christian faith's comprehensiveness, unsurpassability, and centrality are crucial to that enterprise. That is what is truly admirable.

Notes

1. James Burtchaell, *The Dying of the Light: The Disengagement of Colleges and Universities from Their Christian Churches* (Grand Rapids, Mich.: Eerdmans, 1998), 834.

2. Paul Griffiths, *Religious Reading: The Place of Reading in the Practice of Religion* (New York: Oxford University Press, 1999), 3–13.

3. Burtchaell documents this decline in each of his chapters on seventeen different schools. For example, see his account of Gettysburg College's movement from a preponderance to a small minority of Lutherans in *Dying of the Light*, 473.

4. See Burtchaell's description of the waning of chapel and of revivals at Wake Forest in *Dying of the Light*, 369.

5. Burtchaell describes this trend at Ohio Wesleyan University in *Dying of the Light*, 320–23.

6. When I attended a parents' meeting at a Methodist college that my son was attending, an irritated parent asked what the college does when a roommate brings back a date and has him staying overnight in the dorm room, thus depriving the student of her lodging for the night. The student affairs officer avoided any proscription of premarital sex on Christian grounds, but rather said that if this happens repeatedly, the college will act because it deprives the student of her paid-for lodging.

7. A favorite strategy of Burtchaell is to trace the loss of Christian specificity and substance in the mission statements of church-related colleges and universities. See his depiction of Beloit College in this regard in *Dying of the Light*, 98–99. Each college he describes illustrates the same tendency.

8. Burtchaell is particularly critical of pietism as one factor in the secularization process. See *Dying of the Light*, 838–42.

9. Just to cite the well-known *U.S. News and World Report* rankings, Notre Dame is ranked nineteenth among national universities (with one of

the nation's best graduation rates), Baylor is seventy-first and in the top 1 percent of schools with National Merit Scholars attending), Wheaton is fiftieth among national liberal arts colleges (and eleventh in the Franklin and Marshall survey of the college origin of Ph.D.s), Calvin is eleventh among regional midwestern universities (and third among "best buys"), St. Olaf is forty-fifth among national liberal arts colleges (and thirteenth among "best buys"), and Valparaiso is fourth among midwestern universities (and fourth among "best buys").

4
A Call for Diversity

Mark U. Edwards Jr.

In the wee hours of the morning, college and university presidents are given to fretting about formidable challenges. How can we keep up with the exploding growth of human knowledge? How can we attract enough students so that we can do our job and pay the bills? How can we keep our institution affordable to all in a society in which four-fifths of families have seen either decline or stagnation in their real incomes? How can we keep revenues increasing at a rate sufficient to keep up with the rapidly escalating costs of information (books, periodicals, and electronic resources) and cutting-edge technology (computers, scientific equipment, and video and communication equipment), and the expanding need for skilled labor (professors)? How shall we cope with mounting state and federal regulation? How should we react to prospective students and their parents who see education as a commodity, are obsessed with credentials, and fixate on technical training for specific jobs? How should we educate for a society that is becoming increasingly diverse ethnically, racially, and religiously? What should we do with such diversity on campus in an age of identity politics and polarizing debate?[1] Presidents of church-related colleges or universities are bedeviled with an additional, paramount concern: How can we meet these daunting challenges while retaining the Christian calling of our institution?

For the rest of this chapter, I will focus on one example: diversity. Why is it an inescapable and consequential challenge? How might church-related colleges and universities embrace this challenge for the good of its students and the greater society?

"Vocational Schools"

To jolt drowsy audiences back into wakefulness, I sometimes announce that church colleges should be "vocational schools." I am not, of course, advocating that church-related colleges dedicate themselves to courses on welding or hairstyling. Rather, as a Lutheran Christian and heir to the Lutheran doctrine of vocation, I believe that individual Christians have callings and that, by extension, so do institutions of Christian foundation.

The Lutheran understanding of call is well known and easily summarized: all Christians have a Call, with a capital C, to be God's people, and many diverse callings, with a small c, by which they live in faith in God's promise through Christ and in service to the neighbor. Can this be applied to institutions? I believe it can and should, for church-related institutions have missions that stem from, and depend upon, individual callings. For example, Christians founded church-related colleges and universities to express, embody, and facilitate the call to serve the neighbor, in this case, through higher education. To realize individual calls, Christians often build institutions.

The notion of an institutional call draws attention to what Christians intend their institutions to accomplish. It focuses on results,[2] on how Christians seek to serve the neighbor. In what does this service to neighbor consist? First and foremost, church-related colleges and universities are called to educate students and to prepare them for life and work. If a church-related college or university fails in this, it does not matter what else it accomplishes; it has betrayed its call.

Most Christians would agree that church-related colleges and universities are also called to take seriously religion, and specifically Christianity, as an intellectual matter that bears on many other areas of intellectual inquiry. Faculty and students do not relegate religion to the private sphere, nor do they restrict religious questions to classes that explicitly have religion as a subject. Rather, at church-related colleges and universities faculty and students raise religious questions, including matters of ethics and morality, in all sorts of classes, from physics to psychology, from English to evolutionary biology. Church-related institutions of higher education are called, then, to educate their students to think deeply about their own beliefs, those of others, and their bearing on the life of the mind and life in the world. Christian graduates should understand Christian theology, ethics, and history. All graduates should be equipped and motivated to seek the common good and to view life as a call to service.

When it comes to elaborating further on the call of church-related colleges and universities, denominations part ways.

For some, a church-related education should protect students from the evils and temptations of the larger world. Christians founded colleges in rural locations to keep the students away from the allure of urban life. Today, no place is remote enough to insure insulation. Thanks to television and the Internet, the larger society pours into the college community. At St. Olaf we do not have cable in dormitory rooms because we believe that private TV watching weakens community and competes with the values of a liberal arts education. Nevertheless, students equip their rooms with TVs and VCRs anyway. Even if we could ban TV, each room is wired for the Internet, and the Internet conveys the values of our larger society at least as well as television. Soon television programs themselves will come over the digital pipes that currently bring the Internet to each student's room. Our society's unhealthy promotion of individualism, consumerism, and competition cannot be screened out; it must be dealt with educationally.

Another area of disagreement: some expect a church-related college to preach the gospel, catechize youth, and provide a collegial equivalent of congregational life. As a Lutheran Christian I consider this a confusion of missions. A church is not a college. One is called to preach, proselytize, and lead worship; the other is called to educate. Churches seek to nourish faith; colleges seek to deepen a student's understanding of faith and of many other things. Faith is a gift of the Holy Spirit, not a human work and certainly not a work of education. A college of the church may provide opportunities for the Holy Spirit to act, but it cannot take credit or blame for faith or its lack. To be sure, church-related colleges and universities should provide opportunity for worship, prayer, and Christian fellowship in their extracurricular activities. To repeat, however, their mission differs from that of a church. According to Martin Luther, when Christians confuse the work of the "kingdom of the right hand" (preaching the

Word) with that of the left (doing the work of the world), the devil is pleased.

Diversity and Higher Education

There are practical, pedagogical, and mission-related reasons why our institutions will become more diverse. To begin with, the student body of tomorrow will necessarily be more diverse. The U.S. Bureau of the Census projected that in 2030, 40 percent of the American population will be "minorities," a designation, I would add, that shrinks in cogency as their numbers grow.[3] Immigration will account for some of this change, but most will come from higher birthrates among minority groups. Both the immigrants and the large numbers of American children in these groups will need education, including higher education. College students of the twenty-first century will be not only more ethnically and racially diverse but also more religiously diverse as the world's religions take root in America.[4]

Even without these demographic shifts, there are ample pedagogical reasons why colleges and universities will want to become more ethnically, racially, and religiously diverse. As we are reminded by former university presidents William Bowen and Derek Bok, educators have long known that exposure to differences in experience, background, and perspective enriches the learning of all students.[5] This has been confirmed empirically for racial diversity. In their study of graduates of selective institutions of higher education, Bowen and Bok found that both whites and blacks believed that diversity contributed significantly to their educational experience.[6]

Students also benefit enormously from religious diversity. Although we live with the myth of an America rooted in the "Judeo-Christian tradition," the truth is that all the world religions are present here in significant numbers.[7] We live in a shrinking global community where the religions of the world must learn about, and learn to live with, each other. Colleges and universities need to help.

Finally, church-related colleges and universities were founded to serve by educating young adults. Originally, this service may have been intended primarily for the children of the founding ethnic group or religious denomination. Nonetheless, these colleges and universities soon broadened their sense of mission to include others in the larger society, and that call to mission persists. Greater diversity serves the common good.

Diversity, Religious Identity, and Secularization

In parts of the country, especially on the coasts, colleges and universities have become substantially more diverse. This change has been pedagogically fruitful and has benefited society. It has also attenuated the religious character of the education offered. Church-related colleges and universities have become more secular.

Increased diversity accounts for only part of this secular trend. George Marsden, Douglas Sloan, Merrimon Cuninggim, David O'Brien, and James Tunstead Burtchaell, among others, have written about these developments.[8] I have reviewed their works elsewhere.[9] Marsden offers the most magisterial analysis. In his *The Soul of the American University: From Protestant Establishment to Established Non-belief,* he explores the way in which many liberal Christians in the late nineteenth and early twentieth centuries identified Christian ideals with Western civilization and thereby ironically abetted a secularity that Marsden deems hostile to Christianity. Sloan in his *Faith and Knowledge: Mainline Protestantism and American Higher Education* emphasizes the failure of Christian intellectuals and academics to find a convincing way to relate faith to knowledge, especially scientific knowledge. O'Brien in *From the Heart of the American Church: Catholic Higher Education and American Culture* suggests that Catholics, by coming later to the challenge of modern secularity, may be able to learn from the Protestant example and, in a time more hospitable to religion and less enamored of the absolutist claims of Enlightenment reason, may take a different course that preserves their Catholic identity. Although Cuninggim and Burtchaell offer many penetrating observations, Cuninggim is too sanguine about trends in church-related higher education and Burtchaell too cynically pessimistic. Burtchaell is remarkably condescending and unforgiving toward academics and administrators who sought, not always successfully to be sure, to guide their church-related colleges and churches through the white water of twentieth-century secularity and its concomitant confidence in scientific and Enlightenment reason. Several of these accounts, and especially Burtchell's, suffer from a nostalgic view of church-related higher education and an unrealistic appreciation of the changes in the larger society that have buffeted colleges, universities, and the church itself.[10]

As the historian Mark Schwehn has aptly observed, "The 'secularization of the academy' hypothesis is by now not so much mistaken as it is unfruitful."[11] Nonetheless, Christians need to be concerned lest developments go too far. To explain why, we must first consider why some people, including people of faith, question whether colleges and universities should retain a sense of religious calling.

Religion and Higher Education: The "Dark Side"

The social effects of religion have always been mixed. Critics can point to the violence and division engendered throughout Western history by religion. They can call attention to ethnic tribalism (such as we have seen recently in the Balkans), religious intolerance (which was strong in America just a generation or so ago), and Christian practices and beliefs that hindered the search for truth (for example, regarding evolution). For much of the early history of American higher education, Catholics and Jews were excluded from the leading academic institutions, or their numbers were limited by quota. Not surprisingly then, some contend that in our increasingly diverse world, higher education must remain above the fray, relying on procedural values of reason, scientific experiment, and "secular" discourse to allow otherwise exclusive and potentially opposed groups to talk to each other. The academy becomes in their view an important part of the "public square" where secular rationality allows productive, socially beneficial discourse across ethnic, religious, and ideological boundaries.

Such views dominate much of academe. In their extreme form they rule out all claims of fact or moral principle that arise from religious conviction. In a more moderate form, they allow religious ideas and moral claims in academic discourse if these ideas and claims can be justified in secular (rational) terms.

Although the proposed remedy is too extreme, the concerns are justified. Historically, strong communities often foster divisions between insiders and outsiders. They commonly mistreat minorities and nonconformists. On what they see as life-or-death matters, they are inclined to stigmatize those with whom they disagree as not merely mistaken but evil.[12] Student religious groups can exhibit all these tendencies. So can church-related colleges and universities. Religious conviction should not be banned, but its baneful aspects need to be acknowledged and curbed.

The Cost of Secularity

Given this "dark side" of religious community, why should not Christians who wish to be good citizens in a pluralistic society simply embrace the secular model of higher education? To exclude religion from higher education, to capitulate to the insistence that faith belongs in the private sphere, is to treat faith, as the law professor Stephen Carter has put it, like a hobby, that is, as an interesting private inclination that has no, or should have no, relevance when entering the academy or the public square.[13] Such exclusion forces believers either to deny much of the grounding of their moral and intellectual being or to contort their beliefs into an alien form that just happens to fit the "rules" of reason and evidence accepted by the secular academy. These rules, although extraordinarily productive in scientific research, represent only one way of human knowing. Believers must insist that their beliefs, although based in part on different notions of reason and evidence, have a rightful place in intellectual and academic discourse. After all, other convictions that also fail the narrow test of scientific rationality—for example, Marxism, feminism, and laissez-faire economics—are nonetheless considered respectable and are widely advocated within the academy. Religiously based convictions should not be the sole metaphysical claims excluded from academe.

There are also practical considerations. Christians must learn to survive within a pluralistic environment. To survive, much less to flourish, Christians must maintain their distinctive (although among themselves varied) beliefs while living peacefully with difference. Christians need to protect their identity (or identities) against secularism, consumerism, and the effects of the mass media. Becoming socially homogenous by accepting the "secular" rules of the academy is no solution, or at least no solution if churches wish to perpetuate themselves. There is no future in denying the intellectual side of religion or reducing faith to matters of private sentiment. If Christians allow religion to be excluded from the academy, they will be abandoning a precious part of their heritage.

How It Might Be Done: Some Modest Suggestions

As we move into the twenty-first century, church-related colleges and universities will increasingly be staffed and attended by people who differ ethnically, racially, and religiously. In this more diverse world it will be neither possible nor pedagogically desirable to expect staff and students to abandon that which makes them different and blend into the (increasingly shrinking) majority culture. To be fair and accommodating, colleges and universities must become more explicitly than ever communities (or associations) that include and embrace different subcommunities.[14]

College staff and students will need to feel at home in multiple, overlapping groups. They will likely identify most strongly with their family and with their ethnic, racial, and religious communities. Still, other groups will also impart meaning and identity to their lives, such as house or dorm mates, athletic teams, students in a particular major, music ensembles, volunteer organizations, and the like. Finally, they need to identify with the college or university itself, including the institution's commitments to the life of the mind and to the serious consideration of religious belief.

Multiple Overlapping Associations and Identities

To understand how this adjustment might work, we must recognize, with Martin Marty, who cites in support Ernst Gellner, Alfred Schutz, and Michael Oakeshott, that human beings belong to various groups and draw identity in varying degrees from all of them.[15] At one level these various identities may seem contradictory, but they are united in personhood and shifting focus of the individual involved.[16]

Consider, for example, a student who is a middle-class African American from the suburbs, a Catholic in a Lutheran college, a basketball player and choir member, a social work major, and a volunteer for Big Brothers and Big Sisters. She will identify with some groups more intensely than others. For example, she may identify intensely with other African American women. If circumstances force her to choose between loyalty to her African American "sisters" and support for a group of African American men regarding, say, tensions in dating relationships, she would probably choose to support her sisters. In most cases, however, she should experience little tension between her identification with fellow blacks and her identification with other black women. Although Catholic, she may feel little tension with the Lutheran identity of her college until, for example, she encounters a Lutheran woman pastor or debates abortion with a group of Lutheran African American women in her residence hall.

Her other associations may also be defining for her self-understanding but less central. For example, her competition as a basketball player may both sustain her sense of being an athletic person and also provide an opportunity for conviviality with fellow athletes. Her work as a volunteer for Big Brothers and Big Sisters may contribute to her growing sense of vocation as a social worker, the major that she is pursuing. In a dispute with the college administration about reductions in the social work program, she may feel intense loyalty to her fellow social work students, but when socializing, she may spend more time with her basketball teammates. Finally, she may feel distant from, and even a bit dismissive toward, the traditions and values that are regularly celebrated in her college. Yet when visiting home she may nonetheless speak proudly of her college, enjoy getting together with alums from her school, use school connections to find a summer job, and passionately urge her younger sister to apply to "her" college rather than to the local university.

Such multiple alliances and interwoven strands of identity make her who she is. Some are more intense and central; others are more distant but still defining. She is not a walking contradiction; rather, she is a human being who is living in a complexly overlapping world. She is like all the students we educate.

Realizing the Mission

What qualities or characteristics might a church-related college want this student to possess upon graduation? Here are some possibilities, drawing on our earlier discussion of calling. Above all, the college should want her to be well educated and prepared for life and work. If a college fails at this, it has failed as an educational institution, whether church related or not. A church-related college, however, should also want her to be well equipped to think rigorously about her religious and moral beliefs. She should recognize that a religious perspective is intellectually legitimate, whatever the larger, secular society might claim. The college should probably want her to see life and work in terms of a religious calling. The college should expect her to consider the common good and not simply individual interest when taking a stand. The college should hope that she understood and valued community; that she was prepared to volunteer in activities that benefited the larger society; and that she understood the importance of cooperation, civil discourse, and speaking up for the disadvantaged. Finally, if the Holy Spirit chooses to use the college as a means to confirm or strengthen her faith, the college should be delighted. Still, the college should not kid itself that it, somehow, was responsible for this result. This list is not exhaustive, but it responds, I think, to the overarching mission of most church-related institutions of higher education.

How could a church-related college or university achieve such educational results? How does it do so now? In the rest of this chapter I want to suggest some possibilities. More important, I want to urge that church-related institutions of higher education think more self-consciously and deliberately about the goals they wish to achieve and the means to their achievement.

Christian Content

Is there an explicitly (and singular) Christian position on any intellectual or academic matter? In addition, even if it is decided that there *is* a Christian position, why should a Jewish teacher, a Hindu student, or Moslem staff member accept it? Furthermore, does a "Christian" position on any academic matter admit of assessment in terms acceptable throughout academe? What is a professor who has imbibed deeply the values of "academic freedom" and "objective scientific research" at research universities supposed to do with claims that do not follow the generally accepted rules of evidence and proof?

These are hoary questions of church-related higher education. George Marsden in his *The Outrageous Idea of Christian Scholarship* superbly elucidates the issues and refutes the critics who think that religious perspectives have no place in academic discourse. If a Marxist, a feminist, a dogmatic materialist, or a supply-side economist may import metaphysical assumptions into his or her academic work, there is no reason today, with Christianity's hegemonic control over higher education a thing blessedly of the past, that Christians should not be allowed to do the same. Moslems, Jains, Hindus, Jews, Buddhists, and adherents to other religions should also be allowed to add their perspective to the hurly-burly of academic discourse and debate.

Marsden and I do disagree about some epistemological implications of the Christian faith. I have written on this elsewhere and wish here to offer only an observation or two.[17] Marsden has argued that the Christian doctrines of creation and incarnation may have important epistemological implications for how human beings may know and understand the world. He may be right. I, in turn, operating from the Lutheran tradition that tends toward greater "epistemological humility," have suggested that reason, experience, and experiment—means of knowing that Christians share with the secular academy—may be the best, or even the only, tools that human beings have to understand the world. I agree with Marsden that Christian commitment may incline the scholar to certain questions and explain his or her preference for certain answers. I strongly concur that Christian conviction may prevent Christian scholars from accepting, for example, the metaphysical assertion of naturalism that denies "that there exists or could exist any entities or events which lie, in principle, beyond the scope of scientific explanation."[18] Nevertheless, it remains possible for a Christian scholar, I assert, to work within a framework that explains the working of the world solely according to natural causes. To repeat, Marsden may be right about epistemology and Christian belief, but I submit that only reason and experience can show that he is. The real point I want to make is that "epistemological humility," whether Lutheran or not, allows and invites academics of other religious or philosophical persuasions to enter the debate on equal terms. This may be a beneficial accommodation to diversity within church-related institutions of higher education.

This disagreement about "Christian epistemology" illustrates a healthy diversity within the Christian community itself. Christians disagree with Christians on all sorts of important issues. As the sociologist Robert Wuthnow has shown, diversity often divides Christians within denominations as much or more than it divides Christians of different denominations.[19] Although Christian scholars may fruitfully continue to debate whether Christian conviction should influence the content of scholarship, they need to recognize that much of what constitutes Christian education resides not in class content but in educational settings, peer interaction, and mentoring and role models.

Interdependence, Cooperation, and Cocurricular Activities

As I have argued earlier, colleges and universities are made up of multiple overlapping groups that have varying claims on the identity and involvement of students. The challenge for the school is to affirm the worth of ethnic, racial, and religious distinctiveness while finding means to instill in students an understanding of interdependence and of the value of cooperation and service to others. Much could be, and has been, written about ways to affirm identity and difference, from curricular programs, such as multicultural studies, to theme houses. I want here to offer a few brief observations about collegiate activities that bring students together from different ethnic, racial, and religious groups and subtly teach and embody the fact of interdependence and the importance of being mindful of the needs of others.

Consider the making of music by student ensembles. At many church-related colleges and universities there is a tradition of student music ensembles (many of which perform sacred music and thereby reinforce the Christian identity of the institution). These ensembles give students the experience literally of harmonious cooperation. Individual performers subordinate their talents to a common good. Beautiful music is the goal; cooperation without competition is the means. There are no losers, only winners: both the performers and the audience. The whole is larger than the sum of its parts. The students experience the power of harmonious cooperation at such a deep level that it can color their approach to life in general. The experience is deeply educational, although it does not take place in a classroom and may not feel like learning to the students. Yet the lessons, tacit as they may be, can stick.[20] A similar analysis could be applied to athletic teams, although the college must be intentional in devising ways of countering the unhealthy aspects of competition that our larger, secular society encourages and rewards.

Athletic teams and music ensembles are constituted largely on the basis of talent. Athletic or musical prowess is not, as far as I know, in any significant way related to opinions about religion or morality. Such "talent groups" comprise various subgroups that may differ ethnically, racially, religiously, or in many other ways. Yet the talent group unites the subgroups in the pursuit of an overarching goal: to compete on the athletic field or to produce beautiful music. Socially, the baseball team or the choir may include diverse subgroups, but all come together to perform, and in the performance they learn about, and learn to respect, each other. At the very least they experience interdependence. A baseball team cannot succeed without, say, a shortstop. The choir cannot do without the altos. Pluralism can be maintained while still acknowledging interdependence and unity in larger goals. To the degree that this "small scale" lesson is learned and generalized to the larger society—and such generalization is likely to be fitful and complicated—then the college experience is preparing students for harmonious life in a diverse world.

Role Models and the Doctrine of Calling

Role models can exert remarkable influence. Faculty or staff members who are self-consciously living out their baptism in love of God and service to the neighbor through education can have a striking influence on young people who are seeking models for the life that they would like to lead. If the faculty or staff members are willing to talk about their sense of Christian calling, so much the better.

I spoke earlier of the Lutheran understanding of calling. Although Lutherans like to lay special claim to this doctrine, it is, in fact, an understanding of Christian life and service that can be embraced across the denominational and theological spectrum. It is a way of looking at things that can, arguably, be embraced also by Jews or Hindus or Moslems or people of other religious traditions who believe that God is honored when human beings serve one another. Women and men who have no professed religious belief can feel a call to service on other grounds. Church-related institutions of higher education should promote such awareness whenever students are mentored about career choices and future work. Faculty and staff should be encouraged to look at their own work in the college in these vocational terms.

Role models for students are not limited to faculty and staff. Many senior students exert a profound peer influence on first-year and sophomore students. I suspect that the volunteer tradition, the commitment to service, the participation in Bible study and prayer groups, and other commitments and religious activities that characterize most church-related institutions of higher education are mediated from one student generation to the next more by the students themselves than by anything that the faculty, staff, or administration do. Perhaps the best thing that an institution can do is be sure that there is space, encouragement, and funding available to allow the students to "do their own thing" in support of the college's mission.[21]

Overarching Stories

"Talent groups," role models, peer influence, and even a sense of calling can be found in all institutions of higher education. Where, then, does Christian distinctiveness enter in? My answer is, the stories we tell to make sense of who we are and what we do.

Our identity, both to ourselves and to others, often takes the form of a story. When asked who we are, we may first reply with a name — our story's title, as it were. If pressed for more than a name, however, we narrate some part of our life. Our story may be severely abbreviated: we offer up our occupation or, if a student, our major. Such a reply is at best an implicit narrative that depends on the hearer to fill out on the basis of his or her own understanding of the likely story behind that occupation or major. Nonetheless, in our own sense of self and in any more extensive sharing with others of who we are, we tell the story of our life. Our story is always selective; we touch on the "plot changes," the "turning points," the crucial events or revelatory experiences that, to our minds, made us who we are. However brief or extensive, we are our stories.

Communities also find their identity in stories. This is true for church-related colleges and universities and also for the larger Christian community. The defining story of the Christian community is of course the story of Jesus. As is the case for all identity-constructing stories, it has its crucial events or "turning points" that establish Jesus' identity and, by extension, the identity of those people who see Jesus' story as a defining part of their own story.[22]

Stories or narratives may also be used to bind together disparate groups, to braid together diverse strands that constitute today's and, even more so, tomorrow's church-related institutions of higher education. Let me illustrate this point with reference to my college, St. Olaf. The details would change, but the observations should apply to other church-related colleges and universities that are mindful of their constituting, mission-conveying stories.

For Oles, as St. Olaf students are called, the stories come chiefly out of a Norwegian Lutheran past. This Norwegian heritage is celebrated solemnly at Founders Day, November 6, in the names of college buildings, in unusual curricular offerings such as Norwegian and Scandinavian history, and in the story of a group of pioneers who founded a college to help Norwegian immigrants become Americans. Yet it also is recalled with humor and playfulness with such things as the Ole "fight polka," "Um, Ya Ya," and with jokes about lutefisk and lefse. This Norwegian heritage, visibly present in the buildings and rehearsed in the festivals and gatherings of the academic year, gives the college community a sense of grounding in times past and reminds it of those who planned, labored, and sacrificed so that faculty might teach and students learn.

Other church-related colleges will enjoy different ethnic stories and different sets of traditions and practices that can convey the sense of overarching identity to the groups and subgroups that make up the community. Nevertheless, all church-related colleges and universities share the story that provides the core of their identity, and that is the Christian story, in its various denominational varieties. This story can be preached from the chapel pulpit. It can be conveyed by legacy students, who speak of siblings, parents, aunts, uncles, and grandparents who attended the college and what their education had meant to them. It can be shared in informal Bible studies, in personal testimony by students and staff, and in inscriptions on walls. It can be told at matriculation ceremonies and at graduation. It needs to be present but not oppressive, informing but not conforming. If done rightly, even the members of the community who are not members of the founding denomination or not even professed Christians will understand that the religious heritage of their institution and its regular enactment in worship and celebration is a constituting aspect of the school. Whether these colleagues react with approval or disapproval, whether they remain aloof or become engaged as skeptical participants, their own stories will be shaped by community memory and will in turn contribute to the evolving story of the institution. Moreover, if I may be permitted a theological assertion, we need to remember that the Christian story is a community-constituting story; we Christians believe that through the Holy Spirit, our story enacts what it narrates.

Notes

1. See Deborah Tannen, *The Argument Culture: Moving from Debate to Dialogue* (New York: Random House, 1998).

2. Much of the literature of church-related institutions of higher education focuses, unhelpfully to my mind, on inputs, which are expressed in lengthy lists of "marks" according to which a "true" college of the church should be measured. See the literature cited in note 9, especially the works by Cuninggim and Burtchaell.

3. U.S. Bureau of the Census 1997, table 19, page 19, cited in William G. Bowen and Derek Bok, *The Shape of the River: Long-Term Consequences of Considering Race in College and University Admissions* (Princeton, N.J.: Princeton University Press, 1998), 12 n. 51.

4. See Diane L. Eck, *Encountering God: A Spiritual Journey from Bozeman to Banaras* (Boston: Beacon Press, 1994), and Diane L. Eck, *On Common Ground: World Religions in America,* CD-ROM ed. (New York: Columbia University Press, 1997).

5. "Originally, diversity was thought of mainly in terms of differences in ideas or points of view, but these were rarely seen as disembodied abstractions. Direct association with dissimilar individuals was deemed essential to learning. The dimensions of diversity subsequently expanded to include geography, religion, nation of birth, upbringing, wealth, gender, and race." Bowen and Bok, *Shape of the River,* 218–19.

6. "The ultimate test of diversity as an educational policy, therefore, is not whether episodes of friction and misunderstanding occur, but what students think of their total experience after traveling the sometimes bumpy road toward greater tolerance and understanding. On this score, the findings discussed in this chapter speak for themselves. Of the many thousands of former

matriculants who responded to our survey, the vast majority believe that going to college with a diverse body of fellow students made a valuable contribution to their education and personal development. There is overwhelming support for the proposition that the progress made over the last thirty years in achieving greater diversity is to be prized, not devalued." Bowen and Bok, *Shape of the River*, 255.

7. See Diana Eck's Pluralism Project home page (www.fas.harvard.edu/pluralism).

8. George M. Marsden, *The Soul of the American University: From Protestant Establishment to Established Nonbelief* (New York: Oxford University Press, 1994); George M. Marsden, *The Outrageous Idea of Christian Scholarship* (New York: Oxford University Press, 1997); Douglas Sloan, *Faith and Knowledge: Mainline Protestantism and American Higher Education* (Louisville, Ky.: Westminster John Knox Press, 1994); Merrimon Cuninggim, *Uneasy Partners: The College and the Church* (Nashville: Abingdon Press, 1994); David J. O'Brien, *From the Heart of the American Church: Catholic Higher Education and American Culture* (Mary Knoll, N.Y.: Orbis Books, 1994); James Tunstead Burtchaell, *The Dying of the Light: The Disengagement of Colleges and Universities from Their Christian Churches* (Grand Rapids, Mich.: Eerdmans, 1998).

9. Mark U. Edwards Jr., "The College and the Church: Review Essay," *Pro Ecclesia* 7 (winter 1998): 104–9, and Mark U. Edwards Jr., "Christian Colleges: A Dying of the Light or a New Refraction?" *Christian Century*, April 21–28, 1999, 459–63.

10. See Edwards, "Christian Colleges."

11. Mark R. Schwehn, "A Christian University: Defining the Difference," *First Things* 93 (May 1999): 25–31.

12. I developed this argument at length for the case of Martin Luther in Mark U. Edwards Jr., *Luther and the False Brethren* (Stanford, Calif.: Stanford University Press, 1975). The dynamic remains potent to this day.

13. Stephen L. Carter, *The Culture of Disbelief: How American Law and Politics Trivialize Religious Devotion* (New York: Basic Books, 1993).

14. Martin E. Marty, *The One and the Many: America's Struggle for the Common Good* (Cambridge, Mass.: Harvard University Press, 1997).

15. Ibid., 149ff.

16. Ibid., 154. Marty offers three examples, and here is number three: "A third person may be a lesbian activist who, for the sake of focussing her energies, will not be in coalition with men, straight or gay—but in another mode and toward a different end may be an ardent Catholic, restless but still 'there' in a patriarchal and hierarchical men's world. Such people are not being self-contradictory. They are addressing different situations and companies

out of the center of a relatively coherent personhood. None grasps experience whole, but always through a preoccupying mode, with a focused intent."

17. See Edwards, "Christian Colleges." See also Mark U. Edwards Jr., "Called to Serve," in *Called to Serve: St. Olaf and Church-Related Higher Education,* ed. Pamela Schwandt, L. DeAne Lagerquist, and Gary DeKrey (Northfield, Minn.: St. Olaf College, 1999).

18. *The Encyclopedia of Philosophy* (New York: Macmillan, 1967) 5: 448.

19. Robert Wuthnow, *The Struggle for America's Soul: Evangelicals, Liberals, and Secularism* (Grand Rapids, Mich.: Eerdmans 1989); Robert Wuthnow, *The Restructuring of American Religion* (Princeton, N.J.: Princeton University Press, 1988); Robert Wuthnow, *Christianity in the Twenty-first Century: Reflections on the Challenges Ahead* (New York: Oxford University Press, 1993).

20. Unfortunately our students' experience of making music together is becoming increasingly attenuated for most of the rest of us. Where we once heard music only if we produced it ourselves, or at least watched and heard real human beings make music, now through the "miracle" of electronics, our stereo systems or, more isolating yet, our Walkmans, we can experience wonderful music divorced from any immediate human cooperation. At the reflexive level of experience, many of us no longer learn from music the truth of its production: that music asks people to subordinate narrow self-interest to achieve a common goal, that music depends on human cooperation and in that cooperation something is produced that is greater than the simple sum of its parts, and that music with its harmony is at least one appropriate metaphor for the functioning of a healthy society.

21. "Peer influence" probably plays a much larger role in the mission of church-related colleges and universities than most of us are aware. From college choice to college culture to career choice after college, peers lead the way, encourage or discourage, and set the tone. We need to understand better how this works and, where possible, align this powerful source of influence with the college's Christian mission.

22. This is a significant insight of "narrative theology." See, for example, Stanley Hauerwas and L. Gregory Jones, eds., *Why Narrative? Readings in Narrative Theology* (Grand Rapids, Mich.: Eerdmans, 1989).

5

Public Religion and Higher Education: The Role of the Faculty in Maintaining the Catholic Identity of Catholic Colleges and Universities

Charles Zech

In November 1999, the U.S. National Conference of Catholic Bishops (NCCB) approved a document implementing *Ex corde Ecclesiae,* Pope John Paul II's 1990 apostolic statement on Roman Catholic higher education. This was the culmination of more than a half-century of debate over the relationship between Catholic institutions of higher learning and the Catholic Church hierarchy. In 1949, Pope Pius XII initiated discussions that ultimately led to the formation of the International Federation of Catholic Universities. After the Second Vatican Council, Catholic colleges and universities used the federation to dialogue on their mission in light of both Vatican II and the sweeping societal changes of the 1960s.

In a 1967 meeting held at Land O'Lakes, Wisconsin, about two dozen Catholic educators, bishops, and religious leaders met to discuss the role of Catholic colleges and universities. The primary document emerging from that meeting declared that "the Catholic University must have true autonomy and academic freedom in the face of authority of whatever kind, lay or clerical, external to the academic community." It also declared that a Catholic university must be a community "in which Catholicism is perceptibly present and effectively operative."[1]

The Land O'Lakes statement was a major milestone in the history of Catholic higher education in the United States. It firmly put Catholic colleges and universities on record as committing themselves to the highest standards of academic excellence. It was followed by a flurry of changes, including the conversion of the membership of the boards of trustees of most Catholic colleges from consisting of only vowed religious to predominately lay control. Since that time, Catholic colleges and universities have been wrestling with the dichotomy between their need to maintain institutional autonomy and academic freedom and their relationship with the wider church, including the bishops.

Acutely aware that many secular U.S. universities had once been affiliated with various Protestant denominations, and observing the same sort of drift away from their Catholic roots among some European universities, the Vatican began discussions with various experts in the late 1980s. The consensus from these discussions was that relatively few regulations were needed, that they should be general in nature, and that their implementation should fall on the local bishops' conferences. Documents emerging from these discussions were instrumental in shaping John Paul's thinking as he drafted *Ex corde*.

Following the release of the statement in 1990, the U.S. bishops began the task of devising norms that would apply *Ex corde* to the system of higher education in this country. One sticking point was the revised code of canon law that had been published in 1983. With regards to the relationship between the church and Catholic colleges and universities, the code had stated that faculty members must be "outstanding in their integrity of doctrine and uprightness of life." It further required that the presidents of Catholic colleges and universities make a profession of faith and that Catholic theologians receive a mandate to teach from the competent ecclesiastical authority (Canon 812). All of these, of course, are in conflict with the concept of academic freedom.

In establishing norms for the application of *Ex corde*, the bishops devised a pastoral, rather than legalistic, approach. The initial document stressed the importance of trust and cooperation between the bishops and Catholic educators and addressed the issue of a mandate for Catholic theologians as a footnote, indicating it needed further study. In November 1996 the NCCB approved these norms by a vote of 240 to 6. In 1997, however, the Vatican Congregation for Catholic Education rejected the NCCB's norms on the basis that they had not adequately addressed the issues raised by canon law. The document approved by the NCCB in November 1999 specifically addressed these issues by requiring that presidents of Catholic colleges and universities take an oath of faith and that Catholics teaching theology in Catholic colleges and universities have a mandate to teach from their local bishop.

Although the press coverage surrounding the norms for implementing *Ex corde* has emphasized these two issues, others have observed that in focusing so much on questions such as that of a mandate for theologians, the bishops and Catholic educators have overlooked an important point: most of the courses that students at Catholic colleges and universities take are not theology courses. No matter what occurs within a theology department, the Catholic nature of a university depends on the faculty in departments such as English, history, economics, biology, and so forth. Faculty in these departments ultimately determine the Catholic nature of the university through their teaching and research, as the saying goes, not by the answers they give but by the questions they ask. The teaching and research of the entire faculty, not just those few who teach theology, determine the extent to which a college or university maintains its Catholic identity. Rather than arguing over mandates for Catholic theologians, Catholic colleges and universities could better spend their energies assuring that the entire faculty, both Catholic and non-Catholic, feel a connection to the school's Catholic identity and mission.

The Faculty and Catholic Institutional Identity

The remainder of this chapter reports on an empirical analysis of the extent to which faculty at Catholic colleges and universities feel connected to their school's Catholic identity. This is a complex and multifaceted issue. Three measures are analyzed: the willingness of faculty to teach Catholic values across the curriculum; the extent to which faculty try to make a connection between their personal religious faith and their teaching and research; and a bottom-line type issue of how connected the faculty feel to their institution's Catholic mission. Special attention is paid to the impact that faculty development programs and hiring procedures have in shaping faculty attitudes.

Methodology

Two survey instruments were distributed. One was sent to the presidents of 207 U.S. Catholic colleges and universities. It was intended to gather background information on each institution (number of students, number of faculty, religious order affiliation, and so on) and information on curriculum and faculty development programs.

This survey was factual in nature and did not ask for opinions, except for one question that asked the president's opinion of the school's success in developing a faculty that reflected the school's Catholic identity and mission. A total of 153 (73.9 percent) of the baseline questionnaires were returned.

The other survey instrument was sent to faculty at Catholic schools. A random sample of ninety-eight institutions (stratified by number of students and region) was selected. Thirty randomly selected full-time faculty at each school received the questionnaire. The survey asked both background questions (age, race, and religion, for example) and opinions about curriculum issues and the degree to which they identify with their institution's Catholic mission. The opinion responses were scaled from 1 (Strongly Disagree) to 6 (Strongly Agree). A total of 2,930 faculty surveys were distributed (some schools had fewer than thirty full-time faculty members), of which 32 were undeliverable and 1,297 were returned (a response rate of 44.8 percent).

In addition to the raw numerical ratings, faculty were also invited to provide written comments. Reading these comments revealed that the issues raised in the survey not only were timely but also had touched a raw nerve among many faculty. Some faculty, for example, returned unanswered surveys with a note attached that stated, in effect, that this was a very sensitive issue on their campus, and they did not trust our promise that all individual responses would be kept in strictest confidence. Comments on the completed questionnaires struck a number of themes. Some of the comments received reflected on the change in Catholic identity over the last generation. One respondent stated, "We have been negligent about the Catholic character of this college; we took it for granted . . . and are newly aware of the need to study the Catholic character of our institution." Another wrote, "Our college is presently struggling with this problem and challenge. It is a difficult and sensitive area for discussion which was taken for granted for twenty years and is now a problem."

Some respondents expressed the fear that Catholic identity would be equated with religious orthodoxy. One said, "I am strongly opposed to Catholic fundamentalists who admire the methods of Bob Jones University. The search for truth should be open in a Catholic environment, not imposed from above." Another stated, "While it is important to maintain an authentic Catholic character, I feel this effort is often a mask for the most conservative interpretation. A Catholic identity truly representative of the Church and its history would be wonderful. One that subverts true Catholicity in the name of orthodoxy narrowly understood would be tragic."

Some faculty were openly hostile to the notion that the Catholic identity of their school should be important. One respondent said, "To introduce the bias of any religion into education as this survey suggests is totally counter-productive to the higher educational process. You should be ashamed of yourself for even suggesting it." A second said, "I am profoundly disturbed by efforts to assign faculty and the curriculum a role in defining and promoting the Catholic character of any institution. These efforts are ill-advised for they will hinder my institution's ability to be a first-rate university. They will, regrettably, maintain forever the university on a parochial domain. A third said, "I think 'religious character' should be eliminated. It is a drawback to excellence. In time, I believe it will be, as was done over a period of several hundred years at many excellent schools, such as Princeton, Yale, etc."

The comments of some respondents revealed a rift among the faculty at their school over this issue. One stated, "There is a radical split between those who value the Catholic identity highly and those who are indifferent or slightly hostile to it. Unless changes are made, the latter group is going to remake policy and curriculum decisions as time passes." Another noted, "Sadly, there is a core group of faculty who are openly hostile and nothing is done to remedy this."

Some respondents blamed their administration for not taking a firmer stand in defending the Catholic identity elements of their mission statements. One respondent said, "A small number of faculty are committed Catholics. A not-negligible number are anti-Catholic. The large majority are best classified as indifferent to religion of any kind. Thus, promotion of the 'Catholic character' is not to be expected from the faculty. The curriculum more or less reflects this indifference, as does the general ethos of the campus. Indifference to the Catholic character of the institution has been a policy objective of the chief administrative officers and the Board of Trustees." A second stated, "Our administrators do not have enough confidence in their mission to argue for it forcefully. They bend over backwards to accommodate the secular prejudices of lay faculty, and do not support those lay faculty who are given the responsibility of promoting the Catholic mission of the school." A third said, "We, i.e. Catholic colleges, are not doing nearly enough to promote the Catholic character that we represent. Our administrators so often give just token service in this area."

Some respondents tied their school's efforts to promote its Catholic identity with financial issues. One wrote, "There is a tendency of our administration and some faculty to be intimidated by students' attitudes towards not only Christian but Catholic issues. For fear of losing students and tuition, many areas of our mission statement have been compromised." Another said, "We have gone through a period of some twenty years when the college's Catholic identity was hidden because it was viewed as non-marketable." A third said, "The ultra-conservative theology at my current university has alienated me and other faculty and has driven away excellent students. The administration is keeping its head in the sand, hoping not to alienate rich people."

Other comments that were received were consistent with those quoted above in that they revealed that this is a very sensitive and explosive issue to faculty on all sides of the *Ex corde* debate.

A Word on Generational Differences

It is obvious to anyone who has been involved with Catholic higher education over the last couple of decades that there has been a dramatic change in the attitudes of faculty, both Catholic and non-Catholic. This reflects attitudinal changes that have occurred in society at large, but especially among Catholics, concerning the role of authority. Authority in general, but especially religious authority, is arguably respected less by younger faculty than by their more senior peers.

James Davidson and his colleagues have categorized the religious beliefs and practices of three generational cohorts of Catholics.[2] Their study is based on an understanding of that period of a person's life known as the "formative years" and the effect that it has in developing a generational sense of identity. According to this theory, there is a critical stage in a person's development where experiences are especially decisive in exerting a lasting influence on that individual's life. Researchers differ on the precise time frame for the formative year's period. Some believe it could start as early as age thirteen, whereas others extend it to as late as age twenty-five. In any event, the memories from those years live on well into the future. They continue to affect how a person perceives and relates to the world.

By extension, the formative years' theory suggests a collective sense of identity among members of a generation because they shared a common set of experiences. Because the formative years' experiences of each generation differ from those of others, so too will their worldviews and values.

According to Davidson et al., the defining religious moment for U.S. Catholics was the Second Vatican Council and the reforms that followed. They identify three generational cohorts among Catholics: those who experienced their formative years before Vatican II (the pre–Vatican II cohort); during Vatican II (the Vatican II cohort); and after the reforms of Vatican II were in place (the post–Vatican II cohort). These groups are somewhat analogous to the concepts of pre–baby boomers, baby boomers, and post–baby boomers (the so-called Generation X) except that those born during World War II would be included in the Vatican II cohort, and the youngest baby boomers are more closely aligned with Generation X. Each generation's religious beliefs and practices are a reflection of both the general societal and specifically religious events that occurred during their formative years.

The Pre–Vatican II Cohort

The dominant societal events of anyone who reached their formative years during the 1930s and 1940s were the Great Depression and World War II. Among the lessons the youth of this period learned was the importance of society pulling together. Depressions are not ended, and wars are not won, through individualistic efforts. They came to trust institutional authorities and to rely on them. Indeed, in such trying times they had little choice. Authority was viewed as promoting the common good.

Catholics of this era were typically either immigrants or the children of immigrants. They were frequently the victims of religious bigotry. To cope, they joined distinctively Catholic organizations that emphasized the importance of doctrinal orthodoxy and obeying Church teachings. Catholics of this era developed a collective, institutional view of their faith, with respect for both religious and civil authority.

The Vatican II Cohort

Catholics who were born in the period from the mid-1940s to the mid-1950s encountered two distinct, almost contradictory eras, both in the secular and religious worlds. In the society at large, the 1950s were characterized by the calm of the Eisenhower administration, a period when both authority and institutions still commanded respect. They spent much of their formative years in the radical 1960s, learning to challenge authority and question institutions. They went from air-raid drills in their 1950s elementary schools to sit-ins on their 1960s college campuses; from watching Elvis get drafted to fleeing to Canada to avoid being drafted themselves. Confidence in society's authority and institutions diminished as they came to be viewed as part of the problem, not the solution.

There were counterpart events in Catholics' religious climate as well. In the 1950s, they were raised much like the preceding cohort. They learned their religion from the *Baltimore Catechism*. They were taught a very institutional concept of religion. The Catholic Church was "the one true Church." Heaven could be achieved only by an unchallenged following of the church's teaching.

All of this was changed dramatically by Vatican II. Among the impacts of Vatican II was a transformation from an institutional to an individual understanding of faith. Key outcomes included a greater sense of ecumenism among Catholics and a greater reliance on individual conscience. The hierarchical model of the church was not totally discarded, but the laity were given new respect as "the people of God." They were told that they shared in the priesthood through their baptism. They were encouraged to make their voices heard through parish councils and other lay ministries.

The outcomes of Vatican II were reinforced by the 1968 release of *Humanae Vitae*. A large number of Catholics were already using contraceptives, and the report of Pope Paul VI's advisory committee, which had recommended that the birth control decision be left to individual conscience, had been leaked to the public. Catholics were confused. The documents of Vatican II had declared the supremacy of individual conscience, but the encyclical seemed to take the decision out of the hands of the individual couple. Many laypersons openly dissented with the pope, and they were joined by a significant number of clergy. For the first time in recent history, a large number of Catholics were questioning the church's teaching authority.

So the older Catholic baby boomers, who were already part of a generation that was questioning authority in the secular world, were also questioning authority in their religious world as well. They were struggling to mesh the respect for authority and institutions that they had learned in the 1950s with the contempt for authority and institutions that characterized the 1960s. In a sense, they had a foot in both camps.

The Post–Vatican II Cohort

This group includes the younger baby boomers and Generation X, both of whom experienced their formative years in the 1970s or later. These years included scandals (Watergate and, later, Irangate and Whitewater). The U.S. government looked impotent in combating foreign terrorism, including the Iran hostage crisis. The government also exhibited a seeming inability to cope with economic trauma (long gas lines, high inflation, exorbitant interest rates in the 1970s; out-of-control federal budget deficits in the 1980s). All of these continued the 1960s' pattern of distrust of society's institutions. At the same time events occurred that led to lower expectations among this cohort. They experienced technological disasters such as Three Mile Island, Chernobyl, and the Challenger explosion. Corporate downsizing and outsourcing to take advantage of cheap foreign labor limited career opportunities. AIDS emerged as a significant social problem.

There were also changes on the religious scene. Just as in the secular world, organized religion was rocked by scandal, including those involving televangelists such as Jim Bakker and Jimmy Swaggert and the pedophile problem among some Catholic priests.

Of course, by this time the reforms of Vatican II were in place. Although members of this cohort have little direct knowledge of Vatican II, they have felt its impact. They were not exposed to the *Balti-*

more Catechism. Instead, personal responsibility for their own individual faith journey was emphasized. The church was viewed as a tool for helping them get to heaven, rather than as an end in itself. In fact, many place more importance on being a good Christian than on being a good Catholic. They feel free to disagree with church teaching, often distinguishing between God's law and church law. In addition, they are more likely to consider the specific circumstances before determining the rightness or wrongness of an action.[3]

The results of the nationwide survey conducted by Davidson et al. showed post–Vatican II Catholics to be more traditional than Vatican II Catholics in their theological views but less traditional in their ecclesiological views and moral attitudes. A sample of the responses is shown in Table 1. In most cases, Vatican II Catholic attitudes fell between those of the pre–Vatican II and the post–Vatican II Catholics (i.e., a foot in each camp).

It follows from this brief review that generational cohort differences in religious beliefs and practices should be expected among Catholic college and university faculty, no matter what their religion. Younger cohorts are different from their older colleagues in many ways. Still, we might expect to see even a greater dichotomy among faculty members who are themselves Catholic. How this exhibits itself in their attitudes toward curriculum and Catholic identity and what, if anything, can or should be done about it are continuing themes in the analysis that follows.

Because the future of a school's Catholic identity is tied to its younger faculty, it is important to focus on their attitudes. In many ways their attitudes are similar to those of the faculty as a whole, but in other ways (as the formative years' theory would suggest) they are distinctly different. The empirical analysis that follows focuses on those faculty who have been teaching at their current school for ten years or less.

In the sections that follow, faculty opinions concerning the extent to which Catholic values should be taught across the curriculum, the degree to which they attempt to make a connection between their personal religious faith and their teaching and research, and the extent to which they identify with the mission of their school will be examined within the context of four general categories: the individual's

Table 1. Generational Cohort Differences in Religious Attitudes

	Pre-Boomers	Baby Boomers	Post-Boomers
I. Theological Views (Percentage agreeing these beliefs are "very important to me")			
A. Jesus physically rose from the dead	83	65	70
B. Jesus was completely divine like God and completely human like us in every way except sin	75	63	69
II. Ecclesiological Views (Percentage agreeing)			
A. One can be a good Catholic without going to Mass	51	63	73
B. Women should be allowed to be priests	41	61	66
III. Moral Attitudes (Percentage agreeing)			
A. Catholics have a duty to try to close the gap between the rich and the poor	48	48	62
B. It is always wrong to engage in premarital sex	50	22	18

Source: Davidson et al., 1997

personal characteristics; the characteristics of the school; any faculty development efforts that the school has utilized to foster Catholic identity among its faculty; and the impact of the school's hiring policies and procedures. (Only those findings that were statistically significant at the .05 confidence level are reported in Table 4.) Table 2 (faculty development) and Table 3 (hiring policies) show the percent of schools from the baseline questionnaire utilizing some typical programs.

Table 2. Faculty Development Programs and Percentage of Respondent Institutions Employing Each

Program	Percentage
New faculty orientation, including discussion of institution's mission statement	72
Faculty retreats	30
Faculty seminars or workshops focusing on institution's Catholic identity	35
Lecture series for faculty focusing on institution's Catholic identity	24
Annual presidential address devoted to Catholic identity of the institution	22
Specially designated liturgies for faculty	25
Standing faculty committee charged with overseeing Catholic identity of the institution	12
Campuswide publication discussing Catholic identity/mission	20
Reliance on cadre of faculty who offer faculty development regarding the institution's Catholic identity through informal channels	29

Empirical Findings

Teaching Catholic Values across the Curriculum

As might be expected, the question concerning the extent to which Catholic values should be taught across the curriculum evoked some strong comments from faculty in the sample. Some were violently opposed to the notion. For example, one stated, "I am strongly opposed to the restrictions on academic freedom that are posed by concentrated efforts to have any religious doctrine or faith an integral part of courses across the curriculum." Another said, "Catholic identity and values should be discussed in *appropriate* classes (e.g., ethics) but should not be forced upon any professor (maintaining professional freedom in the classroom)." Still another said, "Religion's place is *only* in a religion class that is optional for the student." Others expressed support, at least on a limited basis. One respondent stated, "I do not feel that there is a 'Catholic' physics, chemistry, or mathematics or

Table 3. Recruitment and Hiring Practices and Percentage of Respondent Institutions Employing Each

Practice	Percentage
Identify institution as Catholic in all faculty recruitment advertising	68
Specify a preference for Catholic faculty in all faculty recruitment advertising	2
Specify that faculty are expected to be sympathetic to the Catholic mission in all faculty recruitment advertising	34
Guidelines for search committees indicating responsibility to recruit candidates who can contribute to the Catholic mission	35
Discuss institution's Catholic nature and heritage during interview	69
Ask specific questions of candidate regarding willingness to uphold Catholic perspective on faith and morals in the classroom	19
Distribute copy of institution's mission statement to candidate prior to or during the interview	64
Require candidate to submit written statement reflecting his/her understanding of the institution's mission statement	7
Make specific reference to *Ex Corde Ecclesiae*	6
Require interview with institutional representative charged with monitoring the mission of the institution	23

that it is desirable to have same. But it is desirable to have, for example, papal encyclicals discussed in a course in Sociology." Another said, "The primary purpose of Catholic higher education is development of the intellect. Catholic teachings and values should assist in this process. Catholic teachings, values, experience and tradition stand up well in reasoned intellectual discourse and discernment."

Finally, some staked out a middle ground, arguing that values should be taught across the curriculum but that they need not be labeled as "Catholic." One person stated, "I don't think we need to preach Catholic values but get students in touch with their own self and identity and recognition of the need for values and morals." Another respondent said, "Many of us teach and model Catholic values without labeling them Catholic. The word *Catholic* and its jargon can be a turnoff to accessing the common Catholic values that we do hold and implement." One faculty member probably spoke for the majority when she/he noted, "At my school, there are a few that are deeply interested in promoting Catholic values, a few that present the issue of Catholicism in their classroom, and most could care less."

On the basis of their responses to the numerical survey overall, newer faculty tended to disagree mildly that Catholic values should be taught across the curriculum. Nonetheless, within the overall sample, there were some interesting trends (Table 4). New faculty who were Catholic and older were the most supportive. The same was true for those who taught at a school where 10 percent or more of the faculty were vowed religious and for faculty teaching at liberal arts colleges. Surprisingly (and this is a pattern that also shows up later in this study), faculty teaching at institutions where fewer than 60 percent of the students are Catholic were also more supportive of teaching Catholic values across the curriculum.

Seven faculty development programs were found to influence significantly the attitudes of new faculty on this issue. They were as follows: sponsoring a new faculty orientation on the school's Catholic mission; offering faculty workshops and also a lecture series that focused on the school's Catholic identity; offering annual presidential addresses on the same topic; providing special liturgies for faculty; and both appointing a standing faculty committee charged with overseeing the institution's Catholic identity and relying on informal faculty development efforts to achieve the same goal. Maintaining a standing faculty committee on the school's Catholic identity was the most successful faculty development tool in increasing newer faculty acceptance for teaching Catholic values across the curriculum.

Perhaps of even greater importance for newer faculty is the relationship between various hiring practices and their feelings about teaching Catholic values across the curriculum. Three faculty recruiting practices were found to be related to faculty attitudes on this matter: ensuring that all recruitment advertising specifies that faculty are expected to be sympathetic to the school's Catholic mission; establishing guidelines for all search committees that indicate their responsibility to recruit candidates who can contribute to the school's Catho-

Table 4. Statistically Significant Differences, Mean Values (1 = Strongly Disagree, 6 = Strongly Agree), Newer Faculty Sample

Question	Teaching Catholic Values	Connect Faith and Teaching/ Research	Connected to Mission
I. Personal Characteristics			
A. Religion			
Catholic	3.91	4.18	4.48
Protestant	2.63	3.25	3.62
Non-Christian	2.30	2.51	2.98
B. Age			
Under 40	2.93	3.45	3.77
40–49	3.11	3.45	3.83
50 or older	3.64	3.97	4.29
C. Gender			
Female			4.29
Male			3.77
II. Institutional Characteristics			
A. Vowed Religious Faculty			
Under 10 percent	3.06	3.48	3.71
10 percent or more	3.51	3.83	4.48
B. Percent Students Catholic			
60 percent or less	3.57	3.83	
More than 60 percent	3.13	3.55	
C. Carnegie Classification			
Research	2.70	3.17	3.66
Comprehensive	3.27	3.67	4.05
Liberal Arts	3.50	3.75	4.10
III. Faculty Recruitment and Hiring			
A. Specify Faculty expected to be Sympathetic to Mission			
Yes	3.59		
No	3.15		
B. Guidelines to Search Committees			
Yes	3.57	3.83	
No	3.16	3.58	

Table 4. *continued*

Question	Teaching Catholic Values	Connect Faith and Teaching/ Research	Connected to Mission
C. Ask Candidate about Willingness to Uphold Catholic Perspective			
Yes	3.72	4.24	
No	3.21	3.97	
IV. Faculty Development Programs			
A. New Faculty Orientation on Mission Statement			
Yes	3.42	3.77	4.24
No	3.01	3.37	3.42
B. Faculty Seminars/Workshops on Catholic Identity			
Yes	3.57	3.90	4.43
No	3.15	3.53	3.78
C. Lecture Series Focusing on Catholic Identity			
Yes	3.50	4.36	
No	3.24	3.91	
D. Annual Presidential Address on Catholic Identity			
Yes	3.68	4.48	
No	3.20	3.88	
E. Special Liturgies for Faculty			
Yes	3.57	3.92	4.37
No	3.22	3.59	3.91
F. Standing Faculty Committee Overseeing Catholic Identity			
Yes	3.93	4.15	4.50
No	3.22	3.60	3.96
G. Informal Faculty Development Regarding Catholic Identity			
Yes	3.57	4.00	4.52
No	3.19	3.53	3.81
H. Faculty Retreats			
Yes			4.22
No			3.93
I. Campuswide Publication on Catholic Identity			
Yes			4.25
No			3.96

Note: All differences significant at .05 level.

lic mission; and asking candidates during the on-campus interview about their willingness to uphold a Catholic perspective on faith and morals in the classroom.

Connection between Religious Faith and Teaching and Research

We asked our sample about the extent to which they try to connect their personal religious faith with their teaching and research. The question was phrased so as to make it clear to the respondents that we were interested in the relationship between their personal faith, whatever it might be, and their teaching and research and that the question was not intended for Catholics only. Overall, there was moderate agreement that they do make this attempt.

As Table 4 illustrates, the pattern of agreement on this issue with respect to both the personal and institutional factors was identical to the pattern of agreement for teaching Catholic values across the curriculum. Newer faculty who are Catholic and older and who taught at liberal arts colleges, at universities with vowed religious comprising more than 10 percent of the faculty, and at schools where 60 percent or less of the student body was Catholic were more likely to make this connection.

Five faculty development programs were associated with increasing attitudes toward connecting faith with teaching and research. All five had been shown above to have a significant impact on the willingness to teach Catholic values across the curriculum. They included both new faculty orientations and faculty seminars that focused on the school's Catholic identity; special liturgies for faculty; and both formal standing committees and informal faculty development efforts regarding Catholic identity. Once again, appointing a standing faculty committee charged with overseeing the Catholic identity of the institution was the most effective faculty development tool.

It had been expected that a school's recruiting and interviewing policies would have a significant impact on the willingness of new hires to connect their faith with their teaching and research. Recruiting and interviewing policies that emphasized the importance of the school's Catholic identity and mission would presumably screen out those candidates who did not feel comfortable with this orientation and send an early message to others concerning the school's expectations. Nevertheless, only one recruiting policy had a significant impact: the provision of guidelines to search committees indicating their responsibility to recruit candidates who can contribute to the Catholic mission.

Connection with the School's Catholic Mission

Although the respondents to our survey as a group indicated that they were supportive of their school's Catholic mission, some of those who commented were openly indifferent or even hostile to their institution's mission. One stated, "I am unconnected to Catholicism, and have no desire or interest in its role for faculty or curriculum, or vice versa. The Catholic character is irrelevant to me. I neither disparage it nor promote it." Another said, "I associate the Catholic character with the current patriarchy and misogyny of Roman Catholicism. The Pope and the cardinals have decreed it so. Therefore, I must condemn Roman Catholicism."

Nonetheless, most of those who commented were generally supportive of their school's Catholic mission. Some honed in on the two critical issues. One respondent said, "Very little energy and concern is in place with regards to the type of faculty being hired, that is, the emphasis is restricted to a faculty member's academic credentials rather than insisting also on people committed to the college's religious identity and mission." Another said, "The difficult question is tenure and its expectations. Would you, without fear of a lawsuit, refuse tenure to someone, good in teaching and research, but somewhat hostile to the institution's Catholic heritage?"

If a school values its Catholic mission, hiring and tenuring decisions are crucial. At the same time, however, faculty development programs can be effective in ensuring that the tenured faculty already on board value the institution's mission. As was the case in the preceding analysis, the effect of hiring policies and faculty development programs are considered in this section along with other determinants of support for the institution's Catholic mission.

The sample of newer faculty tended to agree that they felt connected to their school's Catholic mission. Table 4 indicates that newer faculty who were Catholic, older, and female felt more connected to their school's mission. The same held for newer faculty who taught at schools where 10 percent or more of the faculty were vowed religious and for those who taught at liberal arts colleges.

A large number (nine) of faculty development programs were significantly associated with the newer faculty's connection with their school's mission. This was more than for either of the other two measures of Catholic identity studied, indicating that faculty development programs are more successful in affecting faculty connection to the institution's mission than they are in impacting faculty attitudes toward either teaching values across the curriculum or connecting their faith with their teaching and research. The highest rating went to the use of informal faculty development conducted by committed faculty members, followed closely by the appointment of a formal faculty committee on the school's Catholic identity.

Conclusion: Ten Things that Catholic Colleges and Universities Could Do to Increase Faculty Identity with Their Mission

Catholic colleges and universities in the United States are walking a tightrope. As the Land O'Lakes statement made clear, they have "a strong commitment to and concern for academic excellence."[4] At the same time, the vast majority of Catholic schools treasure their Catholic identity and wish to maintain and build on it. The maintenance of an institution's Catholic identity, however, depends on the efforts of the entire faculty, not just those few who teach theology. Yet the faculty's role in embellishing the Catholic identity of an institution is complex and multifaceted. The empirical section of this report has considered it from three different perspectives: the willingness of the faculty to teach Catholic values across the curriculum, their willingness to connect their faith with their teaching and research, and the extent to which the faculty identify with the school's Catholic mission. From this analysis, certain patterns have emerged that have allowed us to identify several actions that Catholic universities can take in order to enhance their Catholic identity without sacrificing their commitment to academic excellence. The following, in no particular order, are ten recommendations for bolstering the faculty's support for their institution's Catholic identity and mission.

Catholic Faculty

In every measure of faculty identity with the institution's Catholic identity and mission that we employed, faculty who were Catholics themselves were more supportive than non-Catholic faculty. Does this mean that Catholic colleges and universities should hire only Catholic faculty? Certainly not. Most faculty can cite examples of non-Catholic faculty members who are more in tune with the institution's mission than are some faculty with Catholic backgrounds. Some have argued that a school needs a critical mass of Catholic faculty. Yet what constitutes a critical mass? Is it 75 percent, 50 percent, one-third? The data from the survey were used to test a quadratic functional form $(Y = a + bX + cX_2)$, which allows the simple calculation of an optimal. That is, we can calculate the value for X when Y is maximized. Setting Y as the faculty members' rating of how connected they feel to their school's Catholic mission and X as the administration's estimate of the portion of the faculty who are Catholic, statistical tools were used to estimate the parameters for a, b, and c. The optimal value for X was then calculated to be 52.5. That is, faculty identify most with their school's Catholic mission when slightly more than half of the faculty are themselves Catholic. This is meant to be just a rough estimate, not a hard and fast rule, for what constitutes a critical mass of Catholic faculty. Clearly, however, a critical mass need not be a substantial majority of the faculty, nor can it be a substantial minority.

Faculty Age and Experience

Older faculty are more connected to their institution's Catholic identity than are younger faculty. One could argue that this is just a stage that the younger faculty are going through, that someday they will be as supportive of their school's Catholic mission as are today's veteran professors. Nevertheless, the formative years' theory argues that this is not merely a stage, that there are permanent cohort differences between the senior and the junior faculty. Although some of the younger faculty may share some of the traditional religious beliefs with their older colleagues, they are much less influenced by formal religious authority. Administrators at Catholic colleges and universities have to take this into account. The more senior professors needed relatively little in the way of faculty development to ensure their commitment to the school's Catholic identity. A greater effort must be spent on developing the younger faculty, an effort that recognizes the post–Vatican II emphasis on the laity as "the people of God" rather than the "one true Church" message of the pre–Vatican II era.

The Role of Vowed Religious

One of the consistent outcomes of this study was the role that vowed religious play. The example set by those faculty who are vowed religious apparently permeates the entire faculty and sets a tone for connecting with the school's mission. Unfortunately, in this age of declining religious vocations, most religious orders are experiencing difficulty in maintaining a significant presence among college and university faculty. Catholic schools need to recognize the impact that declining religious vocations have on their ability to develop and maintain a Catholic identity among their faculty. In addition to the faculty development programs discussed below, Catholic colleges and universities should make every effort to ensure that those few vowed religious who are on campus serve as out-front, visible examples to the rest of the community regardless of their official position (faculty member, administrator, campus ministry, and so on).

Carnegie Classification

In nearly every measure that we used, faculty at liberal arts colleges identified more strongly with their institution's Catholic mission than did faculty at other institutions. Faculty at research universities felt less connected than faculty at other schools. This finding is not surprising, given the types of faculty who are attracted to these different types of schools, but it does highlight the fact that, although all Catholic institutions need to be vigilant in maintaining their Catholic identity, research universities have an especially difficult challenge.

The Role of the Faculty

When it comes to developing a faculty who identify with the school's Catholic mission, our findings show that the faculty themselves can play a crucial role. Two separate approaches stood out. One was more formal: the appointment of a standing faculty committee that was charged with overseeing the Catholic identity of the institution. The other was more informal: the reliance on a group of faculty who took it upon themselves to mentor the other faculty regarding the school's Catholic identity. The two approaches are almost 180 degrees opposite, but they both worked. Unfortunately, to the extent that this informal mentoring is performed by the more senior faculty, the formative years' theory would predict that it is unlikely to be carried on at the same level of competence as the younger faculty move into the more senior positions. Catholic schools should consider appointing a standing committee for this purpose. Still, given the concerns expressed in the comments made by some of our respondents, they must safeguard that this committee does not evolve into a "Catholic orthodoxy police."

The Role of the President

Both the numerical ratings and the faculty comments made it clear that the president of the college or university plays an important role. Faculty who perceive that the president is indifferent to safeguarding the institution's Catholic identity might well eventually become indifferent themselves. It is not enough for the president to make the case for the school's Catholic identity with external groups such as potential donors or the local bishop. The president must be a visible advocate for the institution's Catholic identity on campus as well. We found that one of the most effective faculty development tools was an annual address by the president devoted to the school's Catholic identity. Presidents who make the effort to communicate directly to the faculty on this issue are sending a clear message as to their support and, by implication, their expectations for the faculty.

Faculty Workshops and Lecture Series

Two similar faculty development tools that were found to be effective across the board were the offerings of faculty workshops and lecture series that focused on the institution's Catholic identity. Both of these programs can be effective in conveying the general message that the school's Catholic identity is important. They can accomplish more than that, however. They can also be invaluable tools in assisting faculty to carry out the specifics of the Catholic mission, such as helping faculty understand methods for teaching about Catholic values across the curriculum or strategies for connecting their faith with their teaching and research.

Special Liturgies

The spiritual side of developing a faculty who identify with the institution's Catholic mission is often overlooked. Nonetheless, we found that offering specially designated liturgies for the faculty was an effective means of increasing their support for the school's Catholic identity in all of our measures. Part of what it means to be a Catholic school should involve addressing the spiritual needs of the various elements of the community as well as their material needs.

Faculty Recruitment

Remarkably few faculty hiring policies and procedures were associated with greater faculty support for the institution's Catholic identity. This is striking because the conventional wisdom is that the hiring process is a critical component in building a faculty who identify with the school's Catholic mission. One faculty recruitment process that was found to be effective was providing guidelines to search committees indicating their responsibility to recruit candidates who can contribute to the Catholic mission. Search committees frequently get so involved in evaluating a candidate's teaching and research potential that they might well overlook the candidate's potential for contributing to the Catholic mission. Candidly, some faculty view this aspect of the search as either anti-intellectual or mere window dressing. Unless the search committees are made aware of this responsibility, and it is backed by administrative clout, it is likely to be ignored or at best to receive only token consideration. A second recruiting policy that was found to be generally effective was to ask candidates about their willingness to uphold the Catholic perspective on faith and morals. This sends a clear message early on to the perspective faculty member about the school's expectation.

New Faculty Orientation

It is probably obvious to point out that a faculty orientation for new faculty members that emphasizes the institution's Catholic identity and mission is an effective means of educating faculty about the school's Catholic identity. It also sends a strong signal to those new faculty members about the importance that the institution places on its Catholic identity. Table 2 shows that 72 percent of the schools in our sample presented new faculty orientation that discussed the school's Catholic mission. This approach was used more than twice as often as any other faculty development tool. Those 28 percent of the Catholic colleges and universities that do not employ this tool should reconsider.

Notes

Work on this project was funded by a grant from the Association of Catholic Colleges and Universities. Some of the material in this chapter also served as the basis for the following articles: Judith A. Dwyer and Charles E. Zech, "ACCU Survey of Catholic Colleges and Universities: Report on Faculty Development and Curriculum," *Current Issues in Catholic Higher Education* 16 (winter 1996): 5–24; Judith A. Dwyer and Charles E. Zech, "American Catholic Higher Education: An ACCU Study on Mission and Identity, Faculty Development, and Curricular Revision," *Current Issues in Catholic Higher Education* 19 (fall 1998): 3–32; and Charles E. Zech, "The Faculty and Catholic Institutional Identity," *America,* May 22, 1999, 11–15.

1. "Land O'Lakes Statement on the Nature of the Contemporary University" (1967), 1.

2. James D. Davidson et al., *The Search for Common Ground: What Unites and Divides Catholic Americans* (Huntington, Ind.: Our Sunday Visitor, 1997).

3. William V. D'Antonio et al., *Laity: American and Catholic* (Kansas City: Sheed and Ward, 1996), 84–88.

4. "Land O'Lakes Statement," 1.

6

A Memorandum on the Higher Learning in Catholic America

Robert Sullivan

A generation ago Christopher Jencks and David Riesman published a sociological *tour d'horizon* of American higher education. *The Academic Revolution* offered a crisp evaluation of the state and prospects of Catholic universities and colleges that remains cogent. Its theme was the structures of knowledge and administration on campuses, not the climate of faith, piety, and service. Jencks and Riesman doubted that more than a handful of those institutions would ever join the ranks of what were conventionally deemed the nation's best schools. They were, moreover, unable to discover from informed Catholics any persuasive, commonly accepted answer to the question, "What should be distinctive about a Catholic college?" They judged it "likely if not inevitable" that Catholic institutions would continue to accommodate themselves intellectually and administratively to mainstream standards of higher education, above all to the dominance of "lay professionalism," which for them defined the academic revolution.[1]

As distinguished secular academics, Jencks and Riesman regretted that development because it would reduce the already thin variety within American higher education. Absent an improbable consolidation of resources in a few strong colleges and universities, there was one slight hope that the Catholic institutions could preserve any educationally meaningful identity as church schools. It lay in the ability of the religious orders that founded and in 1968 still conducted almost 90 percent of the Catholic colleges to recruit educable and tenurable men and women in sufficient numbers to enable them to function on campuses as effective cadres of mediation between the worlds of faith and learning. Even should enough such recruits be found, however, Jencks and Riesman doubted whether the adjective *Catholic* "has any real meaning in an era when the character of a place calling itself a 'college' seems wholly prescribed by other established institutions, and especially by the graduate programs of leading universities."[2] They thus defined the basic issue that, first quietly and now insistently, has for a generation confronted Catholic colleges and universities in America: preserving a coherent religious identity while pursuing, and in many cases achieving, academic respectability. Although the passage of time has made American higher education even more consumerist and bureaucratic, the normal forms of governance and administration as well as the construction of academic knowledge are still recognizable as those that Jencks and Riesman described.

Curiously, the diagnosis of *The Academic Revolution* failed to provoke interested Catholics into anything like the recent bout of public, discordant soul-searching about the health of the religious identity of their colleges and universities.[3] The book was reviewed in only a few Catholic journals. The general neglect derived in part from the virtually separate sphere within which some Catholic higher educators then still functioned, but it also reflected the widespread acquiescence in, and in some quarters celebration of, the book's analysis and forecast. At least one reviewer found in it no news for those who "have been reading Catholic journals in recent years."[4] Today most observers, whether they celebrate or indict the transformation of the Catholic academy, seem to rely on basically moral categories of judgment. They dwell on human agency and neglect the existence and effect of structures, particularly the structures of academic knowledge. The increasing intellectual and administrative secularization of America's Catholic colleges and universities was written neither in the stars nor in a conscious design or collective ineptitude, turpitude, and infidelity. More intelligibly and credibly, the twentieth-century history of Catholic higher education is connected with certain fundamental demographic and economic realities, the complications of history, and the nearly irresistible attraction of both the dominant academic and administrative structures of American higher education and the privileged discourses about those structures.

Also weighty was a persistent American conviction about the nature of authentic religion. For many religiously committed faculty and administrators during the late twentieth century, the burden of maintaining the Catholic identity of their campuses depended on preserving and strengthening an ethos of worship, service, and community within which students could be religiously nurtured rather than on establishing any distinctively Catholic academic arrangements, whether organizational or intellectual. Faith for them, in other words, was more about living than about knowing. David Riesman, an equal-opportunity intellectual elitist, scouted the presence of a non- (perhaps even anti-) academic approach to religion in even the most prestigious Catholic institutions: "Today Notre Dame's achievements in science and engineering need to be protected against the spokesmen of a sentimental humanism all the more compelling because it feels itself defeated. It would also be a loss if the insistent rationality that has been associated with the best Jesuit education were dropped in favor of sensitivity training."[5]

A generation later the emphasis on religion as living more than knowing has proved decisive in preserving a lively Catholicism on many campuses, both exclusive and otherwise. A precondition is that the schools enjoy a reliable, overwhelmingly Catholic pool of applicants. Where they exist, where large amounts of money are invested, and where the dedicated pastoral service not only of laypersons but also of numerous sisters, brothers, and priests is marshaled, Catholic colleges have succeeded both in ensuring an attractive ethos of worship, service, and community and in guaranteeing that at least some high administrative positions continue to be occupied by members of the founding religious orders. Even in most of those schools, nonetheless, classrooms, laboratories, and department meetings are largely disconnected from the religious ethos, and there are earnest discussions, both grave and polemical, about how to enhance the Catholic identity of higher education.

As a result of mergers, acquisitions, closings, and the abandonment of religious sponsorship, there are now more than thirty fewer Catholic institutions of higher education than in 1960, and new foundations have virtually ceased.[6] In 2000, the approximately 230 surviving institutions were still clustered in the northeast and the midwest. Even so, enough regional variation exists to complicate, and sometimes even baffle, sweeping generalizations. Collegeville, Minnesota, neither was nor is to be conflated with Fairfield County, Connecticut. Differences in ethos are also palpable. No one could confuse the regimen and atmosphere of Fordham University in New York City with the regimen and atmosphere of the Franciscan University of Steubenville, Ohio. The passage of time, however, seems to have mainly vindicated the crisp evaluation offered in *The Academic Revolution.* The basic structures of Catholic colleges and universities, including the organization of knowledge, appear to be more closely assimilated to prevailing American patterns.

With some noteworthy exceptions, the Catholic institutions were generally prosperous during the 1990s. Their student bodies fairly accurately mirror the embourgeoisement of the mass of the Anglophone Catholic community in America. A plausible case could be made that institutions of higher education are now the most thriving Catholic schools in the United States, though only a few possess formidable endowments and Midas-like development offices. A small number have succeeded in joining the ranks of what are conventionally deemed America's elite colleges and universities. None of them is yet fixed on lists of the luminously prestigious. There are chapters of Phi Beta Kappa on more than a dozen Catholic campuses, up from one, the College of St. Catherine, Minnesota, in 1938. The Catholic University of America was a founding member of the Association of American Universities, and it remains the sole affiliated Catholic university. About a dozen Catholic institutions are research and doctoral universities with enrollments of more than ten thousand. Most are four-year colleges enrolling less than twenty-five hundred students,

Nationwide, more than 670,000 students are enrolled in Catholic colleges and universities, and the majority of them are women. Increasingly, baccalaureate candidates are older than traditional undergraduates, and the number of what were once called "part-time" students is growing. Mainly, those demographics conform to general trends in American higher education. There appear, however, to be two important differences. On one estimate, the aggregate growth in the enrollment of minorities in Catholic colleges at the end of the 1980s was less than 50 percent of the total growth for all private institutions of higher education. If so, the lag stands in marked contrast with the enormous racial diversity that distinguishes Catholic high schools in most urban areas. Coeducation is the rule on Catholic campuses for nearly all men and the great majority of women, but the existence of more than forty all-women's Catholic colleges, about one-sixth of the total, remains an expression of Catholic exceptionalism. Their survival is particularly impressive because the ranks of the orders of women religious have shrunk far more than those of the orders of men, and women's colleges were sometimes unable to rely on even the cooperation of nearby Catholic institutions run by male orders. In some places, there was evidence of virtual institutional predation when men's colleges became coeducational.

Administratively, the essential characteristics of secular institutions are visible in nearly all Roman Catholic institutions. Their governance is legally vested in autonomous, predominantly lay boards of trustees, and the vast majority of their senior administrators, from department chairs up to, and in many places including, presidents, are laypersons. Their faculties are religiously mixed, and religious affiliation generally plays little role in hiring faculty, sometimes even in departments of religious studies or theology. The female and male religious orders that founded Catholic institutions failed to recruit educable and tenurable newcomers to their ranks in sufficient numbers to function on campuses as effective cadres of mediation between the worlds of faith and learning. Almost everywhere, predominantly lay faculty belong to departments that are defined according to one or another academic discipline. With the exception of some departments of theology or religious studies, the principle of knowledge governing each of them is essentially naturalistic, and routine codes of academic freedom obtain. The governance of departments is to a greater or lesser extent participatory and nearly everywhere entails input into or effective control of hiring. On most of America's Catholic campuses, even those with a palpably religious ethos, the triumph of the "academic revolution" is manifest. With the achievement of greater academic respectability, the issue of how, or whether, to preserve a meaningful identity as Catholic colleges is more sharply focused than when Jencks and Riesman wrote.

Because the present condition of American Catholic higher education has deep sources, it is best explored structurally and historically.[7] Beginning in early-nineteenth-century Germany, the research university became the primary institution for generating the multiplying forms of specialized inquiry that in the twentieth century everywhere defined real, objective knowledge.[8] The modern idea of a university was less that of an institution where students imbibed inherited, time-less truths, which were increasingly stigmatized as mere beliefs or opinions, than of one supporting original research conducted within differentiated and self-contained academic disciplines and subdisci-plines. Because of the manifest success and resulting prestige of the researches of the investigators who in 1833 were first called "scientists," knowledge was redefined and increasingly fragmented. By 1900 the most creative and respected scholars, imitating the example of their scientific colleagues, learned to regard as intellectually irrelevant both the philosophical and theological assumptions and implications of their own researches. In the measure that specialization was prized, big questions were sidetracked, even in departments of philosophy.

According to disciplinary naturalism, a field became a proper object of academic inquiry if it admitted the collection of data that could be investigated and explained inductively or analyzed logically, prefer-ably in ways that admitted verifiable (or falsifiable) hypotheses. The academic use of religious ideas was inadmissible if they presupposed or asserted the existence of God. Such ideas could be legitimately studied as historical or sociological phenomena, but no credence could be given to their ultimate supernatural implications, which were at best metaphors for social relations and at worst residues of a basically prelogical cast of mind.[9] In the English language, the resonance of such disciplinary naturalism was captured by the words *agnostic* and *agnosticism*, neologisms suggested in 1869 by T. H. Huxley, the most redoubtable champion of Charles Darwin's principle of natural selec-tion. At the end of the twentieth century, those attitudes were the touchstones of the graduate programs in the natural and social sciences and humanities of all leading universities in the north Atlantic rim. There, as Jencks and Riesman pointed out, the faculty of American Catholic colleges and universities, or at least their dissertation supervisors, were educated.

Eighty-three years after Thorstein Veblen wrote, it is still commonly felt to be outré to analyze the higher learning in America as a business, but a business it is, as Martin Marty recently reminded us, and a busi-ness it was decades before Veblen.[10] There are some constants in American culture. In canon law and daily practice, the orders of sisters, priests, and brothers who founded, built, and within living memory still governed most of the nation's Catholic colleges and universities were the anchors of their churchly identity. Their hegemony over Catholic higher education exemplified functional differentiation long before the concept existed. With the exception of the Catholic University of America, which has an immediate juridical relationship with the American bishops and the Holy See, and a few colleges sponsored by dioceses or diocesan orders of sisters, the formal connection between America's Catholic colleges and the hierarchical church ran through the superiors of the religious orders to the competent Roman authorities. Formally, the local bishops of most of the dioceses in which those institutions lay exercised only an indirect authority, monitory not supervisory. Then as now, the working of informal arrangements is another matter. Many religious, especially those occupying administrative positions within the schools, were captains of instruction and occasionally of erudition: dedicated, intrepid, commanding, and frequently visionary. More often than not, their educational roles derived from their religious profession or clerical state rather than from a primary vocational decision of their own for scholarship, science, or administration. Their notions of how higher education should be conducted tended to draw on available models. Well into the twentieth century, the Jesuits, the largest order of higher educators, maintained an elaborate scheme of early modern European provenance. In the case of the newer orders that reinvented themselves as higher educators in the United States while creating the bulk of its Catholic colleges and universities, there were models confected from, first, European memories, and, then, routine American practices. Nowhere was corporate self-reinvention ever definitive. It became a process.

From the start, with the founding of Georgetown in 1791, securing a market share was of critical importance to those captains of instruction. By the late nineteenth century there finally existed a network of institutions that allowed the majority of college-bound American Catholics to choose Catholic institutions. Because of strong religious convictions and, often, loyalty to particular schools, there were always aspiring young Catholics for whom there was only a Catholic option. They were never sufficiently numerous to guarantee an adequate constituency for Catholic higher education in the United States. Always and almost everywhere, students had to be recruited and competitors matched or trumped. Sometimes those competitors were Catholic.

The orders jostled one another for enrollment, frequently at close range. Thus the Augustinians founded Villanova just outside Philadelphia in 1842, and within a decade the Jesuits were building a rival, St. Joseph's, a few miles away within the city. Whatever the benefits to prospective students of such internal competition in maximizing choice and controlling prices, its intellectual costs to American Catholicism were, as Jencks and Riesman insisted, cumulative and exigent. Internal competition long prevented Catholics from creating their own academically prestigious colleges and universities. It also obviated the possibility, first, that the bulk of the intellectually ablest and most ambitious Catholics could be educated in Catholic graduate schools and, later, that most such scientists and scholars could spend their careers teaching and doing research in Catholic institutions. The competition among the religious orders ensured that there would never be a viable alternative for Catholic academics to the dominant naturalistic and disciplinary concept of knowledge taken for granted in leading universities.

By 1900 the curricula of many Roman Catholic colleges already had a strongly professional (or preprofessional) and commercial bias. Educational entrepreneurship, the precondition of institutional survival, necessitated it. There was also an anxious discussion of the drift of college-bound young Catholics toward competing non-Catholic institutions. The effort of some Catholic higher educators to convince the American hierarchy to prohibit Catholics from attending non-Catholic colleges failed. Philip Gleason suggests that "the crux of the difficulty seems to have been that the college men were unwilling to give the archbishops meaningful control over their institutions, or even to guarantee that they would meet minimal qualitative standards."[11] Mutual suspicion between diocesan bishops and the religious orders was already an old story in 1215. Throughout the twentieth century the imperative to preserve effective institutional autonomy, even in relation to the Catholic hierarchy, fostered a large measure of competition in the marketplace of Catholic higher education.

Until the second half of the twentieth century, the core population from which the Catholic schools drew belonged to the still upwardly mobile but already Americanized classes rather than to those that were either destitute or ancestrally prosperous. Such students, or their parents, could afford to pay some tuition, if not always room and board.

The social range within the core population is suggested by the difference between arrangements for the undergraduates in the two Jesuit colleges in Massachusetts. Until the 1950s the men who attended Boston College, both when it was located in the South End of Boston and after its move to the city's edge, commuted, whereas even in the 1840s those who went to the College of the Holy Cross in the smallish city of Worcester, forty miles to the west, lived on campus. Into the 1950s, all American Catholic colleges were cheaper to run than comparable non-Catholic institutions, much as Catholic missions to Africa were cheaper to run than their Protestant counterparts. Everywhere, a striking level of cost-effectiveness obtained because of the often heroic self-abnegation of the members of the religious orders who did the bulk of the teaching and administration. They were vowed to poverty and to chastity, received only subsistence, and lived in community, virtually always available for all manner of tasks. They were "living endowments" whose existence long seemed to obviate any need to raise adequate dollar endowments. Because costs were held down, it was possible for the Catholic institutions to undertake enough improvements to remain competitive with other private and even public colleges. Religiously, educationally, and economically, the orders were integral and irreplaceable on Catholic campuses.

As early as 1900 some of the consistent features of twentieth-century Catholic higher education in America were visible, including the imperative of preserving effective institutional autonomy, the necessity of competing for students, and dependence on the vowed religious, both to compete effectively and to preserve a Catholic institutional identity. The threat of secularization was also widely canvassed a century ago. Catholic sensitivity to secularizing and Americanizing pressures was galvanized by the rise of the regional and professional accrediting agencies, which were meant to prevent the imposition of uniform federal standards and controls like those which the laicizing states of Europe mandated. The involved and piecemeal Catholic acceptance of secular accreditation encapsulated another consistent feature of the twentieth-century history of Catholic colleges and universities. Following a lag, they largely tended to adapt to dominant secular models. On Catholic campuses, for example, the differentiation of higher education from secondary education was not complete until the 1930s.

An equally important example of the slow but eventual assimilation of secular forms by Catholic institutions is the acceptance of the modern research university as the premier form of higher education. The new concept of knowledge conveyed by the new kind of university was not highly marketable among Catholics, except for those studying medicine, law, engineering, and commerce. Their universities were slow to develop creditable doctoral programs in the natural and social sciences and the humanities. It is suggestive that a Protestant minister received the first Ph.D. awarded by a Catholic university in the United States. Hypothetically, neo-Thomism, by papal decree the official philosophy of the Catholic Church after 1878, might have enabled Catholic academics to refine if not quite reject the new concept of knowledge. Informing the philosophy was the premise that human wisdom had been perfected by 1274 when St. Thomas Aquinas died. Thereafter the path to the higher knowledge lay in habituating minds to his concepts and categories so as to foster in them a spirit of creative imitation. Although discovery conceived of as concerted, original academic research was not intrinsic to the neo-Thomist revival, it was early on involved with the new concept of knowledge. Establishing accurate and authoritative editions of the works of Aquinas and the other medieval doctors required an erudite scholarship that could be acquired only in research universities. The curriculum vitae of the preeminent Catholic historian of medieval thought, Etienne Gilson (the Sorbonne, Strasbourg, Harvard, the Collège de France, Toronto, and so forth), was perhaps uniquely grand, but it hints at the unintended assimilative potential within the revival of Scholasticism.

At the conceptual level, moreover, neo-Thomism was a philosophy more than a theology. Assuming that there existed a division between the "natural" and the "supernatural," it yielded a spacious domain of pure nature *(natura pura)* governed by unaided human reason. It was a territory largely safe for the pursuit of knowledge defined according to the principles of disciplinary naturalism. Although jealous in matters of theology and doctrine and technical philosophy, the hierarchical church was disinclined to meddle in the domain of *natura pura*. An instructive book could be written on the chastening impact on modern official Catholicism of the remorseless attention paid to Galileo's condemnation by the Roman Inquisition. It might be titled *Not Burned, but Always Wary*. The Vatican's determination never again to be seen as stifling the advance of legitimate natural science, the core of *natura pura,* helps to explain why neither of Charles Darwin's great revolutionary books, *Origin of Species* and *The Descent of Man,* joined the *Zoonomia, or the Laws of Organic Life* of his grandfather, Erasmus, on the *Index Librorum Prohibitorum.*[12]

A European episode in the relatively painless accommodation of official Catholicism to theories of human evolution illustrates that cautious policy and also sheds light on the entire twentieth-century history of Catholic higher education in the United States. In 1909 the University of Cambridge, Charles Darwin's alma mater, celebrated both the centenary of his birth and the golden anniversary of the appearance of the *Origin.*[13] The Catholic Church was then in the throes of the modernist controversy, which culminated in a papally inspired hunt for and repression of supposed theological deviants so encompassing and intransigent that it extended even to cardinals.[14] Responding to an invitation from Cambridge, the academic council of the Catholic University of Louvain (Leuven) in Belgium, then the one really distinguished Catholic university anywhere, voted to send a delegate to the celebration. There Henri Dorlodot, a priest, the head of the geological institute at Louvain and a corresponding member of the Geological Society of London, delivered an encomium that seemingly annexed St. Augustine to the cause of Darwinism. It annoyed some Francophone Catholic antievolutionists, on whom Canon Dorlodot later imperiously turned: "If the great Doctor [Aquinas] had belonged to the Rectoral Council of this University in 1909, he would have decided, as did our Deans, that for the sake of the honor of religion the Catholic University could not abstain from joining in the celebration at Cambridge."[15]

At a time when theologians faced sometimes indiscriminate harassment, Dorlodot went back to direct his institute, outspoken but secure. Even before there was a full-fledged Catholic research university in America, the concept of knowledge founded on disciplinary naturalism was established at Louvain and acquiesced to by the Vatican authorities. Decades before the *Index* was abolished in 1966, as long as scholars and scientists respected some clear theological and philosophical boundaries, certain moral teachings and sociopolitical positions, and a few conventions of etiquette, the official church was effectively willing to concede the autonomy of their disciplines and the legitimacy of disciplinary naturalism. Apart from the study of theology, which itself was being transformed into just another academic discipline, twentieth-century Catholicism everywhere failed to discover an alternative concept of knowledge, one that drew on the distinctive intellectual traditions of the church to advance higher learning. It is a failure of imagination that Catholicism shares with the rest of Christianity and Judaism.

A history of the reception of Galileo's inquisitorial condemnation in America's elite institutions of higher education would be equally instructive. It might be titled *Always Warier, Even If Not Burned*. An animus against denominational control was virtually a birthright of the American research university, and the perception of Catholicism as the apotheosis of ecclesiastical dominance and dogmatism focused the animus. Andrew Dickson White, founding president of Cornell, first president of the American Historical Association, and ambassadorial eminence, lived very long and indulged freely in the awkward but revealing indiscretion that belongs to the doubly venerable. They can announce what others of similar mind only prudently think or whisper. In 1896, White finally published a historical polemic whose argument he had debuted in 1869. Underlying *A History of the Warfare of Science with Theology in Christendom* was the conviction that disciplinary naturalism defined authentic knowledge, particularly in the university. Only the laicization of academic institutions and the instruction and research they supported enabled the intellectual emancipation from "theological control" that was the precondition for the progress of knowledge, what White called "Science."[16] It followed that the researches of "sober-minded scholars" always regulated whatever limited intellectual content religion possessed. Anything more cognitively ambitious was "theology," essentially obscurantist and repressive speculation, the ghost of the primitive dogmatic casus belli. Nine years later White was roseate about the future and even more indiscrete: "More and more the thinking and controlling races are developing the power of right reason; and more and more they are leaving to the inferior and disappearing races the methods of theological dogmatism. More and more, in all parts of the civilized world, is developing liberty of thought; and more and more is left behind the tyranny of formulas."[17]

Andrew Dickson White wrote at what was perhaps the high point of an unthinking, sometimes racist equation of the institutional and theological aspects of religion with the incorrigibly primitive. In 1906, a year afterward, the Carnegie Foundation for the Advancement of Teaching, the progenitor of TIAA-CREF, was founded to help provide pensions for professors retired from private, nonsectarian colleges. Any assistance was denied to those who had taught at schools tightly connected to a religion or with a religious qualification for their trustees. The ban included all Catholic institutions. It is difficult to calculate either how long or how intensely many respectable American secular academics assumed Catholicism to be antithetical to intellectual excellence, even to bare honesty. For some who were liberal minded and politically active, there was a low, steady suspicion of Catholicism that particular issues or events could inflame.[18] For others, however, the animus seems to have been a habit of mind so ingrained as to be unself-conscious. Thus, one of the most sophisticated and accomplished Americanists of the mid-twentieth century lauded, without perceptible irony, Andrew Dickson White as one of the "promoters of the secular university" whose strategy "was not one of militancy but of quiet persistence and partial accommodation . . . [uninterested] in making the tension between science and religion the source of unnecessary antagonism and struggle."[19] It is a suggestively capacious notion of "quiet persistence and partial accommodation."

Whatever the exact strength of anti-Catholicism in American intellectual life, Catholic academics and the colleges and universities where they taught were routinely stigmatized. They reacted variously with defensiveness, emulousness, and what used to be called "status anxiety." American Catholics have historically been in tension and oscillation between a sense of exclusion (or exclusiveness) and a desire to belong. For most of the twentieth century, both the tension and the oscillation affected the direction of higher learning in Catholic America. Intellectually and institutionally, the desire to belong finally proved to be the more powerful drive. Before the end of the 1950s American Catholic academic inferiority was already a watchword on Catholic campuses. The election in 1960 of a Roman Catholic as president of the United States segued into the ecclesiastical opening achieved by and ascribed to the Second Vatican Council (1962–65). Efforts to uplift Catholic colleges and universities by mainstreaming them were energized. Whether or not it was bliss to have been alive then, a world rich in new possibilities seemed to be dawning.

Not all stigmas, however, are fictive. In 1937, Robert Maynard Hutchins, president of the University of Chicago, gadfly of American higher education, and the one secular mandarin of the period whom many Catholic academics found simpatico, charged that their institutions "imitated the worst features of secular education and ignored most of the good ones." He meant, in Philip Gleason's words, that those colleges and universities "were as much tainted as all the rest by . . . athleticism, collegiatism, vocationalism, and anti-intellectualism, but they failed to emulate their non-Catholic counterparts in dedication to research, to high academic standards, and to inculcating good work habits."[20] Even when allowance is made for the hyperbole and caricature that are the gadfly's stock-in-trade, Hutchins's indictment captures the intellectual failure of the one serious attempt to elaborate and institutionalize a credible, distinctively Catholic alternative to the concept of knowledge embedded in disciplinary naturalism: the neo-Thomist revival.

Decades before 1937, philosophy "according to the mind of St. Thomas," i.e., his Renaissance and baroque expositors and commentators, had been imposed by the Holy See as the official Catholic philosophy. At least in America, however, undergraduates rarely studied Aquinas's own works even in translation. Rather, the interpretations and glosses of his epigoni were summarized for them, usually in dreary manuals and textbooks. Into the 1950s, "integration" through one or another variant of neo-Thomism seemingly possessed in the Catholic academic milieu some of the grail-like allure and elusiveness that would later mark numerous secular interdisciplinary academic projects. A heavy load of course requirements in philosophy and the apologetics that passed for theology fell on every undergraduate in every Catholic college in America, creating the appearance of unique academic coherence. The requirements impeded the spread of the elective system within Catholic institutions, but it is at least arguable whether they went very far in integrating the worlds of faith and learning on campuses. Subversive questions were obvious and sometimes voiced— What did hylomorphism have to do with chemistry? What did suspicion of moneymaking have to do with economics?

Religion was an even more fundamental problem for the revival. After World War II, neo-Thomism continued to be a philosophy taught to undergraduates in lieu of a developed Catholic theology, not as its prolegomenon. The very lack of religious specificity that made neo-Thomism appealing to a secular-minded educator such as Hutchins also limited its capacity to provide an intellectually and imaginatively compelling foundation for Catholicism. Privately, some learned European scholars of *echt* Thomism scouted the textbook variety as a kind of Catholic rationalism potentially corrosive of Christian orthodoxy.[21] It appears, moreover, that many who were deeply involved with American Catholic projects of higher education saw religion primarily as a matter of sharing in a pervasive ethos, of living more than appropriating a body of doctrine. Often distinguished by transparent faith in Christ, intense devotion, and humbling asceticism, their version of Catholicism partook of the practical, moral, and personal notion of religion that Alexis de Tocqueville famously ascribed to the "influence of democracy on the action of intellect in the United States."[22] The 1960s added a salutary, balancing emphasis on the social imperatives of Christian faith, but often the quest for justice was itself essentially moralizing in its inspiration and its implications. It was thus powerless to mitigate the secularization of academic knowledge and administration. In one important way, the quest for justice perhaps accelerated that movement. To the extent that in some orders a ministry centering on social justice was taken as worthier than one in higher education, the contracting talent pool of potential academics and educational administrators within those orders further shrank.

Before the exhilarating, liberating, and wrenching adjustments that overtook American Catholic colleges and universities after 1960, evidence existed that there the worlds of religion and learning were rather loosely connected. Twenty years earlier, some prominent American neo-Thomists launched an unsuccessful rearguard campaign to reverse and interdict the use by Catholic practitioners and patients of psychoanalysis and similar forms of depth psychology, all of them in some measure irreducibly secular maps of the human inner life. The reaction poignantly testified to the precarious hold of neo-Thomism on Catholic minds and imaginations. Many American Catholics embraced those new therapeutics of the soul because they seemed more plausible guides to the contours of the self than the one-dimensional voluntaristic faculty psychology found in textbooks propounding the official philosophy. Equally telling was the rapid collapse of curricula organized around neo-Thomism after its official status lapsed during the 1960s. The subversive questions of students and professors of chemistry, economics, and other disciplines came home to roost, but Catholic colleges and universities even now retain heavy formal course requirements in theology or religious studies as well as in philosophy. Typically, both function as privileged departments rather than as the unmoved movers of some higher academic integration. In the wake of the disestablishment of neo-Thomism, there is no distinctively Catholic consensus about the goals and structure of undergraduate curricula. Catholic institutions ranging from Alverno College, Wisconsin, to St. Anselm College, New Hampshire, have framed original and effective undergraduate core programs, but their basic academic organization mostly presumes departments or preprofessional programs organized according to the conventional principles of disciplinary naturalism.

One of the primary objects of the neo-Thomist revival was to exclude personal experience as a theological category. As if in a predictably opposite and equal reaction, with the declension of the official philosophy, experience became the paramount category in much of American Catholic religion, catechesis, and even academic theology. Thus few who still await middle age can easily grasp all the lush, clichéd repertoire of Catholic jokes derived from the lost system of education and the religious ethos that sustained it. For such younger people, David Lodge's Catholic romans à clef belong to a cultural world nearly as remote as that of *Middlemarch*. It was the formative religious environment of their parents or grandparents. More seriously, for two decades most Catholics have arrived as undergraduates on Catholic campuses strikingly innocent of many of the doctrinal rudiments of Catholicism: variously well disposed and observant, or instinctively compartmentalizing their lives, or alienated from they know not quite what, or participating in that moving and ecumenical contemporary American religious drama, trying to restore what they imagine to be a betrayed tradition. By now, some of them are Catholic faculty members at Catholic colleges and universities, and their religious situations appear to display a similar variety. Something of the kind is said to be observable on many Protestant campuses that retain a strong denominational ethos.

The twentieth-century institutional history of Catholic higher education may have been even more supportive than its intellectual history of the desire to join the American mainstream. After World War I the greatest period of enrollment growth in its history occurred, but the depression of the 1930s saw financial emergencies or debacles, as well as a few closures, which exposed the precariousness of much of the earlier expansion. During World War II many all-male campuses were kept open by officer training programs, which, in addition to integrating them religiously as never before, taught their administrators how both to work with the federal government and to solicit federal money. The wartime experience prefigured the profound assimilative consequences of the federal assumption of the burden of funding big science, institutionalized after 1950 in the National Science Foundation. Just as Catholic colleges and universities began to receive and solicit public money in growing amounts, the judiciary, following the Supreme Court's lead in *McCollum v. Board of Education* (1948), was making constitutional doctrine out of the stringent interpretation of the no-establishment clause propounded by Leo Pfeffer. The late 1960s saw the conjunction of a growing reliance on government funds, a fundamentalist interpretation of the separation of church and state, and a widespread sense that a new age of American Catholicism was dawning. Taken together, they powerfully furthered the institutional secularization of many Catholic colleges and universities. Even when the winds of that particular constitutional doctrine abated, the leadership of most Catholic institutions showed little appetite for attempting a revanche.

As usual, the forces of the academic marketplace also exercised a strong assimilative influence. When the Korean War ended, American Catholicism and its institutions of higher education were poised to participate in the spreading affluence and general consensus that marked the next decade of national life. The huge expansion in the student population fed by the GI Bill affected Catholic colleges and universities, though less impressively than in the 1920s. It also intensified the competition among them to attract students. As in the first half of the nineteenth century, the majority of American Catholics attending college were choosing non-Catholic institutions. A long period of steady growth, often haphazard and wasteful, ended in the late 1960s, to be followed by another cycle of widespread retrenchment and in some cases pronounced institutional vulnerability. As a result, Catholic colleges and universities adopted an even more competitive and assimilating stance while also trying to come to terms with the ramifying changes within the church that followed the Second Vatican Council. It was an environment that demanded not only innovation but also improvisational policy making.

Within the religious orders that conducted most of the Catholic institutions, a cadre of specialized educational administrators began to emerge during the 1950s. Before then, the office of college or university president was often linked to that of religious superior or in the gift of such a superior. There was never an abundance of academically prepared religious equipped by temperament and ability to govern successfully in the rapidly changing circumstances of late-twentieth-century Catholic higher education. It is difficult, furthermore, to discern any well-developed, effective systems of evaluating, training, and tracking religious to become chairs, deans, provosts, and even presidents. The economy of Catholic colleges and universities was becoming more fully monetary, and the scope of hiring was widening and opening (everywhere the percentage of faculty members who were lay and salaried was growing). No distinctively Catholic style of or approach to academic administration emerged. Those charged with such management had to discover or devise for themselves compasses with which to navigate the sea change. Many of the ablest of them succeeded because they astutely copied instruments of government that seemed to work in secular institutions. Others muddled through or floundered. Their inadequacies would have damaging effects on the coherence and élan of some institutions into the 1990s.

More successful were concerted efforts that began in the 1950s to educate members of the religious orders up to the higher, more specialized standards that obtained in American academic life. During what proved to be the last phase of an unparalleled harvest of vocations to religious life and the ministerial priesthood, the academic quality of the sisters, brothers, and priests who belonged to the orders sponsoring colleges and universities dramatically improved. As Jencks and Riesman suggested, there was into the late 1960s still hope that something approaching that rich harvest might last indefinitely. They wrote, however, as the supply of recruits to the orders was diminishing and vowed religious were leaving in unprecedented numbers. Except for technical issues of governance and management, apparently systematic consideration was rarely given, either then or later, to studying and trying to cope with the complex implications of this demographic change for the future of the religious identity of the vast majority of America's Catholic colleges and universities.

During the next few years most of the nation's Catholic colleges redrafted their charters in ways that deprived the founding religious orders of direct control over governing boards. The results were disparate. In some cases, the institutions became not only legally but also really secular, but in others the founding orders retained effective general control, and the lay boards almost seemed to serve as a barrier against the intervention of external ecclesiastical authority. Two aspects of the change in structures of governance are noteworthy. Only a few schools that redrafted their charters observed the requirements of church law governing the alienation of ecclesiastical property, yet there were at the time no audible public complaints about that omission from either local bishops or the competent Roman dicasteries.

Intrachurch theological disputes in those years cast a long shadow on the relations between the administrators of Catholic colleges and universities and higher ecclesiastical authority. During the 1950s there were efforts in America to devise a theological justification for official Catholicism developing beyond the negative teaching on religious liberty and church establishment contained in the Theodosian Code (435 C.E.), a development finally decreed at the Second Vatican Council. In response, elements in the Roman curia, clinging to the traditional thesis and at once ascendant and threatened, moved strongly against those Americans, as they had a few years before against a group of eminent European theologians whose scholarship seemed to undermine the neo-Thomist revival. That forty years later Philip Gleason described this demarche as an exercise in "raw ecclesiastical power, wielded in utter contempt of academic freedom" suggests how deep and fresh were the wounds it left even among judicious American Catholic intellectuals.[23]

A collective memory of the episode was later reinvigorated by a few spectacular rows over academic freedom. A sense of injury apparently still conditions most senior educational administrators' attitudes and approaches toward the Roman authorities and even the American bishops, many of whom appear to harbor corresponding suspicions of their own. Particularly important was the case of the Reverend Professor Charles Curran, a moral theologian at the Catholic University of America who dissented, inter alia, from the condemnation of artificial means of contraception before and after it was renewed in the encyclical *Humanae Vitae* (1968). The Curran affair went through several permutations and ended in civil litigation after he was removed from the university's theological faculty in 1989. On Catholic campuses and elsewhere during those years, issues of theological authority and reliability merged with the issue of maintaining (or restoring) institutional Catholic identity. In June 1967 an invited group of prominent Catholic educational administrators and others met at a resort in Wisconsin called Land O'Lakes. They issued a brief statement that began with the ringing declaration that "to perform its teaching and research function effectively the Catholic university must have a true autonomy and academic freedom in the face of authority of whatever kind, lay or clerical, external to the academic community itself."[24] They also insisted that the academic discipline of theology could, by stimulating on campuses "an interdisciplinary dialogue that will be total," preserve everywhere a meaningful Catholic intellectual identity.

The merger of the theological and identity issues endures to frame most present-day American discussions of Catholicism and higher learning. In the media, a remarkable amount of attention has been given to *Ex corde Ecclesiae*, Pope John Paul II's 1990 apostolic constitution on Catholic higher education, largely because of the protracted, continuing effort to frame norms for implementing it in the United States. (One search engine turned up 2,990 items *sub voce* on the Internet.) Rich and in many ways creative, the document is at once a source and a symptom of the recent bout of public, discordant soul-searching about the health of the religious identity of Catholic colleges and universities, above all in the United States, home to the largest group of such institutions. The burden of the current debate about the papal document and its mode of implementation, however, is reductionist, assuming that on Catholic campuses the issues of theological authority and reliability are interchangeable with the issue of maintaining or restoring institutional Catholic identity. Usually lost in the shuffle are the various structural issues that I have tried to describe here, particularly whether academic knowledge must still be organized according to the principles of disciplinary naturalism and whether Catholicism can somehow be realized as a coherent religion with inescapable cognitive dimensions, realized in that way first on Catholic campuses for students and then beyond for alumni and alumnae. The resolution of the debate about the American norms for *Ex corde Ecclesiae* presumably involves the same complex and often subterranean negotiations that have marked the last decade. Until the underlying structural issues are fully engaged, however, the maintenance or restoration of institutional religious identity in American Catholic colleges and universities is likely to remain as uncertain as the "interdisciplinary dialogue that will be total" which academic theology was expected to stimulate on campuses.

Notes

1. Christopher Jencks and David Riesman, *The Academic Revolution* (Garden City, N.Y.: Doubleday, 1968), 375.

2. Ibid., 398.

3. The literature is enormous and predictably uneven. Taken together, Michael J. Buckley, *The Catholic University as Promise and Project: Reflections in a Jesuit Idiom* (Washington, D.C.: Georgetown University Press, 1998); James Tunstead Burtchaell, *The Dying of the Light: The Disengagement of Colleges and Universities from Their Christian Churches* (Grand Rapids, Mich.: Eerdmans, 1998); and David J. O'Brien, *From the Heart of the American Church: Catholic Higher Education and American Culture* (New York: Orbis, 1994), convey the range of diagnoses and prescriptions. It may be worth considering why priests and other men seem to dominate published discussions of the fate of Catholic identity on Catholic campuses.

4. Richard Horchler, "Education and Meritocracy," *Catholic World* 208 (October 1968): 38.

5. David Riesman, "Commentary," in *From Backwater to Mainstream: A Profile of Catholic Higher Education,* by Andrew Greeley (New York: McGraw-Hill, 1969), 171.

6. These paragraphs summarize Tomas M. Landy, "Demographic Snapshot: Catholic Higher Education, 1960–1990" (paper presented at Saint Louis

University, May 9, 1997), a persuasive longitudinal analysis. I am grateful to Professor Landy (College of the Holy Cross) for a copy of his essay. Central elements of my analysis are confirmed by Melanie M. Morey and Dennis H. Holtschneider, "Relationship Revisited: Catholic Institutions and Their Founding Congregations," report issued October 1, 2000, by the Association of Governing Boards of Colleges and Universities. It studies the administration of 172 Catholic colleges and universities in the U.S.; summary available at www.agb.org.

7. The indispensable history into the 1960s is Philip Gleason, *Contending with Modernity: Catholic Higher Education in the Twentieth Century* (New York: Oxford University Press, 1995), on which my own historical summary depends. The subsequent period is addressed in Alice Gallin, ed., *American Catholic Higher Education: Essential Documents, 1967–1990* (Notre Dame, Ind.: University of Notre Dame Press, 1992); Alice Gallin, *Independence and a New Partnership in Catholic Higher Education* (Notre Dame, Ind.: University of Notre Dame Press, 1996); and Alice Gallin, *Negotiating Identity: Catholic Higher Education since 1960* (Notre Dame, Ind.: University of Notre Dame Press, 2000).

8. Here and elsewhere I incorporate sections of Robert E. Sullivan, preface to *Higher Learning and Catholic Traditions* (Notre Dame, Ind.: University of Notre Dame Press, 2001). Laurence R. Veysey, *The Emergence of the American University* (Chicago: University of Chicago Press, 1965), remains basic for the American side of that transatlantic history; it is most recently traced in John H. Roberts and James Turner, *The Sacred and the Secular University* (Princeton: Princeton University Press, 2000); for a comparative context, see Sheldon Rothblatt and Björn Wittrock, eds., *The European and American University since 1800* (Cambridge: Cambridge University Press, 1993).

9. A classic expression of the contrast between an attentive if reductionist notion of the cognitive status of religious ideas and a notion of them that is dichotomous and essentially dismissive is found in Emile Durkheim, review of *Les fonctions mentales dans les sociétés inférieures,* by Lucien Lévy-Bruhl, and of *Les formes élémentaires de la vie religieuse,* by Emile Durkheim, *L'Année sociologique* 12 (1909–12): 33–37.

10. Thorstein Veblen, *The Higher Learning in America: A Memorandum on the Conduct of Universities by Businessmen* (New York: B. W. Huebsch, 1918); cf. Martin Marty, "Secularization and the Academy," *Sightings,* August 14, 2000 (online document available from the Martin Marty Center at the University of Chicago Divinity School).

11. Gleason, *Contending with Modernity,* 25.

12. *Index Librorum Prohibitorum SS. mi D.N. Pii PP.XII* ([Vatican City]: Typus Polyglottis Vaticanis, 1948), 121.

13. My account summarizes Harry W. Paul, *The Edge of Contingency: French Catholic Reaction to Scientific Change from Darwin to Duhem* (Gainesville: University Presses of Florida, 1979), 93–97.

14. Noteworthy on the subject are Gabriel Daly, *Transcendence and Immanence: A Study in Catholic Modernism and Integralism* (Oxford: Clarendon Press, 1980); R. Scott Appleby, *Church and Age Unite: The Modernist Impulse in American Catholicism* (Notre Dame, Ind.: University of Notre Dame Press, 1992); and Marvin R. O'Connell, *Critics on Trial: An Introduction to the Catholic Modernist Crisis* (Washington, D.C.: Catholic University of America Press, 1994).

15. Henri de Dorlodot, *Darwinism and Catholic Thought*, trans. Ernest Messenger (London: Burns, Oates and Washbourne, 1922), 87, as cited in Paul, *Edge of Contingency*, 97.

16. Andrew Dickson White, *A History of the Warfare of Science with Theology in Christendom*, 2 vols. (New York: D. Appleton, 1896), 1: xi–xii, 414–15.

17. Andrew Dickson White, *Autobiography of Andrew Dickson White*, 2 vols. (New York: Century Co., 1905), 2: 571.

18. John T. McGreevy, "Thinking on One's Own: Catholicism in the American Intellectual Imagination, 1928–1960," *Journal of American History* 84 (1997): 97–131.

19. Richard Hofstadter, "The Revolution in Higher Education," in *Paths of American Thought*, ed. Arthur M. Schlesinger Jr. and Morton White (1963; reprint, Boston: Houghton Mifflin, 1970), 277; cf. Peter Novick, *That Noble Dream: The "Objectivity Question" and the American Historical Profession* (Cambridge: Cambridge University Press, 1988), 321–22.

20. Gleason, *Contending with Modernity*, 247.

21. Laurence K. Shook, *Etienne Gilson* (Toronto: Pontifical Institute of Medieval Studies, 1984), 301.

22. Alexis de Tocqueville, "How Religion in the United States Avails Itself of Democratic Tendencies," in *Democracy in America*, 2 vols., trans. Henry Reeve, ed. Phillips Bradley (New York: Vintage Books, 1956), 2: 21–29.

23. Gleason, *Contending with Modernity*, 282.

24. Gallin, *American Catholic Higher Education*, 7.

Part III
Personal Reflections from the Front Line

7
Religion and Public Education
James C. Moyer

Several years ago I was working in our summer student orientation and registration program, where faculty help all first-time students complete their first registration. A professor from the English department observed to me near the end of the summer that religious studies was still "an undiscovered jewel." What she meant was that many first-time freshmen avoided religious studies courses because they did not know what such courses at a public university were like. Despite extensive advertising efforts, that often remains true. Nevertheless, the department has thrived, with an annual average of more than sixty majors and one hundred minors, about thirty graduate students, and more than eighteen hundred students enrolled in its courses each semester. Equally important is that the Department of Religious Studies has earned a strong reputation with a variety of constituencies —including diverse religious groups—both on and off campus.

History of the Department of Religious Studies

The story of the Department of Religious Studies at Southwest Missouri State begins in the 1930s when about one hundred students met on their own on Wednesday nights because they were interested in Christian ministry. These students contacted the president of the university and requested formal classes in religious studies. The president invited a local Presbyterian minister to teach such classes. In 1939, Dr. F. W. A. Bosch began a modest religious studies curriculum. It included Old Testament history, Prophets, New Testament, homiletics, and Sunday school pedagogy. Because the classes violated the separation of church and state, they were discontinued in 1949. In the 1950s, several religious groups established campus ministries that soon developed Bible courses offered off campus through their own accredited religious colleges. The 1963 yearbook advises: "These [Bible] courses are accredited by Southwest Missouri State and apply toward a degree as transfer credit from William Jewel College." By the late 1960s, the Baptist Student Union was teaching an average of four hundred students per year. That represented more than 5 percent of the current student body. Several other religious colleges also offered courses through campus ministries of their own. The volume of student interest led the administration to investigate the founding of a department of religious studies. After considerable study and consultation, the university sought a legal opinion from the state attorney general because no other public college or university in the state of Missouri offered religious studies courses through a regular department. The result was a strong positive endorsement, and in 1969 the university hired Dr. Gerrit J. tenZythoff to develop a department. Dr. tenZythoff had earned his Ph.D. from the University of Chicago and had been teaching history at Ohio State University. He brought not only immediate prestige and credibility to the new department but also an abundance of people skills. He teamed with his wife, Elisabeth, to charm even the most vocal opponents. At the time, some talked seriously of taking the university to court to determine whether the department violated the separation of church and state. Dr. tenZythoff, however, wisely did two things that carried the day for the department. He spoke to many community and religious groups and won their support. Even more important, he asked the qualified campus ministers who had been teaching courses for their own religious colleges to offer courses through the new department. Although this was risky, it assured a loyal team of teachers who became the best advocates for this new department to their own religious constituencies. When a consultant did a feasibility study for the adding of a religious studies major, he marveled at the department's carefully cultivated relationships with various religious constituencies.

The 1970s were a time of tremendous growth for the university, and total enrollment nearly doubled. The department could not meet student demand. It added a minor in 1972, and the first tenure-track faculty member arrived in 1973. By 1981, the tenure-track faculty totaled eleven, and departmental enrollment approached fifteen hundred. In 1982, the department added a major in exchange for a reduction in the number of religious studies courses that met general education requirements. A master of arts degree rounded out the program in 1994.

Several observations about this history are in order. First, many students in the Ozarks are genuinely interested in religion, and that interest is ultimately what led to the founding of the Department of Religious Studies. Second, the administration concluded that people were willing to take risks to meet student demand and begin a department of religious studies. Third, Dr. tenZythoff built the department as a complement to campus ministries and used their leaders as his first teachers. This created excellent rapport with, and support from, many religious constituencies. Fourth, Dr. tenZythoff's skills with people created a unique team of religious studies colleagues who invested time and personal attention in their students. This legacy, though modified by new leaders and the passage of time, continues today without significant change.

Recruiting Students

The recruitment of students is an ongoing effort. The department must work closely with the enrollment management team to recruit majors and minors from the pool of prospective students. This effort includes calling and writing prospective students as well as assisting in campus visitation days. The numbers gained are small, however, because only a few students each year declare religious studies as their major at the outset of their college career.

Even more important is the recruitment of current students to a first class in religious studies. This is a challenge because there are at least five misconceptions about religious studies courses in a state university.

First, there is a general ignorance about the difference between confessional education (seminary or religious college) and the academic study of religion, or learning *about* religion in a state university. Unlike history, English, and mathematics, religious studies courses are still relatively uncommon in public education. Much of the department's publicity is devoted to explaining what religious studies is and is not.

Second, many students still consider it illegal to teach religion in a state university. They confuse it with religious indoctrination, which is illegal. In 1963, however, the Supreme Court in *Abington v. Schempp* encouraged the academic study of religion, and today more than 60 percent of the "secular" universities in the United States offer courses that deal with religious issues.

Third, some students think religious studies courses are only for religious people. Students often say this, believing such courses are promoting religious faith. All students, whether religious, agnostic, atheistic, or apathetic, would benefit from the study of religion for numerous reasons, not the least of which is the impact of religious issues on all peoples throughout history.

Fourth, other students think religious students set the curve, assuming that practicing religious students know more than they do. This is possible but unlikely. Rather than rewarding students for personal religiosity, the Department of Religious Studies evaluates them on the results that good reading, writing, and study skills should produce. Frankly, the content of the courses is often significantly different from the religious instruction religious students receive elsewhere. Parochial school graduates have never compared their religious studies courses to their parochial school courses.

Fifth, and finally, some students believe religious studies courses force one to become more religious, and others think they force one to abandon faith. Because the goal of the courses is education, not indoctrination, students become more educated rather than more or less religious. The department hopes that all students will become more thoughtful in their religious faith, or in their lack of faith, as a result of their taking courses from the department.

Therefore, recruitment efforts are best targeted directly to the students themselves, keeping the above misconceptions in mind. Admitted freshmen receive a letter before their registration inviting them to take a religious studies class. This group includes only the undecided freshmen, not those who have declared a major so that departments of decided majors can do their own advising. The letter explains what the academic study of religion is and promises a good experience with the teachers and department courses. The letter concludes with some persuasive comment such as "Don't be a religious illiterate."

The department encourages faculty to participate in the university's student orientation and registration program (and a sister program for transfer students). This program is designed to help the beginning students register for their first schedules. This summer program includes a special track for parents. Called the "Faculty Chat with Parents," the session avoids recruiting, but the net result is that being helpful to parents, along with responding to their interest and curiosity, has the potential to encourage their sons and daughters to enroll in religious studies courses.

Five Religious Studies Department lower-level courses may be used to meet general education requirements. These courses are "Introduction to Religion," "Paths of World Religions," "The Literature and World of the Old Testament," "The Literature and World of the New Testament," and "Religion in America." Because these courses are only some of several course choices to meet the general education requirements, the department must constantly advertise these courses and recruit students for them. At SMSU, the best way to do this is through word-of-mouth advertising from students who have good experiences in religious studies courses. Each of the professors invests time in students, personalizes courses for them, and helps them succeed. This does not mean the courses are easy. In fact, students often comment that they work harder because they are challenged and stimulated by the excellent pedagogy.

Another important way to advertise is to work with advisors across campus. Religious studies faculty actively seek opportunities to explain their course content to other advisors. These activities include attending and participating in the Advisor Forum with other advisors and learning from professional advisors about what courses should cover and how to help students succeed.

Professors also work with the public to explain what the academic study of religion is. This work includes speeches to community and religious groups and media appearances, including a biweekly five-minute radio program titled "A Religious Studies Notebook." In particular, religious studies faculty work closely with all campus ministries. This effort includes explaining what the academic study of religion is and how it differs from campus ministry, speaking to their groups when invited, and working together to keep overly zealous religious groups from inappropriately propagating their faith. Some of the explanation is conducted in a large group (annual appreciation luncheon), but most of it occurs in small groups, especially with directors and staff members who are new. One new director of a campus ministry remarked on the difference between his experience at SMSU and an earlier experience at another university where the religious studies department was his biggest adversary. We have found it productive to proffer a departmental welcome to campus ministers and to clarify with them our different but complementary roles.

In short, the Religious Studies Department works to make friends and allies of every constituency as far as this is possible. Yet it remains possible—even likely—that education may produce change that is not welcomed by everyone. Therefore, the olive branch must always be extended even if it is not accepted.

Usually the best way to recruit new majors and minors is to look at students who have had one or more courses in religious studies. If they really enjoy the courses and do well in them, they may be recruited to be a major or minor in the department. Usually the fundamental question that arises as these students try to decide is, "What can I do with a religious studies major?" Obviously some students will go into a religious career, but many need to understand that religious studies, like other liberal arts majors, helps to develop communication and critical thinking abilities, sensitivity to others, and a whole range of skills for which most employers are looking.

Challenges for the Future

Unsympathetic, Hostile, or Ineffective Administrators

Administrators on all levels could wreak havoc on any successful department of religious studies. A president or any upper-level administrator could systematically dismantle a successful department in such ways as freezing tenure-track positions or not authorizing replacements, curtailing or eliminating all nontenured or part-time positions, diminishing the budget, or deciding that religious studies courses do not fulfill general education requirements. At present, more than 90 percent of the department's student credit hours come from five courses that may count in two categories of the university's general education–humanities requirements. Removing those options would devastate the department and eliminate the most effective recruiting tool for new majors, minors, and graduate students. Even an ineffective head or chair could unwittingly spark a decline in a successful department of religious studies.

The administrative challenge can be met in several ways. Every administrator needs to be educated about what religious studies is and is not. Faculties must never assume that the education of the dean, vice president, or president is complete, and they must faithfully pursue new ways to describe what the department offers and accomplishes. Another effective response is for religious studies faculty to be team players within the university and to support other departments and new initiatives whenever possible. This does not mean blind support, but it does mean that the administration can generally count on the department to support its academic vision. A third response is to make good things happen frequently and to be sure administrators hear about those things. The bottom line is that a department (and its chair) must always seek to work well with the administration. This should also assist in the appointment of an effective replacement for the chair when that becomes mutually agreeable to both administration and faculty.

Budget Shortfalls

This deserves its own category. These days most departments are being asked to do more with less budget. This may mean a diminishing of the budget for such reasons as fewer students and less tuition, economic slowdown, or financial mismanagement. Good departments always require money, in part because they must be labor intensive. Some pundits predict fewer and fewer dollars available for higher education and urge us to devise new ways of educating students. Right or wrong, any retrenchment will certainly hit religious studies departments harder than such departments as English, mathematics, communication, or history.

This challenge is particularly difficult to address. In addition to practicing frugality, every department needs to have an effective fundraising effort that could make up some, or even the majority, of any shortfall.

Decline of Interest in or Hostility toward Religion

College students today are increasingly interested in religion, and the increase of enrollment in SMSU's Department of Religious

Studies reflects that interest. Religious curiosity waxes and wanes, and any substantial decline of interest will negatively impact departments of religious studies. When several TV evangelists were exposed in the 1980s and society became negative toward them, we noticed that some people associated religious studies with them and kept their distance. Such things are rarely measurable, but it is clear that student interest in religious studies is cyclical. Departments cannot control these cycles, and it is impossible completely to counter a shift in popular interest in religious studies. Continuous effective advertising targeted to students as well as excellent teaching and learning in classes can help to minimize the impact of these cycles.

Changes in Church-State Laws or in Interpretations of Them

Although the changes may not be predictable, it is possible that various groups could lobby effectively to change the laws and interpretations that currently permit and encourage the academic study of religion. One need only look at twentieth-century examples in other countries to see this in action. Religious freedom is a precious freedom, and so is the right to study religion academically without censorship. This freedom can be maintained only by a vigilant citizenry. Religious studies faculty should take every opportunity to educate all constituencies about this.

Opposition by Various Constituencies

Some constituencies can be especially vocal in their opposition to departments of religious studies. One such incident occurred at SMSU when several hostile local religious leaders demanded that a tenured professor be fired. At issue were the professor's alleged "progressive" views, which conflicted with the cherished beliefs of the opposition. The department responded quietly with many one-on-one lunches, explaining academic freedom in the state university and how it differed from doctrinal statements signed by faculty members at a religious college. The department weathered that storm even though the affirmative action officer worried about the effectiveness of a low-key, behind-the-scenes defense. One religious leader appealed all the way to the president of the university. Happily, the department was able to make its case, and the professor survived and is still teaching.

Another significant constituency is the group of students who take religious studies courses. Complaints from a variety of students are inevitable. Each one must be handled individually. So far, the SMSU department has been able to acknowledge these complaints and satisfy them with diplomacy. Nevertheless, perceptions are just as important as the facts, and a student could make unsubstantiated charges that later prove to be false. A generation of goodwill and effective public relations can go a long way to diminish the credibility of such charges.

Insensitive Faculty or Unqualified Faculty

A disgruntled faculty member could try to destroy a successful program. Such a person might be a faculty member denied reappointment, tenure, or promotion. For example, when the SMSU religious studies chair had to tell a faculty member that his application for tenure had been denied, the chair requested the department's most senior faculty member to attend the meeting. His assistance was invaluable, and he took another hour after the meeting to absorb the candidate's complaints and hostility.

Although hard to envision today, it could be that the pool of well-trained and qualified religious studies professors will dry up. Without well-qualified faculty, it is possible someone without adequate qualifications could mishandle a situation, have it explode, and cause irreparable damage. Obviously unqualified faculty should never be used. It is important always to try to keep the dialogue open with the newest and least-experienced faculty so they can talk about how to handle explosive situations. In addition, experienced mentors at SMSU are paired with all first-year faculty to help them become effective teachers and colleagues.

Obviously, every situation is unique, but I hope this glimpse of the religious studies department's experiences at Southwest Missouri State University will be helpful to others who work in the field of religion and public education.

8
The View from
the University Chapel

Alison L. Boden

The task of college and university chaplaincies is obvious: to promote religious practice. Or is it obvious? And if the promotion of religious practice actually is the function of chaplaincies, what are the methods, criteria, and goals for its realization?

At many (but not all) denominationally related institutions, chaplaincy programs are expected to enable the academic community to live as faithfully as possible in accordance with the precepts of the sponsor's religious tradition, usually broadly translated and with exceptions granted for those who are not members of the founders' tradition. Public colleges and universities, meanwhile, do not have institutionally supported chaplaincies but rather are host to religious organizations funded by outside sponsors such as dioceses, adjudicatories, and national organizations such as Hillel, Intervarsity, or the Muslim Student Association. Generally, these groups have relatively well-defined objectives in keeping with the tenets of their faith traditions, although there are imaginative—and occasionally contentious—interpretations of how the objective might be lived out (an emphasis on community service, the religion's culture, scriptural study, social action, worship, and so forth). I write from the perspective of a chaplaincy program at an urban, private university that has no particular religious affiliation. My staff and the programs that we oversee are not charged with the promotion of a particular religious tradition; our mandate is to enable spiritual growth and exploration for all members of the university community, whether or not they identify with any formal tradition. In this sense the "obvious" function of chaplaincy programs still sits very easily with us. At the same time, however, there is nothing obvious at all about our mission, and for two reasons. The first is the relationship of our students to religion, and the second is the relationship to religion of the secular institution of higher education.

As many commentators have noted, large numbers of today's students have no real religious affiliation or education. Some have intentionally avoided it; others were raised by parents who were disaffected with their own traditions, skeptical of religious institutions, or wished to avoid the religious question because of their interfaith marriages. The result is that many students are religiously uninitiated and illiterate. Like most of humanity, however, they are spiritually hungry. They are religious seekers, although many prefer to distance themselves from concepts such as "religion" and "the religious." Innumerable students have sat in my office and said, believing themselves to be absolutely original in their self-description, "You know, I'm not religious, but I'm very spiritual" and "I don't subscribe to any particular tradition, but I find my own truth in a blend of many of them, in things that really speak to me." The "shopping around" aspect, the pick-and-choose nature of such intentionally constructed cosmologies and practices certainly angers many who have dedicated themselves to particular religious traditions and who resent what they understand as a kind of pilfering from spiritual passersby. The trend is rooted in two additional aspects to the religious rootlessness of many students — anti-institutionalism and individualism.

The anti-institutionalism is born of a disaffection with establishment structures, with organizations that smack of inherited validity or authority. (One might argue that validity and authority—particularly concerning religious institutions—can never be truly inherited, but that is not on the minds of those students who think this way.) What is valuable and worthy is what is evaluated and reconstructed in the moment, based on personal experience, personal revelation (a term very familiar to old-fashioned religion yet newly appropriated by young seekers), emotional connectedness, and, sometimes, ritual novelty. Underlying their attitudes is the conviction in students that meaning is made outside of the structures that have traditionally supplied it. This includes organized religion, and it sometimes also includes the university itself as purveyor of knowledge, status, and power. What is institutionalized has been corrupted, is not trustworthy, cannot be

reshaped to fit a new era, and can only be captive to previous generations' (outdated) understandings of what is to be valued and pursued.
The individualism that pervades postmodern culture has been commented upon extensively. It will be mentioned again before this chapter is through, but let me say now that I do not think it is inherently
a bad thing (as many in the religious communities do assert). Neither
is it necessarily a new thing. Its negative manifestations, to my mind,
on the topic of young adult faith development, involve its seductive
suggestion that ultimate meaning cannot only be articulated but
achieved alone. "Lone rangers" surf the religions as they would the
Web to see what they can glean for themselves as Truth. Their Truth
need not be relevant to anyone else, neither should it be applied to
anyone else (a preventive measure lest others' truths reciprocally be
applied to the seeker in question). Accountability is to be warded off,
for although it would be quite fine to know that others are responsible
to one's own spiritual sense of right and wrong, one would be im-
measurably diminished as a human being if one were obligated to meet
the requirements of another person's notions of right and wrong.
One's humanity would be fenced in, and the ultimate indignity of a
limit on one's self-expression would prevail. In short, the Self would
be absorbed into something larger, something beyond one's personal
control, some directive principle with the potential to override one's
personal choices. If one is not in control of one's choices, what value
is there in living? Certainly, then, one has become a pawn to another's
ideology/theology.

Thus the search for ultimate meaning takes on new forms. Many
students will conduct their search in the classroom, registering for
courses on religious and spiritual traditions far from those of their
families, hoping to find (in the midst of an innocent academic experience) some tools for understanding the cosmos and their own place
in it. Others will place their faith in other institutions or ideas, ones
that nurture a sense of ultimate meaning and even codes of ethics
without overt reference to cosmologies or belief systems. In a recent
course called "Human Rights in Islam, Hinduism, and Christianity,"
some of my students' comments and papers revealed a deep and lovely
search for a source for human dignity that could—possibly—be separated from the religious traditions in question. So many of them were
believers in social justice; the eye-opening experience for them was to

compare their ideas of justice with those expounded in the religions in question, to see the similarities and differences. Yet many approached the course with a foundational belief in justice before any belief in the tenets of the traditions under consideration. Their sincere faith was in certain notions of goodness, fairness, truth, equality, and freedom. Most of these beliefs squared off perfectly with portions of the course's religious content, but connecting their justice concerns to religious practice was the furthest thing from the students' minds. Ultimate meaning and fulfillment for human society was to be found far from the religions and deep in the bosom of the international legal community's deepest yearnings for its common life.

At least there was a sense of a common life! One very troubling thing about the individualistic sentiment in young adults' spiritual meaning-making is its denial that such meaning can be found in community. The denial is not so much one of commission but omission— it is not an intentional negation of community as much as an ignorance of its reality and potential. There is little sense of a corporate project, of peoplehood, of a cloud of witnesses. If any, the social justice believers come closest to a sense of community, as many know their work to be a very definite project done in invaluable tandem with partners who share the same goals and contribute either expertise or sheer decibel level to an effort that is, alone, unsustainable. Nonetheless, many students persist in believing that ultimate reality will be coopted only if divined in community—that those in power in the particular community will foist oppressive or unrealistic interpretations upon the whole that have little personal meaning to individuals. These students' perceptions are based on certain instances of historical fact, unfortunately. Yet they play, also, into fears that individual choice will be compromised if group allegiance is sworn. I am continually struck by how often students will claim that personal choice is the measure of human freedom, capability, success, and self-knowledge. I do not mean to write in these sentences against the importance of self-determination but rather to suggest that one (liberal humanist?) understanding of what it is to make choices becomes the standard of measure of everything, including metaphysical and religious truth claims.

The denial of the importance of community in their spiritual meaning-making is perhaps the greatest obstacle to students' success in their questing. I sense that what they are really yearning for is community—is communion—with some element of transcendence. They want, on the deepest level, to feel connected to a quality of holiness that exceeds their abilities to name or define or grasp but that they are convinced is absolutely real. They sense that there is a numinous presence suffusing all that they see and know; they believe themselves to be inherently a part of this chain of being, and they want to strengthen that sense of connectedness to it.

Perhaps, then, it is no wonder that at the same time that individual seekers are constructing their own systems of understanding themselves in such numinous relation to the world, religious participation is rising on many campuses. New religious organizations are sprouting up while many of the long-established ones enjoy increased student numbers. Parachurch organizations have enjoyed particular success for several decades. Now the "historic" churches' ministries are seeing a welcome upswing. Part of this trend might simply be a return to more "normal" rates of participation after the nadir of the seventies and eighties, but the majority has to do, I would say, with a contemporary pan-cultural emphasis on spirituality, which solid numbers of students still interpret along institutionally religious lines. Whether the routes that students choose are traditional or nontraditional, the ultimate goals are the same: meaning, rootedness, connectedness, and self-understanding.

In the face of all this, the project of chaplaincies to promote religious practice becomes somewhat less than obvious. The situation is further complicated by the often ambivalent, multilayered relationship to religion of the secular institution of higher education. If Jerusalem and Athens once were wed, they now are divorced and on relatively amicable terms, having realized some irreconcilable differences. There have been visitation rights for the ousted Jerusalem, with chaplaincies maintained on many campuses, although with greatly decreased financial and moral power. Other institutions have opted for a total separation, ended their chaplaincies, and substituted an administrative position responsible for oversight of students' religious activities. The "successful applicant" for most of these jobs is someone knowledgeable about the practices of various religions, committed to enabling students to meet their own worship and fellowship needs and skilled at higher education administration. In other words, the moral and ethical authority of an authentically religious presence has been eliminated. Some institutions have done just this in response to the very strong (and independent) moral power of previous chaplains. The increased presence of minority religions on campuses has been answered in many ways, with some institutions committing financial resources to a number of chaplaincies, each responsible for its own constituents. Others have assigned all religious communities to one chaplain, and some have used the situation as further justification for making religious affairs a secular category within student services administration. Some campuses have endeavored to "overcome"—to deny—their previous religious affiliation whereas others seek to build upon it, to expand the base to include all in the multireligious community. In the end, at many campuses religious life is considered an "extra," an optional way of spending some of one's time, an add-on to the basic mission of the institution, something that some people seem to feel that they need for themselves.

In a recent address to newly arrived undergraduates, a senior member of my institution's political science department informed our eighteen-year-olds that, fortunately, the university would not advocate any particular religious perspective. He was right, and I agree that, for our private, secular institution, such an action would be inappropriate. His comment continued as follows: "Not only is there a powerful imperative at Chicago to stay away from teaching the truth, but the University also makes little effort to provide you with moral guidance. Indeed, it is a remarkably amoral institution. I would say the same thing, by the way, about all other major colleges and universities in this country. . . . I would bet that you will take few classes here at Chicago where you will discuss ethics or morality in any detail, mainly because those kind of courses do not exist." I respectfully beg to differ. Moral and ethical issues suffuse the content of courses taught across the curriculum. Students who grapple with the Oresteia, with just-war theory, with Reubens, with languages, with cell biology, and with a host of other topics throughout the departments find themselves considering profoundly moral and ethical issues, guided by the faculty members who represent the institution. Morals and ethics undergird our subjects and work and lives, whether we choose to acknowledge their elephant-in-the-room presence or not.

Although many universities (my own included) do not overtly instruct its members in appropriate religious and ethical perspectives, they convey very clear moral and ethical perspectives all the time. No institution is perfectly monolithic in the messages it endorses, but the overarching vision remains one of an anthropocentric (rather than theocentric) vision of the universe, one in which the human being is as close an entity as anything to that nebulous category of "the sacred." One is likely to learn of the primacy of academic pursuits above all others. The "life of the mind" is the holy activity. Some departments or faculty members, as described above, may teach the uncompromising necessity of competition without compassion, of self-improvement or self-betterment with no responsibility to other persons. Some encourage self-enrichment at the knowing expense of other persons. Some teach the acquisition of knowledge for the betterment of societies, for the promotion of justice and peace. Some teach the acquisition of knowledge for its own simple sake, with tacit instruction on living both well and moderately, on striving for fulfillment in things other than things. It is—all of it—consciously articulated ethical and moral instruction.

A metaphysical position undergirds each of these perspectives. It is not necessarily religious, but it contains its own kind of cosmology and soteriology. It places the human being in a very distinct position vis-à-vis the rest of existing (religious folks would say "created") matter. It gives firm instruction on how one is to view other persons, the existence (or not) of a divine element in the cosmos, what value is to be accorded to specific human beings and on what basis, and which activities are "good" or "proper" or "just." The religions have very definite opinions on these matters as well, with understandings based on anything from salvation history to a cycle of rebirth. No wonder Jerusalem and Athens shook hands and agreed that they had grown apart over time, rather than together.

Individualism is also advocated by many of our institutions of higher education. One hears more and more often of students who cannot—and even will not—participate in group projects that will be graded. They do not wish to compromise their sense of control over their academic remuneration. They do not wish to be part of a corporate effort to do as well as possible, fearing that some members of the group will be academic liabilities, dead weight that prevents them from earning the best grade possible. They seem to have no understanding that the professional work that they eventually will do, and the societies and families in which they will continue to live, are all corporate projects, strivings for common goals and goods. Numerous colleges and universities have done their part to reinforce these attitudes in students, encouraging them to consider each course grade, in-class conversation, or lab experiment a chance to best others and come out on top. Competitiveness in tertiary education is not new, but a particularly fierce spirit of self-concern, combined with a deficient sense of community and of mutual responsibility, seems to me never to have been stronger. It is a manifestation of what one of my colleagues describes as "the sufficiency of private virtue"—the idea that those who fail at any or all things do so because of personal moral flaws, flaws that contribute to poor decision making. If other students do not succeed, it cannot be because of factors beyond their physical and emotional selves. They obviously lacked certain talents and moral priorities. Success and failure are traceable to individual ethical make-up, so one need not feel badly that others may not be doing well. One is not responsible to others, and joint projects force a person into an unnatural partnership with others whose determination and moral make-up may not equal one's own. An exception to this scenario exists in some business programs, which teach that financial and professional self-advancement are often enhanced by teamwork. The goal remains, however, very definitely self-enrichment.

What is the faithful and appropriate response of chaplaincies to the scene that has been described? How do they even promote religious practice on campuses that intend to be nonreligious, not to mention "amoral"? This very conundrum is the reason for the church/academy divorce.

I once told the general counsel at my university that I thought the chapel's role was to serve as "the conscience of the institution." He flinched at the very suggestion and said that no portion of the university could serve as its sole conscience. I have come to agree with him on that score but continue to maintain that the chapel ought to be a significant source of conscience for the institution. A number of voices provide balance and correction and challenge, and featured among them should be that of the religious community.

This task is not a change of focus for chaplaincies, which have always (at their best) asked potent questions of their institutions in order to prompt self-examination and growth. Some recent initiatives have centered on institutions' investments; twenty years ago the concern was South Africa, whereas today numerous chaplaincies are urging their administrations to divest from companies that do business with Myanmar or that use sweatshop labor. This kind of project certainly involves a movement away from pure religious practice and advocacy but is organically related to it. In addition to investment portfolios and major policies, chaplaincies today are in a position to help universities consider their more subtle—and perhaps more pervasive—levels of ethical and moral instruction. A new version of an old calling, then, is for chaplaincies to challenge their university communities and their individual members to name the belief systems by which they operate. Chaplaincies are in a unique position to keep the institution and its members asking themselves, What values are we practicing, teaching, and refuting? What can I learn about myself in light of what I value? Are these indeed the things I wish to espouse, or is there a disjuncture between what I say and do?

A second fresh manifestation of an old calling is for chaplaincies to keep the practice of religion a critical category of self-reflection in academic communities. I have been informed many times, overtly and covertly, that, in the words of one administrator, "the Chapel is not central to our University's mission." I understand what she meant: the chapel does not have a formal academic component. We do not offer courses for credit, as do the departments; we do not confer degrees. People do not come to the university to practice religion; they come to be certified in their fields. Fine. Nonetheless, the religious traditions offer rich (I believe the richest) systems by which to discern one's deepest convictions, priorities, challenges, nuisances, hopes, and potential. Ethical systems exist by which to explore codes of conduct; principles concerning relationships with other people, with a deity, and with nature; and principles concerning charity, warfare, peacemaking, justice, mediation, compromise, ultimate reality, and the meaning of living and dying. They offer some of the most potent challenges to the continuing racism, intellectual and cultural elitism, sexism, and classism in higher education. Real participation in a religious tradition never comes easily; those who vacation in a religion to see what it might offer them will never touch the riches that it holds. There is accountability to self, to others, and to a firm system of ethics for living in the world that can be neither understood nor truly practiced in a short period of time. Chaplaincies invite persons to come and stay awhile, long enough to understand the lens through which the tradition views the self and the self-in-relation. If universities exist solely to offer intellectual credentials, then no—chaplaincies are not central to the university's mission. But if colleges and universities exist to create educated citizens prepared for leadership in diverse and challenging public fora, chapels and chaplaincies are not incidental to such institutions' missions. The very clarification of those missions is a primary task of chaplaincies. If the role of religious programs needs new clarification as the next millennium begins, so perhaps does that of academic institutions. Religious offices offer challenging and supportive contexts and criteria for such discernment.

These related projects of prompting critical self-reflection and promoting religious and spiritual practices and criteria for such self-reflection are implemented in many ways. Regularly offered worship—liturgy and sacrament, religious community and fellowship—are intended to spur potent consideration of the values, commitments, and beliefs of those present, along with providing spiritual food and nurture. The great questions are carried out of the sanctuary and into residence halls, classrooms, living rooms, and student centers, where conversations and groups are convened, questions and convictions are engaged, and, one hopes, religion and intellectualism are melded in whatever unique way has integrity for each participant. Important thinkers—religious, political, scholarly, activist—are invited to speak in chapels to fellow travelers who also endeavor to find spiritual meaning in the banal, the horrid, and the beautiful. Some people's spirits respond more deeply to music or drama or art than to the spoken word. For them are choirs and plays and exhibits and guest artists from various cultures and traditions to bring the sacred to vibrant life. Others will finally face the ultimate concerns of being-human-in-community by leaving the university, perhaps on a trip organized to introduce them to other cultures' ways of living righteously. Perhaps that trip will keep them very close to home, yet in another universe of experiences and moral assumptions. Both are invaluable. All are intended to be catalysts of critical self-understanding, personally and institutionally.

Some words must be said about the effect of the "business" or "corporate" environment on colleges and universities and the resulting implications for chaplaincies. Today, some corporations fund whole departments or endow faculty positions, particularly those whose research serves to profit the corporation's particular industry investments. Have they, effectively, purchased the department for their own research and development? Simultaneously, at many institutions each unit (academic or not) is charged with its own fund-raising, either through student recruitment to the department or through facilities rental (such as chapels for weddings and other events) or grant writing or committing salary money to development personnel. The end effect of such initiatives is a campus-based version of the globally and nationally growing gaps between the rich and the poor. Although some departments (often the professional schools—law, business, medicine) are able to bring in money through big enrollments, student-paid tuitions (rather than institutionally supported grants), and wealthy, generous alumni, other units eat the scraps off the master's table. Chapel programs, for instance, are usually among the losers. Charged with bringing in income yet financially or structurally ill-equipped either to hire fund-raisers or to charge tuition (and how many times on a summer weekend can the chapel be rented for weddings?), they become part of the poorer relatives on campus. Simple spiritual presence is not enough. Programs that cost money must be initiated if the chaplaincies' objectives are to be met. While some departments spend without consideration, others must, in the new era of earning one's keep, cut staff, work with outdated equipment, or pare back programming to a mere representation of a responsible presence on campus. Chaplaincies are likely to be very negatively affected by this trend and yet remain in a "strategic" position to comment upon it. That net worth should come to equal real or institutional or human worth is an affront to the religions' teachings and to the original spirit of the educational enterprise. Providing a critically religious voice on these developments is a key challenge for chaplaincies in the years to come.

In 1995, a group of Asian academics active in the World Student Christian Federation met in Bangkok to consider the religious challenges posed by the corporate climate to universities' missions and cultures. Their draft statement declares, "It has to be asked whether the instrumental understanding of higher education as skills training in the service of the economy does not dangerously threaten the concept of education itself." They lamented the emergence of "curricula designed for commercial rather than human considerations." They concluded, "If the instrumental and commercial view of education is allowed to prevail, not only will the ideal of higher education be eclipsed, but we shall see the shrinking of the spirit of enquiry and free speech, and ultimately the suppressing of the human spirit as the university becomes a tool of the global economy."[1] The drafters of the statement went on to encourage those working with religious organizations on university campuses to challenge the notion that truth (in the form of knowledge) is a commodity to be bought and sold as a tool for self-enrichment and to continually remind all members of academic institutions that they will be held responsible for the moral use of what they learn and teach and know. The situation that they describe exists far beyond the Asian context and is, in its religious ramifications, of primary concern to chaplaincies in every tradition and region of the world.

More and more one hears laments from many in academic communities that a sense of spirituality has been lost in the institutions as they fashion themselves into hives of purely intellectual endeavor. I both agree and disagree. I do sense that the professionalization and commodification of education have led to an overly strong emphasis on academic achievement, but the spiritual component remains vital because many of the human beings who are delivering and receiving these educations continue to search (sometimes in spite of themselves) for a life of the spirit to accompany the life of the mind. On a deep level they understand that the two need not be divorced in order to flourish and that such flourishing might be more possible if the two are intimately joined. As described above, the starting points of the search for spiritual meaning are very diverse, and the end point may be a place that is "very spiritual" without being necessarily religious. The task of chaplaincies to enable transformation to spiritual maturity becomes more interesting, challenging, and important in these circumstances.

What, in this context of innumerable spiritual starting points, could possibly be the criteria for spiritual maturity? What would spiritual maturity look like in the face of such spiritual diversity? Is consensus necessary or achievable? The answer certainly cannot rest in the particularities of the religions' truth claims, although each tradition may well have its own criteria for that. Should it rest in a general and high level of education about religious and spiritual traditions and in the seeker's making the wisest educated choice among them, given her or his spiritual personality? Should chaplains be about helping individuals to know themselves and then to make wise choices from the menu of religious and spiritual traditions? Must it all be, again, about the level of exercise of personal choice? I once heard an eminent scholar state that religious freedom does not truly exist because children are so often instructed by parents as to belief systems and religious truths. How could these young persons ever truly come to a place of free choice in religion when early teachings will certainly have left some mark, some spiritual assumptions, some trace? I do continue to wonder at the (liberal, advanced capitalist) assumption that moral agency is identical with a radical self-determination born of "neutral" origins, as if those were possible.

To be spiritually mature is, to my mind, to have a conscious, reasoned, reflective, practiced life of the spirit. It is the ability to maintain a critical and informed perspective on one's own belief system as well as on others'. It is the ability to withstand assault without withering, to be strong enough to change in response to constructive challenge, and to be able to challenge others without disrespect or defensiveness. The rest is detail—and it is the rich part, the particular teachings and perspectives that lend life its profoundest meaning. Chaplaincies offer seekers tools with which to ferret out the noumena under the clutter, tools for unearthing the meaning in whatever tradition they make their home.

A major objective in forming spiritually mature students (and others) is the goal of creating citizens for multireligious societies. Religion has a role in conflicts the world over, and basic education and maturity could be helpful in articulating what are and are not the authentic religious contributions to those conflagrations. But on a more mundane yet perhaps more influential level, many universities and colleges work hard and commit scarce funds to create opportunities for their communities to explore and understand various cultures and perspectives, believing this to be a part of the education of the total person-as-citizen for a multicultural society. The same commitment needs to prevail in terms of forming citizens for a multireligious society. In addition to whichever particular religion's instruction may be their mandate, chaplaincies are also called to prepare students to enter as adults a country that may have a majority religion (Christianity) and its religious philosophy, but one that constitutionally makes room for practitioners of all faiths and none to coexist on equal footing. The fastest-growing religion in the United States is Islam (Muslim student groups are, likewise, the fastest-growing religious groups on many campuses). The next generation of leaders and voters needs to have a basic education about different religions and a foundation for respect for all traditions, both those with long histories (such as Islam) and those newly arrived. This mandate is about much more than classes in comparative religions, which religion departments may offer handsomely. It calls upon chaplaincies to teach students how to live and work together practically, to model ways for sharing power and communities, and to embody respect. Students need to graduate from colleges and universities knowing what basic questions to be asking in order to live fairly in a multireligious society; they need to have had modeled for them options for what intentional and substantive dialogue might be like. Student religious leaders who form intentional relationships with one another will, by that simple act, educate by example the rest of the student body. Along the way they will, we hope, come to understand their group's or others' teachings on responsibility to fellow citizens, on social justice, and on lives of right social relationship and learn to respect the varying truth claims at the center of the various religions. The challenges offered by beliefs that differ significantly from one's own, if we have done our job well, will not be a source of division but of greater opportunity for learning and grist for responsible lawmaking, much as there may be continuing disagreement about such things as equal civil liberties for those who are female or gay or atheist. Much is at stake; the formation of spiritually mature citizens for a multireligious society will make a decisive difference in how this country responds to public moral issues, to continuing diversification of the population, to the needs of those growing poorer in the midst of boom economies, and so on. In short, whatever social issues come to the fore, a generation of students who have learned how to dialogue across and to respect difference in religious truth claims, without expecting to water down their own deepest beliefs, will be invaluable.

This may sound good (it does to me), but its implementation by chapel programs is complicated and difficult. It centers on chaplaincies' abilities to bring together the different religious organizations on campus and to help them form the relationships through which they begin to dialogue and learn and challenge and change. Interreligious programming can be established; it will be successful if it works with issues that are of genuine interest and importance to students. For example, my campus has had success with what we call our Interreligious Festival for the Earth, an afternoon of drama, pageantry, and food in which (among other things) the various religions' creation stories are told through the use of massive puppets and figures. It is held close to Earth Day and taps the interests of our many students who care about the environment plus those who engage in religious practice. Interreligious worship, on the other hand, is not of interest to the majority of our students. They consider it essentially impossible; the particularity of the way that different traditions simply pray can not be accommodated in the same moment and space. Interreligious worship is understood to have the worthy intention of spiritual unity, but in the end it becomes an impoverishment of real worship and essentially a Protestant talk fest.

Thus interreligious community is attempted through programming. To a certain extent it is passive community building in that many of the students present have been lured into participating because of their interest in a secondary subject, such as the environment. The simple building of interreligious community is not of interest to many of them. Efforts to call together a council of student religious leaders have not been successful, and the offering of money to groups that plan events with others can seem like purchasing pluralism. Even those students who come with a real interest in creating an ongoing, formal relationship between religious organizations have been unable to name for themselves what is at stake in creating such a structure, and no one wants simply another meeting to attend. Identifying what really is at stake for the students can come only from the students. My own concern for the shaping of citizens for multireligious societies is tremendously compelling for me but cannot be foisted upon the students. For them, to date, intentional interreligious community is simply a good idea, like flossing one's teeth. It is undeniably good for us, but it is a time drain, an extra thing to remember, one that rarely gets done. Our campus seems not to be alone in seeking motivation for interreligious associations; a recent study by Wellesley College of institutions across the nation reported that the majority of those with no multireligious programs were lacking them because of "no interest."

Thus the religious organizations are thriving independently, but not together. I am consoled, however, to know that real and meaty encounters between religious and seeking students happen all the time in classrooms, dining halls, and dorm rooms. Chaplaincies are not the only source of encounter, to be sure, but still they are charged with fanning and nurturing the flames that already exist. They can also provide the guidance that will keep such encounters healthy and substantive so that they will avoid the quality (as one Hindu student describes it) of "religious pluralism as group hug." He is right to be dissatisfied with interreligious relationships that reach for mutual affirmation before or instead of real understanding, that avoid grappling with differences, or that reduce the content of the relationship to lowest-common-denominator vacuousness. He and his colleagues are right to want interreligious fellowship that has integrity or no such posturing at all. Naming and embodying the terms of that integrity is a major challenge for the years now before us.

The religious and spiritual landscape at colleges and universities today is far from arid; it is vibrant and growing. The range of foundational assumptions and beliefs and the discourse, models, and methods used in articulating and encouraging religious growth may look quite different from previous decades. The goals, I believe, are the same as ever: spiritual meaning, rootedness, connectedness, and self-understanding. These are then broadened to be understood in concrete relationship to people of all religious traditions. If the project of chaplaincies is made more complicated, it remains extremely satisfying. Chaplaincy is, at its heart, accompaniment. When the way becomes winding, challenging, or newly traveled, the journey certainly is interesting. Under these circumstances, promoting religious growth requires creativity, continual education, resourcefulness, patience, humor, and faith.

Individuals are accompanied, but so are whole institutions, which similarly grow into new roles, partnerships, and manifestations and which embody, as much as a person, a complex of moral and ethical assumptions that guide its behavior. Like individuals, colleges and universities should be prompted by chaplaincies to clearer articulation of their deepest values, prompted to finer self-understanding and sense of meaning. In the end, we seek to create scholars who are equipped not simply with knowledge but also with wisdom. They will be, we hope and pray, people of expertise and conscience, skill and vision, and proficiency and ethics. Not only are chaplaincies as relevant as ever, they have never been more important.

Note

1. Draft statement, University Concerns Group, available from the World Student Christian Federation, 5 route des Morillons, 1218 Grand-Saconnex, Geneva, Switzerland.

9
The College President as Spiritual Leader

Edison O. Jackson

As an educator, my spirituality is the context, the backdrop, that serves as the canvas on to which all of my life's activities are painted. The portrait that comes forth, more often than not, is clear and in focus because of this context of spirituality. Many of my colleagues in higher education have created a dichotomy in their lives, making a clear distinction between their professional lives and their spiritual lives, if such exist. This dichotomy forces them to create two very distinct personalities. So, in some ways, they end up being two very distinct individuals.

Although many things have happened to those of us who are spiritual that can create a dichotomy between the spiritual and the professional, such a division becomes very difficult for people to maneuver and to deal with because it takes a lot of psychological energy to create two personalities. So I have found a level of comfort in just being one person. Let me share with you a statement that I made in my interview when I was a candidate for the presidency of Medgar Evers College. When the screening committee had finished with all the questions they had for me, they then asked, "Would you like to make a comment?" I said to them, "First, what you see is what you're going to get. This is not a false image that I'm putting forth. Secondly, I am spiritual. I am not religious, but I am spiritual, and that is what will inform my behavior and the quality of the decisions that I will make."

As president of Medgar Evers College in Brooklyn, New York, it is a great honor to serve the people of the college community. The students are individuals who seek to improve their lives and the quality of life in their community through higher education. Leading a public

urban institution through the demands and challenges of today's society is a demanding task. Guiding the predominantly black, female,
older students, many of whom have family and work responsibilities,
calls for a level of sensitivity and responsiveness in leadership that
acknowledges the special needs and aspirations of the population.
In order to be an effective leader, I must present myself to the college community as a whole person, one who is composed of body,
mind, and soul. I am, indeed, a human being with physical qualities
and needs, an academic who studies, writes, and periodically teaches
courses on campus, and I am also a person who is critically aware of
the centrality of my spirituality as the guiding force in my life. To be
intellectually honest, I must consider the impact of my spirituality in
my total being and, therefore, in my role as college president.

A Personal Reflection

I am from a family of twelve children who grew up on a farm
in Virginia. From my earliest recollection, the church was an integral
part of the life of my family. There were always blessings of meals and
family prayer. We even prayed in the wake of dangerous conditions
such as thunderstorms. My father was a deacon in the church, and my
mother served as president of the church's missionary society. Attendance at church each Sunday was a must, and all of the children were
involved in church activities. This was not atypical behavior in the
community; it was a way of life. Church activities were not burdensome. They were activities that we looked forward to and found en-
joyable.

I made the decision to join the church at age eleven. In the tradition
of my church, once a young person reached the age of reason, he or
she was encouraged to make a formal and public commitment to the
church and to offer his or her life to God. I was accepted by the
church, baptized, and made a member of the fellowship of the church.
Interestingly, when I went forward to join the church, others followed
me, including my cousin and the young girl who would later become
my wife.

Today my wife, my adult children, and I are all very much involved
in the church. So too are my brothers and sisters and their families.
Within our large extended family structure, there are four ministers.

The church has always been the cornerstone of our lives, and God has been good to me and my family. Our lives have not been characterized by any negative or tragic behaviors; we have lived relatively trouble free.

In my professional life, I just marvel at the way God has worked through people as conduits for blessings. I became dean at a community college in New Jersey at age twenty-six after being recommended for the position by my thesis advisor, who was offered the position but was unable to accept. Although it was not my plan to go into administration, I thought I would try it for a few years. Then, with good people mentoring me and opening doors for me, I went on to obtain a doctorate while working in New Jersey.

After a few years in New Jersey, I journeyed out to California, a place where I knew no one, to explore job possibilities. The venture turned into a great experience. I was soon selected as president of a college to which I had no intention of applying when I went to California. Furthermore, educational assessment had become a major issue in California at the time, and, to my credit, I had been significantly involved in educational assessment in New Jersey. With this background, I soon became an expert on the topic. In addition, based on my work with United Way of New Jersey, the California branch of United Way presented me with the service award that I had earned. This immediately provided me with a level of recognition and credibility that was of tremendous benefit to me in my life and work in California.

Coming to New York was the last thing on my mind. My children did not like California, however, and my aging parents as well as other family members were on the East Coast. My wife encouraged me to pursue the presidency of Medgar Evers College. My experience in California had made me a very attractive candidate, and within two months of my interview at the college, I was the new president. I returned to the East and was again close to family members. In a sense, I had come back home.

Realizing that my family is a wonderful gift from God, as in all aspects of my life I let the spirit guide me in family matters and decisions. One morning I was out running, and I had this thought that I needed to call my daughter and say "I love you" because she was moving into a new arena and was not sure that we were pleased with her move. Although the spirit was heavy on me to call, there was a negative spirit saying, "Oh, you are foolish for making this effort." The spirit of God, however, was saying, "Go ahead and call." So I decided to call. I know that the call was the thing that made her day, as well as many days after that, because she is a "daddy's child" who loves to receive affirmations from her father. It was the spirit that kept driving me and saying, "Call." After I called, the voice that spoke to me was gone because I had answered and responded.

In guiding my children, I listen to the spirit and teach by example. Being from a very large family, I have always shared whatever I had with others. For my children, giving and sharing with others comes naturally. My son often cooks for his wife and young child. I, too, enjoyed preparing meals to assist my wife when our children were growing up. Modeling of behavior allows a parent to teach by example. When a person's preaching is different from his or her living, it is hard for children to follow. My children are very loving and spiritual individuals. Both are involved in the church. I did not have to tell them to believe in God, nor did I do a hard sell about religion and spirituality. They came to believe because they saw the manifestation of God in our lives.

My wife has always allowed me to pursue my professional goals and has placed her own career second to mine. Yet she has been richly blessed in her life. As a teacher, she has always had the opportunity to take an educational position in whatever location the family has resided, if she so desired. She is my greatest counselor, and I find that she has an intuitive sense about what is right. She is, for example, very good at assessing people and will sometimes say, "That person is not good for you." I used to resist that when we were first married. Now, I do not resist it because she is usually right and because I realize that the spirit sometimes speaks to us through others who serve as channels.

I have always practiced the notion that there are some things on which I can focus. Still, there are other things that I will not deal with because I know that God will take care of them. I have learned to listen to the spirit and to practice doing what the spirit leads me to do. In California, for example, where there was a very difficult board of trustees, the spirit would guide me in dealing with the board, and I would be successful. In my life, I am not in charge. I am only an instrument, a channel.

My job at Medgar Evers College, like all my previous positions, is not a traumatic experience for me. I do not worry about being able to carry out the role or about being secure in the position. Professionally, I believe in being prepared and in doing my part; the rest I leave in God's hands. Sharing my life in the spirit with the college community comes naturally to me. I hope, as I lead the institution, that I can make others aware of their own spirituality and the powerful ways in which being spiritual can enrich their lives.

Challenges of Today's Society

While education in the nation has become more secularized, society faces some of its greatest challenges. In discussions with students at the college, they speak of some of the problems facing our Brooklyn community and, indeed, society as a whole. In recent weeks, students have shared their concerns with me about the plight of unwed teenage mothers and the children they bring into the world; poverty; the marginalization of people of color; and destructive behavior on the part of young people.

Teen pregnancy has produced children who are often less influenced by family units. Receiving limited instruction and guidance from the family through religious activities, educational advisement, and community involvement, many have not yet been socialized into moral values and beliefs. Comparative research of the economic results of the changing family structure shows that less-traditional family units tend to earn less money than traditional units. In addition, families forced into poverty often create poverty-stricken neighborhoods, have offspring who develop poverty-driven survival strategies, and have access only to those educational institutions that lack adequate resources.[1]

The marginalization of people of color continues to be a societal problem. Blacks and Latinos suffer disproportionately high poverty rates, and racial minorities tend to be concentrated into their own political subdivisions. Related to the politics of race, students are also concerned about the limited number of men enrolled in our college, a college founded to help empower a predominantly black community.

History leads us to know that the dearth of males on campus is not explained by simply saying that minority males have a hard time realizing the importance of obtaining a higher education. Racial and ethnic issues raise serious moral and ethical questions not only in our own American society but also worldwide.

We have witnessed unrest and growing destructive behavior on the part of our youth. In the wake of the Littleton, Colorado, Columbine High School violence, society has been called to recognize that even in middle-class suburban environments with adequate educational resources, hatred and anger still take root in the hearts of people, and depression affects all people, regardless of race or social class. Interestingly, as we see the power and benefits of the technology, technological advancements can also lead to corruption by exposing young people to unbridled knowledge and unwholesome values. It is believed that many young people who engage in destructive behavior obtain information to feed their negative thoughts and interests from high-technology sources.

American education was founded to build and sustain moral and religious values. A half century ago, many colleges and universities were still headed by presidents who were preachers. Prayer, devotional Bible reading, and chapel survived throughout the first half of the twentieth century, even in many nonsectarian institutions of higher education.[2] No one was ashamed to speak the gospel. I believe that young people were more grounded then because they were guided by leaders who understood the power and importance of morality and values. Students understood that religious and spiritual values give you beliefs and a sense of belonging so that when there are problems in life, you do not have to be thrown forever. You might have temporary setbacks, but you do not become destroyed by them. Educators helped their students to develop a sense of resolve. There was no dichotomy between spiritual development and education.

The secular system of education that we have now is designed to create a dichotomy between education and spirituality. Secular forces do not ask for a moral or spiritual emphasis in education. To the contrary, they ask for a complete separation of education from religious and spiritual teachings. The result is that the schools now help to produce many young people who have no religious and spiritual identity or commitment.

The Pew Research Center for the People and the Press conducted a national survey of religious identity based on telephone interviews with 1,975 adults aged eighteen to twenty-nine. The results showed that fewer young people say grace before meals, attend religious services on a regular basis, or express a belief in God than do people in older age groups.[3] Moreover, a number of university and college officials say that students today, for the most part, lack basic religious training. Although students realize that it is not easy to make moral decisions, they do not have the moral grounding on which many older adults have drawn.[4]

Humanity needs more than secular ideas and secular values. It needs faith, moral values, and the spiritual commitment that seeks truth and goodness. If moral and spiritual values are not taught at home or at school, and if young people do not attend church, then where will they get these values? The secularization of education has proved itself unable to deal with the problems of this society. There is need for a renewed moral and spiritual emphasis in our world, our society, and in education. Otherwise, civilization will be in danger.

The President's Perspective

The challenges and demands of today's society are very complex and formidable. Yet I believe that the spirit of God gives us strength and confidence to deal with whatever problems may confront us. It also gives us peace and hope. When the spirit speaks to us, we receive a boldness and courage to move forward in our lives knowing that we are doing what is right. The inner voice gives us a sound mind.

There are always negative spiritual forces that can take control of our lives, and there is always the temptation to listen to one's carnal self. We all have demons to fight. As we read in the Bible, you must "put on the full armor of God so that you can take your stand against the devil's evil schemes" (Ephesians 6:12).[5] As a human being, my goal is to keep my life filled with the spirit of God. I do not allow negative thoughts to inhabit my mind. Thoughts too often can become reality. Many difficulties in society result from negative thoughts and selfish, unloving behaviors. Satan is rampant and powerful, but the power of God surpasses all influences and understandings. The affirmation of positive thoughts is so powerful in terms of our physical existence and spirituality that it clearly speaks to me about the power of the mind and the notion of listening to one's inner self. All of us have this capacity that sometimes gets neutered as we go through the educational system. As leader of an educational system, I focus on helping people grow in positive thoughts and spiritual values.

We might perhaps envision at least three types of college presidents. First, there might be a college president who does not believe in a divine being or in spiritual life. Obviously, this person will not see the need to be a spiritual leader. He or she may even consider spirituality to be primitive, superstitious, and misleading. Second, we might find an educational leader who has some religious understandings and spiritual leanings but cannot see any useful way of exerting spiritual or moral influence on students and others in the institutional setting. This individual attempts to isolate the spiritual life from daily leadership responsibilities. Finally, there is the president who sees God as the center of his or her life and uses intellectual abilities, creativity, and social passions to seek the greatest good in all realms of life.

If a president is a spiritual person, his or her spirituality will establish the context from which all thoughts and actions flow. It will be the basis for interpreting all aspects of leadership. Often, with intellectuals, a dichotomy between the professional life and the spiritual life is suggested when professionals are spiritually noncommittal and objective in pursuing professional goals and activities. Yet the educational leader is at once a spiritual person and a professional, and, for me, this means there can be no incongruencies, no dichotomy. I believe that the spiritual nature must dominate the educator's entire life, thus bringing about a synthesis of the spiritual and the professional life. The individual who is spiritually mature realizes that once he or she attempts to separate the spiritual from the other aspects of life, his or her spirituality loses meaning and becomes irrelevant. To give wholly and sincerely of ourselves requires that we encounter all aspects of life with that which is the center of our being, spirituality.

Regardless of how educators profess spirituality or the lack thereof, there is all indication that humankind has deep within a great hunger, one that cannot be completely satisfied by any natural or earthly entity. For the spiritual person, however, there is a power and providence that is a great source of comfort, hope, and joy. Those who have not come to this understanding will continue to search. We live in a world that could never have been constructed by human nature. The intellection behind the formation of the universe is one of infinite power and majesty. The educator must teach and counsel against that background. As leader of an institution of higher learning, I have no difficulty in reconciling my finite understanding with the acceptance of a divine power.

The President's Method with Students

Although I have found that academics often create dichotomies and find it difficult to reconcile their spiritual lives with the professional arena, I do not see that most college students have created this dichotomy. Even though they may not be religious, they know the hunger within for something greater than the natural realm of things. Thus, when there is talk on campus about spirituality and the goodness of God, it resonates well with them. Personally, I have found that when I affirm for a group of students on campus that God is the center of my life, their faces light up. Why? I believe that many of the students are saying, "He has spiritual inclinations just as I do, and he is the president of the college." So my personal affirmations speak to a modeling of behavior, a modeling of living.

Part of what I try to do is to show that being spiritual and being connected to the Creator allows me to do what I could not do on my own. I want students to see that one who is spiritual will express hope when everything is dark and it does not appear that there will be any resolution. The spiritual person will have a sense that the difficult times are transitory and that he or she does not need to become locked into that transitory period, which could conceivably become a permanent state of mind. The strategies for living are much simpler.

When I talk to students about the importance of my spiritual life, I speak deeply and sincerely. My message to students is that the president of the college is one who allows the Almighty to dictate his behavior and one whose spiritual nature is the central force in his life. I try to convey the sense of our need to be connected to some power that is greater than ourselves. What we can do through spirituality we cannot do on our own.

I sometimes relay the story of the man and his young son who were walking along a path when they came upon a large stone. The boy turned to his father and said, "If I use all my strength, I can move this stone." He pushed and pushed at the stone with all his might but could not budge it. He then said to his father, "I used all my strength, but I could not move the stone." The father looked at his son and replied, "No, son, you did not use all your strength because you didn't ask me to help." I do not speak to any particular religious belief when I talk with students. I simply want them to come to a realization that as they struggle and push as hard as they can that spirituality will bring them comfort and peace and will allow them to do things that otherwise they would not be able to do. My hope is that they develop a spiritual nature and, along with it, strategies for being in the world, but not of the world.

Today, unless an institution has a religious affiliation, we do not teach those strategies in schools. In my own way, as college president, I try to help students realize some of the spiritual values that can help them in day-to-day living and in meeting the challenges of life. This is my ministry as president.

Students need spiritual grounding in dealing with all the problems in their lives, and they need spiritual guidance in finding answers to the questions that trouble them. God is faithful to his word, but we do not always understand this. Part of what I try to do is to help people to understand that the faithfulness of God is something onto which we all can hold. What we have to learn as a people is that there are times when we just need to be quiet. We do not need to do anything even though everything around us is chaotic. We just need to be still and listen to the spirit. Then there are times when we must move out and act. As I work with college students, I convey spiritual ideas of hope, self-worth, and love. In doing this, I hope to provide words of inspiration, supply bases of intellectual thought, and help students recognize their own gifts so that they can minister to others.

Providing Words of Inspiration

Words are very powerful. Words can encourage. They can destroy. They can crush. They can inspire. In my experience as president of a public college in a large urban community, many students have come up to me after a speech or they may have come years later and said, "You know, your words encouraged me, and they kept me going." I would wonder to myself what it was that I said, all the time understanding that every person has his or her own ears. I believe that God has fixed it in some way that students hear what they need to hear. The spirit moves in a way that makes the speaker simply an instrument. I have spoken at churches and have had people come up afterward and say, "You know, that was just the message I needed." When they articulate what they heard, I say, "That's not what I said. That was not my intent." Nevertheless, the spirit moved them to compute for themselves in a special way what they needed to hear. That is why it is important to have some understanding of an audience and its needs. Such knowledge can help a leader to focus better on the message that might be most helpful to a particular group. Although many of today's students have no particular religious affiliation, they can be spiritually uplifted by the positive and encouraging words of an institutional leader.

Supplying Bases for Intellectual Thought

The idea of spirituality from a leadership position in an academic institution is more important than in some other places because students are introduced to new ideas and are encouraged to explore new horizons. Often they have to release themselves from their old thoughts and views of life. If there is not something that is very central to their lives and if they are not grounded in personal values, they will have no foundation on which to stand as their traditional notions are attacked or uprooted.

When a philosophy professor says, "There is no God," how will students participate in that type of discussion? Without spiritual grounding, young people and older students as well can become troubled. In science classes, where students learn that science has given people control over much of the environment, students with a spiritual understanding will know that science has erected a framework within which truth and goodness must be sought and moral choices must be made. In the social sciences, students will reflect on the idea that we are all children of God and inescapably bound to each other. Thus, we must love and minister to our brothers and sisters. In seeking solutions to social problems and issues, students can be guided by moral and spiritual values. From the expressive mode of the humanities, students can relate to the intuitive, symbolic, and even spiritual nature embedded within all of us. In any area of academic or personal life, students can rely on spiritual values and understanding for guidance. Through my spirituality, I hope to convey to students a model for dealing with aggressive secularism in education today. If students see that their president, having accomplished all that he has in terms of academic credentials and achievements, is spiritual and believes in a divine being, it helps them to confirm their own inherent spirituality.

Helping Students to Use Their Gifts

When a college president speaks out about spiritual values, it sets a tone for the institution. Sharing spiritual reflections is part of my ministry at Medgar Evers College. As students begin to see my role in ministering to them, and as they begin to gain a deeper understanding of their own spirituality, I hope also to encourage them to minister to others. Being led by spiritual beliefs means sharing the life of the spirit with others. Thus, students must learn to use their gifts to minister to others.

Each student is unique and possesses special gifts and talents. The challenge is to get students to know that they have gifts and to know that they are special. Recently the college held what was called the Medgar Man Summit. It was an event convened to address the issues facing black males on the campus as well as in the larger community. As president, I gave the opening remarks for the conference and set the spiritual tone. I spoke to the young men about their need to find their gifts. I told them about their uniqueness and how they should not devalue their gifts but instead ask, "What is our mission?" "Why were we put here?" In essence, I wanted them to consider how they can minister in their own special and unique ways to a world that is sorely in need of the very special gifts and contributions that black men have to offer. I encouraged the young men to put their gifts to work while creating an atmosphere of cooperation and hope. Discovering and valuing gifts are important to the spiritual life.

I try to have students understand that even if they do not believe in God, the universal laws still apply. Humans are a species above all other animals. Therefore, we have special and unique gifts, which are in keeping with the universal plan. We all need to feel this. Those in the Christian tradition have a basis for understanding just how special they are. As a Christian minister once said, "If we profess that Christ is our savior, we should not have feelings of inferiority about anything because we have new birth, new life. Our life is one of untold worth because we share in a divine life."

Views on Spirituality and Higher Education

Those in leadership positions in higher education must search to impart those ideals that, irrespective of religious traditions, can be applied universally to build morals, values, and ethics. Although one may argue with a religious denomination, there are some basic ideas that transcend denominations. There is a need to focus on those universal ideals of spirituality that can be made a part of higher education and that can bring a certain degree of cohesiveness to the education process and to the lives of students.

How can spirituality be made a part of higher education in a cohesive manner? Because spirituality, including religion, is an important aspect of society and, for many, an important personal experience, it should be given meaningful inclusion in higher education. Even within a public institution, there should be opportunities for extracurricular religious and spiritual expressions. Opportunities might also be made available for multifaith discussions and celebrations in order to identify common understandings and to acknowledge basic values shared in a pluralistic learning community. A recent conference on religious pluralism, spirituality, and higher education sponsored by the Education as Transformation Project of Wellesley College found tremendous support for acknowledging the importance of spirituality in the lives of college students.

Furthermore, students should be able to look formally at religions of the world as an important intellectual study through appropriate course work. Students should have the opportunity to discuss and reflect thoughtfully on the ideas of religion and spirituality in the academic setting just as they are encouraged to study other aspects and accounts of humanity and the world. Allowing students to engage in religious and spiritual discussion, celebration, and nonsectarian study of religion may help students to acknowledge the importance of spirituality in human existence and to identify shared moral values.

Discussion of major ethical issues departmentally, schoolwide, and campuswide can also help the college to find a way to share within an intellectual context spiritual truths and values. There students and faculty who have varied religious or moral traditions, even those with no religious affiliation or belief, can build understanding and a sense of commonality with regard to the solution of problems that must be dealt with by the educated community in the society. In addition, professors might use moral and ethical issues in the current and historical context of their disciplines for discussion and critique by students.[6]

As students explore moral and ethical issues, it is important for them to have some notion of how these ideas can be applied to their own lives. As a spiritual leader, I like to use the idea of planting seeds and harvesting. From my early years growing up on a farm, the law of harvest was very clear and meaningful to me. We plant and we reap. If we plant sparingly, we reap sparingly. If we plant seeds abundantly and cultivate our crops, the harvest can be rich. It is important to let students know that they must use their education and their gifts to plant good seeds wherever they go. This can relate to their family lives, their jobs, their academic pursuits, and their community involvement. Along with the idea of planting seeds, I talk to the students about the need to serve and give back, particularly the need to serve the local community of which they are a part. This means giving of their time, talents, skills, and knowledge to serve others and to help empower others. The harvest from their activities can be very bountiful.

Perhaps the universal value that speaks loudest in all this is love. The challenge of the spiritual person is to love the divine creator and to show faith in this belief through love of his or her earthly brothers and sisters. The spiritual life is the life of love. Students can practice reaching out to others in love through both extracurricular and curricular service projects in the college community and beyond. They can also become involved in social justice initiatives. The role of spirituality in the civil rights movement in the United States during the 1960s and 1970s, for example, is well known and even discussed in the professional literature.[7]

Recently I organized faculty and staff to seek ways to demonstrate love for students. There must be growth in concern for students and their welfare. An all-out effort to improve registration procedures was initiated during the current academic year. The idea was to make the process less burdensome and complicated for students. In addition, great stress was placed on being courteous and helpful to students.

The new emphasis prompted one student to remark, "Were employees given raises? Why is everyone being so nice to me?"

The college is also discussing ways to serve and show concern for students in a more holistic fashion. Not only are teaching faculty necessary in the education process, but counselors, psychologists, and social workers are also important in attending to the needs of students. Our students have many problems and needs, both personal and academic. We must, therefore, be a nurturing and caring community, a community of love. For me, this love of members of our institutional community is rooted in love of God and knowledge that the worth and dignity of each individual is granted to him or her as a child of God. It is my belief, furthermore, that those who are loved will, in turn, show love for others. These students who have been loved will go forth to plant the seeds of love in their communities, their families, and their workplaces.

For me, it is heartening to see the secular intellectual community beginning to explore the role of spirituality in our lives. We are beginning to see that although forces of society have been successful in secularizing education, the spiritual nature of humankind is so powerful that higher education must acknowledge its existence and value. Note, for example, the growing number of studies and projects designed to explore the connection between spirituality and health.[8] Scholars of today are informing us from their own academic stances that humans are indeed spiritual beings. This is something that has been known through history from religious and intuitive perspectives.

Concluding Statement

As a college president who is a spiritual leader, I believe that if students and faculty have no spirituality, no morality, and no sense of purpose, they might be prone to use their education and knowledge for destructive purposes. Instead of having a sense of commitment to sharing and lifting people up, they can easily become the oppressors. Thus, I strive to create a spiritual umbrella over the college. According to one of Newton's laws, two objects cannot occupy the same space at the same time. Following this law, goodness and evil cannot share the same space at the same time. What I have tried to do as president is to bring spiritual goodness to what I do and to how I manage the institution so that evil will have less opportunity to manifest itself. This is the challenge.

In the New Testament, Jesus gives us the Lord's Prayer and says, "Lead us not into temptation" (Matthew 6:13).[9] Who is he talking to? I believe that if the leadership is not rooted and grounded in spirituality, and for me personally, it means in God, Jesus Christ my Savior, then the vision seen is cloudy. Sometimes a person's vision is cloudy because he or she sees with the natural eye rather than the spiritual eye. It is the divineness of the vision that makes it clear. It is difficult for a person to lead and to create a vision when he or she is grounded in the natural forces and senses.

My vision as college president has been created out of my spirituality. I just get ideas. They come when I least expect them. That is why I can listen to a discussion and expound upon the ideas presented because those ideas create in my head a broader vision, one that is not of me. When you know it is not of you, you do not allow yourself to get in the way of that which is coming forth. You get out of the way and do not take credit for it. I do not take glory in what I do, but rather glorify the Doer. My goal is to be an instrument for love, truth, and goodness with the college community.

Notes

1. J. A. Johnson et al., *Introduction to the Foundations of American Education* (Boston: Allyn and Bacon, 1996).

2. W. A. Nord, *Religion and American Education: Rethinking a National Dilemma* (Chapel Hill, N.C.: University of North Carolina Press, 1995), chap. 2.

3. Pew Research Center for the People and the Press, *The Diminishing Divide: American Churches, American Politics* (Washington, D.C.: Pew Research Center, June 1996).

4. J. Neibuhr, "Colleges Setting Moral Compasses," *New York Times,* August 4, 1996, Education Life section.

5. *Good News for Modern Man: The New Testament in Today's English Version,* 3rd ed. (New York: American Bible Society, 1971).

6. Neibuhr, "Colleges," 3.

7. A. D'Lena "Studying Faith in the Civil-Rights Movement," *Chronicle of Higher Education* 44 (1997): A10.

8. For example, H. G. Koenig, L. K. George, and B. L. Peterson, "Re-

ligiosity and Remission of Depression in Medically Ill Older Adults," *American Journal of Psychiatry* 155 (1998): 536–42; J. S. Levin and H. Y. Vanderpool, "Is Religion Therapeutically Significant for Hypertension?" *Social Science and Medicine* (1989): 29: 69–78; and D. Van Biema, "A Test of the Healing Power of Prayer," *Time*, October 12, 1998, 72–73; *Spirituality and Medicine Awards Presented for Psychiatric Residency Training* (Washington, D.C.: National Institute for Healthcare Research, April 1998); *Eight Schools to Receive Award for Spirituality and Health Courses* (Washington, D.C.: National Institute for Healthcare Research, November 1998).

9. *Good News for Modern Man.*

Part IV
Religion and Home Education

10

Religion, Schooling, and Home Education: Past and Present

James C. Carper and Brian D. Ray

Robert Michaelsen, among others, has argued that religion in America takes two general forms. In an influential essay published shortly after the U.S. Supreme Court's controversial decisions in 1962 and 1963 regarding prayer and devotional Bible reading in the state school system, Michaelsen drew a distinction between "America's two religions," which he labeled "A" and "B." He described the former as *denominational* (others use the terms *ecclesiastical, particularistic,* or *private*) and the latter as the *common faith*—those beliefs, myths, and assumptions that function like a religion in the life of the nation. Some scholars have used terms such as *civil religion* or *public religion* to describe this faith. Like particularistic faith systems (which may be nontheistic and functional as well as theistic and doctrinal), religion "B" provides answers, often implicitly, to first-order questions such as "What is the nature of the cosmos?" "What is the essence of human nature?" "What constitutes moral authority?" and "What is the chief end of man?"[1] James Skillen, Richard John Neuhaus, and Robert Linder, among others, have asserted that our civil religion is rooted primarily in two sources that are often in tension—Protestant Christianity with its emphasis on revelation and transcendent authority and the Enlightenment tradition with its emphasis on rationalism and the human experience.[2]

Both religions have played a role in shaping the American educational landscape from colonial times to the present. Given that both address "Big Questions," it should come as no surprise that the role of religion in American education has been a source of considerable controversy, particularly with the advent of public schooling in the middle decades of the nineteenth century. While formal schooling arrangements have certainly been affected by debates regarding the place of religion in American public life and education, as we shall see, so has the family's educational role. Indeed, religious motivations have been the primary force behind the resurgence of home schooling since the 1970s.[3]

Early American Education

Prior to the central, transforming event in the history of education in the United States—the genesis of compulsory, state-supported and -controlled common schooling between 1830 and 1860—the religious diversity that characterized overwhelmingly Protestant colonial and early national America was matched by an equally rich diversity of educational arrangements. With few exceptions—namely, when they were unable or unwilling to care for their children—parents fashioned an education for their offspring that was consonant with their religious beliefs. Education was primarily the responsibility of the family, not the state.[4]

For the better part of the seventeenth and eighteenth centuries the family was the principal unit of social organization and the most important educational agency. As historian Stephen Mintz and anthropologist Susan Kellogg point out, "Three centuries ago the American family was the fundamental economic, educational, political, social and religious unit of society. The family, not the isolated individual, was the unit of which church and state were made. The household was not only the locus of production, it was also the institution primarily responsible for the education of children, the transfer of craft skills, and the care of the elderly and infirm."[5]

In general, then, parents bore the primary responsibility for teaching their children (and often those from other families who had been apprenticed or "fostered out") Christian doctrine, vocational skills, and how to read. That responsibility was not always carried out equally or effectively. According to historian Jan Lewis: "The effectiveness of home schooling varied depending particularly upon region and gender; literacy was much higher in the North than the South, and for males than females."[6] Although many seventeenth- and eighteenth-century white parents sent their children to school for short periods of time—at least in the northern colonies—much education took place in the household. Indeed, a majority of colonial children may have acquired rudimentary literacy skills at home.[7]

In contrast to current schooling arrangements, the colonial mode of schooling was unsystematic, diverse, unregulated, and, for most colonial children, a discontinuous experience. The initiative for school attendance resided with parents, not the state. Furthermore, schooling in colonial America was not as controversial as it is today. In great measure, this was because most schools mirrored the religious beliefs of their patrons and, like churches, were expected to assist parents in the education of their children. They were to complement rather than supplant parental educational efforts in the home.[8]

The diversity of educational institutions and the blurred line between "public" and "private" schools were the most salient features of colonial schooling. The educational landscape was dotted with a variety of institutions: from Puritan town schools in New England; to Lutheran, Quaker, Reformed, and Anglican schools in the middle colonies; to old-field schools in the South. Classifying these schools as purely "public" or "private" is problematic. As historian Bernard Bailyn asserts: "The modern conception of public education, the very idea of a clean line of separation between 'private' and 'public,' was unknown before the end of the eighteenth century." To most colonials, a school was "public" if it served a public purpose, such as promoting civic responsibility. Public education did not necessarily require public support and public control.[9]

Toward the end of the colonial era the family began to lose its position as American society's most important economic and social unit. The slow shift of family functions, including education, to non-familial institutions occurred initially in the settled areas of the eastern seaboard. According to Mintz and Kellogg,

> By the middle of the eighteenth century, a variety of specialized institutions had begun to absorb traditional familial responsibility. To reduce the cost of caring for widows, orphans, the destitute, and the mentally ill, cities began to erect almshouses instead of having such cared for in their own homes or homes of others. Free schools and common pay schools educated a growing number of the sons of artisans and skilled laborers. Work-

shops increasingly replaced individual households as centers of production.[10]

While parents increasingly looked to schools to carry out what had once been primarily a family function, the colonial approach to education continued virtually unchanged throughout the late 1700s and early 1800s. Despite proposals for more systematic, state-influenced schooling offered by such luminaries as Thomas Jefferson and Benjamin Rush, the colonial mode of schooling suited to the Protestant pluralism of the period persisted well into the nineteenth century. Whether sponsored by a church or not, the vast majority of schools at this time embodied some variation of Protestant Christianity, and parents decided whether or not children would attend them.[11]

Protestantism and Public Schooling

The middle decades of the nineteenth century marked a period of intense educational debate and reform that led to major changes in educational beliefs and practices in the United States, namely, the genesis of the modern concept and practice of public schooling. Distressed by the social and cultural tensions wrought by mid-nineteenth-century urbanization, industrialization, and immigration (which included a large number of Roman Catholics from Ireland) and energized by what historian Carl Kaestle has called the values of republicanism, Protestantism, and capitalism, educational reformers touted the messianic power of tax-supported, government-controlled compulsory schooling. Common schools, they believed, would mold a moral, disciplined, and unified population prepared to participate in American political, economic, and social life.[12] Some reformers viewed the common school as a substitute for the family. Horace Mann, for example, often referred to the state and its schools as "parental." Private schools, on the other hand, were often cast as undemocratic, divisive, and inimical to the public interest.[13]

As Alexis de Tocqueville recognized in the 1830s, and several generations of historians have since confirmed, public schooling was nurtured by a robust evangelical Protestant culture that emerged from the Great Awakening of the 1730s and 1740s and was nourished by the Second Great Awakening—a series of religious revivals stretching from the late 1790s through the Civil War. With few exceptions, notably several Lutheran and Reformed bodies, which opted for schools designed to preserve cultural and/or confessional purity, Protestants were generally supportive of common schooling. Indeed, many were in the vanguard of the reform movement. They approved of early public schooling because it reflected Protestant beliefs and was viewed as an integral part of a crusade to fashion a Christian—which, to the dismay of Roman Catholics, meant Protestant—America.[14]

Rather than countenance sharing public funds with Roman Catholic schools, such as requested by Bishop John Hughes in the early 1840s in the face of Protestant practices of the New York Public School Society (such as using the King James version of the Bible), or schools associated with Protestant groups, most evangelicals united behind the "non-sectarian" (in reality pan-Protestant) common school as the sole recipient of tax monies for education. Catholic schools and those of other dissenters from the common school movement were therefore denied not only legitimacy but tax dollars as well. To a significant degree, then, latent anti-Catholicism, rekindled by the immigration of the 1840s and 1850s and Roman Catholic bishops' assertions of missionary intent in the United States, closed prematurely the debate on whether the education of the public could be accomplished by a variety of schools reflecting diverse moral and religious viewpoints funded by tax dollars or required the creation of a government school system embodying a supposedly common belief system with a virtual monopoly on the public treasury—in other words, an educational counterpart to the traditional established church.[15]

While the common schools, by means of Bible reading without comment, prayers, and the ubiquitous McGuffy Readers, taught the beliefs of nondenominational evangelical Protestantism, the civil religion (religion "B") of nineteenth-century America, the Sunday school stressed particular tenets of the various denominations (religion "A"). This educational arrangement of "parallel institutions" was satisfactory to most Protestants. In sum, the public school became the vehicle for transmitting the common faith, and the Sunday school communicated denominational particulars.[16]

By the turn of the century, around 90 percent of elementary and secondary school students in the United States were enrolled in public schools. Of the remaining 10 percent, approximately 65 percent were in Roman Catholic schools. Others were enrolled in Protestant-sponsored institutions (e.g., Lutheran, Reformed, or Episcopal) or unaffiliated private schools. The line between public and private schools had been clearly drawn and widely accepted. Furthermore, in response to Catholic demands for their share of tax dollars to support the kind of education they deemed appropriate for their children, states had forbidden the once common practice of providing tax monies and land grants to privately controlled schools.[17]

Nineteenth-Century Home Education

Although school enrollment was almost universal for children ages seven to twelve by the late 1800s, not all nineteenth-century parents depended on schools to teach their children. For economic, religious, pedagogical, and geographic reasons, some children were educated to a greater or lesser extent at home. Edward Gordon and Elaine Gordon point out that during the better part of the 1800s, literature on "domestic" or "fireside" education was widely available to those interested in the "family school" movement.[18] We do not know how many children were taught at home by either parents or relatives. Several, however, we know much about. In addition to the oft-cited eighteenth-century luminaries such as Washington and Franklin, well-known nineteenth-century figures who were taught by their parents include Thomas A. Edison, who was instructed at home after school officials labeled him "addled"; Andrew Taylor Still, a colleague of abolitionist John Brown and founder of osteopathic medicine, who was largely educated by his father; and Alexander Campbell, founder of the Disciples of Christ, who received part of his education from his father. Lesser lights, such as Daniel Dawson Carothers, chief engineer of the Baltimore and Ohio Railroad from 1904 to 1909, who received his primary schooling from his mother before attending an academy, may be eventually "discovered" in obituaries, memorials, diaries, and family records.[19]

Conservative Protestant Responses to the Secularization of Public Education

In addition to the well-known efforts on the part of such states as Wisconsin, Illinois, and Oregon to regulate or outlaw non-government schools on the grounds that they were a threat to national unity and public discussions of similar ideas in other states, the late

1800s and early 1900s also witnessed the gradual decline of evangelical Protestantism as the dominant theme in America's public religion and the growing influence of the Enlightenment pillar of our civic faith.[20] Pointing out the disruptive effect on American Protestantism of, among other things, Darwinism, higher criticism of the Bible, the fundamentalist-modernist controversy, and growing cultural and religious diversity, sociologist James Davison Hunter argues, with only slight exaggeration, that in the course of roughly thirty-five years (ca. 1895–1930), "Protestantism had been moved from cultural domination to cognitive marginality and political impotence. The worldview of modernity [often termed secular humanism or civil humanism] had gained ascendancy in American culture."[21]

Public education was affected, albeit gradually, by this shift in America's public religion. For example, prior to the Supreme Court's ruling on Bible reading in *Abington Township v. Schempp* (1963), eleven states already forbade it on the grounds that it was a "sectarian" (religion "A") practice. Furthermore, Bible reading in some form was probably practiced in less than half of the nation's public school districts.[22] Christianity also became less visible in the public school curriculum after the turn of the century. For example, in his analysis of the religious content of American history textbooks, Charles Shannon documents a gradual shift from a Christian or theistic worldview to a more secular, "democratic" orientation between 1865 and 1935.[23]

Although the Supreme Court's controversial decisions regarding prayer and Bible reading merely marked the culmination of at least a half-century-long process of "de-Protestantization" of public education, many conservative Christians have interpreted the official removal of these symbols of the evangelical strain of the American civic faith as "yanking" God out of the public schools. Rather than making the schools "neutral" on matters related to religion, they have concluded, these decisions contributed to the establishment of secular humanism as the official creed or religion "B" of American public education and the relegation of Christianity to religion "A" status. This belief has, in turn, led them to scrutinize public education to a greater extent than ever before. Once among the crusaders for the establishment of public education, conservative Protestants are now, ironically, among its most vociferous critics. Many have awakened to the fact that public education is now officially "agnostic" vis-á-vis Christianity.[24]

Since the mid-1960s, these disgruntled dissenters have responded to the "established church" and its "secular" theology in a variety of ways. Many have tried to reincorporate theistic symbols and perspectives in the public schools through, for example, proposing Ten Commandments displays and discussions of intelligent design in science classes. Others have protested the use of curricular materials that they believe advance a secularistic worldview, as in the widely reported textbook controversies in Mobile, Alabama; Kanawha County, West Virginia; and Hawkins County, Tennessee.[25]

Others have forsaken their historic commitment to public education and the "parallel institutions" educational strategy and founded dissenting Christian academies, which, like earlier Roman Catholic schools, have occasionally been faced with intrusive state regulation. Since the mid-1960s, evangelical Protestants and their churches, few of which are affiliated with mainline Protestant denominations, have established more than ten thousand Christian day schools with a current enrollment of more than one million students. Once thought to have been mere segregation academies, the vast majority are now racially integrated and increasingly attractive to minority parents who desire a strong academic program within a Christian context.[26]

The most radical dissenters, "educational anabaptists" if you will, have gone one step further. Since the mid-1970s, a growing number of parents have abandoned institutional education in an attempt to restore education to its purest form—parents teaching their children at home. Although parents' motivations for returning to an educational arrangement that was common in the 1600s and 1700s are many and varied, the vast majority have acted primarily on religious convictions.

Radical Dissent: Home Schooling

There has been conspicuous growth in home schooling from an estimated 15,000 school-age students in the late 1970s to 1.5 to 1.9 million in the fall of 2000. In terms of many demographic traits, home school families are "average" American families. Nevertheless, a significant and growing range of diversity exists with respect to characteristics such as ethnicity, income, and parent education level. In terms of religious affiliation, about 80 percent would identify themselves as "Bible-believing" Christians. Three-fourths of them are from traditional religious backgrounds (especially Baptist, independent or fundamental evangelical, independent charismatic, Assembly of God, Lutheran, Methodist, Pentecostal, Presbyterian, Reformed, and Roman Catholic). In addition, many of the other 20 percent claim some form of particularistic religious belief.[27] How important, though, is religion to all of these families' home schooling?

The contemporary home school community and environment—its literature, its leaders, its rank and file, its debates, its key issues—are permeated with religious overtones and undercurrents, regardless of whether the individual actors claim to be personally religious. Indeed, modern home schooling is religious in warp and woof. This is consistent with the condition of which observers of the education scene have been aware for ages, namely, that all education is religious, regardless of whether proponents of a particular educational offering claim otherwise. Not even the allegedly value-neutral state-run schools of modern America are genuinely so.[28] Parents who home school certainly believe that education is interwoven with religion, with ultimate meanings and concerns.

A key distinction of parents who have chosen to maintain a unique closeness to their children and the primary influence over their children's education rather than send them away to be under the tutelage of others is that they realize there really is no clear distinction between "particularistic faith" and "public faith" when it comes to the education of children. They know that values, beliefs, presuppositions, and worldviews are inherently and inextricably a part of the whole curriculum of a child's life. We think the case can certainly be made that the experience and view of a hardy majority of home schoolers is that in the realm of educating children one should look with suspicion, as Mary Douglas has noted, on anyone who declares that "there are . . . two kinds of reality or process" (i.e., the private versus public).[29] We come to this conclusion based on at least three sources of evidence: the research literature on home schooling, literature written by and for home schoolers, and our personal and varied experiences with home school families across the country.

Religion at the Core

The evidence that religious convictions are the key to parents' reasons for home schooling is rife in the research. Both quantitative and qualitative methodologies and local, state-specific, and nationwide studies (not only in the United States) have consistently produced findings that religious beliefs are at or near the core of reasons for why most people home school. Several examples provide a flavor of what researchers have found.

Jane Van Galen writes that her so-called Ideologue parents she studied in the mid-1980s are Christians who have specific values, beliefs, and skills that they want their children to learn. They want their children to comprehend traditional subject matter and conservative biblical doctrine, learn a conservative political and social perspective, and understand that the family is the most important institution in society. Likewise, Gayla Batterbee reports that the most common reason parents state for home schooling is to impart Christian values. Echoing Batterbee, Shirley Breshears asserts that the main reasons for home schooling include teaching family values and morals that are Bible-based and God-centered and wanting the Bible or Christian teaching to be an integral part of their curriculum. In like vein, Norma Linden concludes the most common reason for home schooling in Texas for most parents is that they think the public schools impose on children an ungodly, humanistic philosophy and too many negative influences.[30]

Many studies, like the preceding, document the centrality of traditional religious beliefs to parents' rationales for home schooling. Furthermore, many other studies suggest that even those who may not associate themselves with ecclesiastical religion do have religious beliefs at the core of their reasons for home educating their children. For example, anthropologist Mary Anne Pitman finds that two of the three broad categories of home schoolers are religious—Christian and New Age. Likewise, sociologist Maralee Mayberry finds that although there is a wide diversity of values and beliefs within home education there is a strong emphasis on the religious. In Indiana three of the five reasons most frequently cited for home schooling are that parents want to control the moral environment of the child, that parents want to control the social environment of the child, and that parents desire more contact with their children. Research shows that concerns about the social contacts of their children and the desire to be with their children greater amounts of time are driven by these parents' religious beliefs, their convictions about key issues in life and how to live their lives in a way that is consistent with their convictions.[31]

A large body of research substantiates that it is religion, be it doctrinal or functional, that motivates these parents. For example, John Fegley finds that religion is very important and that other values such as morality and protection from negative influences (which are both directly linked to parents' religious beliefs) are probably equally important. In her nationwide study of a "secular" subpopulation of home schoolers, Sonia Gustafson finds that four of the seven main reasons for home schooling are all related to beliefs about fundamental issues (i.e., moral atmosphere, social atmosphere, religious education, and negative influence of others from outside the family). Simply put, scholars from a variety of disciplines have found that religion and morality (and related "safety" issues) are key reasons for these parents' decisions to home school their children.[32]

Even research from other nations reveals the importance of religious beliefs to home schoolers. This can be seen in Wendy Priesnitz and Heidi Priesnitz's study of home schoolers across Canada, Terry Harding's exploration of home-based education in Australia, and Paula Rothermel's work in the United Kingdom.[33]

Although motivations for home schooling vary and researchers may use sundry terms (e.g., morality, ideology, culture, and character) while explicating why parents home school, religion—in the sense of individuals' particularistic faith systems—is at the core. Research clearly shows that these parents are working to have a personal, direct, and lasting impact on their children's lives through religiously driven education. As an illustration of this, one might read Tracy Romm, who delves into the home schooling of eight families in Atlanta who represent a variety of religious and ethnic backgrounds (e.g., African American, white/anglo, Muslim, Christian). He finds that these parents, "representing a variety of ideologies and motivations, are concerned primarily with the character-building function of education . . . [referring to] religious or moral traits and to mental abilities that serve to preserve the distinctive qualities of each individual child. Schools are rejected as the referent for this process; they are viewed as serving more as a force for social conformity than as a protector of individual integrity." These parents maintain that "the strength of the nation rests in the ability of the individual to act from his own convictions, and that home-based education is best suited to allow the unimpeded development of these." Romm concludes, "In a sense, all home schooling parents are ideological in that they want to instill strongly-held beliefs in their children and want to maintain some measure of control over outside influences that might compete with their attempt to transmit these." The theme is clear throughout Romm's work: religious beliefs—that is, faith systems, be they traditional or functional—are central to the rationale for and execution of home schooling.[34]

The fact that most home schoolers are evangelical, independent, or fundamental Christians by no means indicates that the others are not religious or that religion plays an insignificant part in the others' home schooling. For example, we think there has been a significant growth over the past five years in the number of Roman Catholic families who are home schooling. We have already mentioned research that notes the involvement of New Age adherents, and several broad surveys have revealed that consequential (and increasing, we surmise) numbers of Jewish, Mormon, and Islamic parents are home schooling their children. It is also important to remember that some of the first people encouraging a return to home- and family-based education in the 1970s were not those emphasizing ecclesiastical Christianity but did have personal belief systems that drove their views about education.[35]

The second area of evidence suggesting the centrality of religion to contemporary home schooling is a burgeoning literature that acts as a support to home schoolers and an advocacy of the practice. Like the research literature, these writings are replete with references to religion and core philosophical beliefs. Our years of reading popular home school magazines such as *The Teaching Home, Home Schooling Today, Practical Home Schooling, Home School Digest, Home School Court Report, Seton Home Study School, Growing without Schooling, Home Education Magazine,* and the *Narrow Path* show us that religion, be it doctrinal or functional, is ever on the mind and flowing through the ink of those writing in these magazines. Visits to Web sites and chat rooms of home school organizations, aficionados, and electronic media corroborate what we have seen in the print magazines.

Finally, our own experience substantiates the claim that religion is an extremely important part of the home school community. Between us, we have been studying and interacting with home schoolers for a total of nearly twenty-five years. Our repeated observations convince us that religious concepts explicitly and implicitly inform and drive the educational choices and pedagogy, political activity, and social behavior of the majority of home school parents and their students. In addition, questions related to religion occupy the time of these people, collectively. We offer two examples. One of the first groups with which I, Ray, became familiar in the early 1980s that was very actively promoting home schooling was a New Age group; every piece of literature that I received from them (and it was a lot) was riddled with religious (or as they preferred to call them, spiritual) references.

Likewise, we have both watched the debate, largely internal to the home school community, over whether home school organizations should limit leadership or participation to members of a particular faith. There have been and are organizations and publications that emphasize that they are advocates only of home schooling and that they support all home schoolers. There are others to whom it is important that they are run or managed by only those of a particular faith or belief system. For example, many of these are organizations run by Christians who try to operate in a way and promote only ideas and products (e.g., in their magazines or at conferences) that are consistent with a biblical worldview. This is a key aspect of both of these types of organizations' (and their participants') worldviews. If an organization claims it is only for home schooling (as if no belief about home schooling or any other issue could ever be important enough to dissuade the organization's members from association with the person holding the belief, however unappealing), then it is saying that the cause of home schooling is either more important than or can be separated from other issues or beliefs. Those who tend to promote and participate in the faith-based organizations are positing that one's core belief system about the "Big Issues" in life (e.g., an adult's and his or her children's relationship with God) is inseparable from education. These people are, furthermore, arguing that these beliefs are so fundamental to education that they must be nurtured and protected at most times that home schoolers associate with one another in organized ways. They are not saying, as do some of those home schoolers who disagree with them about organizational leadership, that neither they nor their children should associate with home schoolers—or others, for that matter—who do not agree with their basic religious beliefs. This historical circumstance within the home schooling community mirrors the difficulty of embracing or negotiating a common faith and a means of transmitting it within the educational arena at large. We present this issue not to judge the wisdom of either side in the debate but simply to suggest that the entire home education community is very religio-sensitive. In this sense, in fact, it is just like the other worlds of education, state-run and private schools.

Parents involved in this debate who are unwilling to set aside their core beliefs realize that—even if someone convinced them that it was a desirable thing to do in a particular situation—there is no realistic way to separate the private aspects of their faith from the public aspects of their faith when it comes to making decisions about the nurture and education of their children. For example, behaviors such as where to educate their children, with what pedagogical practices to educate their children, and how to train and develop discipline in their children all stem from private faith. As life and worship for ancient (and some contemporary) Jews were inseparable, philosophy/religion and education were and are inseparable for both ancient and contemporary Homo sapiens. Furthermore, most home school parents know that they cannot separate private and public aspects of their and their children's religious lives as they go about all aspects of life within their communities.[36]

Parents, Not the State, Choose the Worldview

A growing percentage of parents over the past thirty years have made a fresh and keen analysis of the underpinnings, the root philosophy, and the pedagogy behind the education of children (including their own education) in state-run, institutional, common schools. These parents, and many of those who have "come close" to choosing home schooling, recognize that all education is private in the sense that it happens within an individual's mind and heart *and* that all education is public in that what has taken place in every individual's mind and heart has, inevitably, a bearing on other persons who are part of the public life of a community or a nation. Those who have elected home schooling have decided to keep in their own hands the effects of religion on education rather than to relinquish their children to the religion of the state and of those who are strangers to their children and strangers to their religion, their relationship with God, and their beliefs about the ultimate concerns in life. In other words, they have rejected the new "established church" and its theology.

Public religion in public (state) schools is of a certain persuasion these days, and, as we have noted, it was of a different persuasion in days gone by. Several scholars have asserted that today's state schools express (or *promote*) a secular religion that posits that the supernatural is irrelevant. Home schoolers who recognize and are firm about their own faith know, as one might paraphrase Michael Bauman, who writes about morality and law, that those who object to morals-based education would have to raise the same objection to all education whatsoever, including the education that they themselves support. These parents know that all education (including that in state schools, private schools, "secular" or "for-all" home schooling, and their own home schooling) is inherently religious. They know the private becomes the public even if it is not now so. Many of them explain that they are preparing, truing, aiming, and launching their arrows, their children, into the public world where their once more-private religious life will become much more public. In effect, these parents' "pedagogy is a political act or, as one mother put it, 'the personal is the political.'" Likewise, when it comes to these parents' and these children's religious beliefs and practices, considering that a personal faith system may be either nontheistic and functional or theistic and doctrinal, the private clearly impinges upon the public.[37]

Mayberry, Knowles, Ray, and Muchmore find

The central issue around which the prevalent social movements of the era rally is individuals' right [sic] to defend particular worldviews to which they are committed. . . . In many ways, the home school movement has goals similar to other social movements. The family, an important site of private life, stands in contrast to public institutions, and it offers individuals a protective environment in which to maintain and propagate their particular values and beliefs. . . . The home school movement, perhaps to an extent greater than other movements of the era, exemplifies the principles of individualism and self-reliance, and the attempt to live in a way that is consistent with one's world-view. . . . [In one sense,] the home school movement acts in response to the "colonization" of the family by institutional forms such as public education. It protects family values and beliefs from state intrusion while simultaneously expanding the personal rights of parents by permitting them to adopt freely chosen life-styles.[38]

Home schoolers know that education is innately and pervasively religious. This is why a majority of them began home schooling; it remains why many continue to home school; it evolves into being an important reason for many of them who started for other reasons that ostensibly had nothing to do with religion (e.g., not wanting their child to get involved in drugs or premarital sex, wanting a more child-centered pedagogy, desiring an atmosphere of less competition and mean-spiritedness, avoiding violence in schools). In sum, even today's home schoolers who would claim no denominational or ecclesiastical religion—however liberal, libertarian, agnostic, or atheistic—join the others as educational anabaptists who are all expressing their particular religions as they engage in the personal, familial, unique, and, ultimately, social and political act of teaching, training, and instilling beliefs in their own offspring via parent-led, home-based, and family-based education.

Notes

1. Robert Michaelsen, "The Public Schools and 'America's Two Religions,'" *Journal of Church and State* 8 (autumn 1966): 380–84. See also Richard A. Baer Jr., "Why a Functional Definition of Religion Is Necessary if Justice Is to Be Achieved in Public Education," in *Curriculum, Religion, and Public Education Square*, ed. James T. Sears with James C. Carper (New York: Teachers College Press, 1998), 105–15.

2. James W. Skillen, *Recharging the American Experiment* (Grand Rapids, Mich: Baker Books, 1994); Richard John Neuhaus, *The Naked Public Square: Religion and Democracy in America* (Grand Rapids, Mich: Eerdmans, 1984); and Robert D. Linder, "Civil Religion in Historical Perspective: The Reality That Underlies the Concept," *Journal of Church and State* 17 (autumn 1975): 399–421.

3. Warren A. Nord, *Religion and American Education: Rethinking a National Dilemma* (Chapel Hill, N.C.: University of North Carolina Press, 1995); and Richard A. Baer and James C. Carper, "'To the Advantage of Infidelity,' or How Not to Deal with Religion in America's Public Schools," *Educational Policy* 14 (November 2000): 600–621.

4. Mark A. Noll, *A History of Christianity in the United States and Canada* (Grand Rapids, Mich: Eerdmans, 1992), 7–81.

5. Stephen Mintz and Susan Kellogg, *Domestic Revolutions: A Social History of Family Life in America* (New York: Free Press, 1988), xiv.

6. Jan Lewis, "Mothers as Teachers: Reconceptualizing the Role of the Family as Educator," in *Education and the American Family: A Research Synthesis,* ed. William J. Weston (New York: New York University Press, 1989), 126.

7. For a thorough account of education in colonial America, see Lawrence A. Cremin, *American Education: The Colonial Experience, 1606–1783* (New York: Harper and Row, 1970).

8. Carl F. Kaestle, *The Evolution of an Urban School System: New York City, 1750–1850* (Cambridge: Harvard University Press, 1973), 1–27; and Maris A. Vinovskis, "Family and Schooling in Colonial and Nineteenth Century America," *Journal of Family History* 12 (1987): 19–37.

9. Bernard Bailyn, *Education in the Forming of American Society* (New York: Norton, 1960), 11.

10. Mintz and Kellogg, *Domestic Revolutions,* 23.

11. Lawrence A. Cremin, *Traditions of American Education* (New York: Basic Books, 1977), 50.

12. Carl F. Kaestle, *Pillars of the Republic: Common Schools and American Society, 1780–1860* (New York: Hill and Wang, 1983), 62–103.

13. Alan Carlson, "Will the Separation of School and State Strengthen Families? Some Evidence from Fertility Patterns," *Home School Researcher* 12 (1996): 1–2. See also Charles L. Glenn Jr., *The Myth of the Common School* (Amherst, Mass.: University of Massachusetts Press, 1988); and E. Vance Randall, *Private Schools and Public Power* (New York: Teachers College Press, 1994).

14. Alexis de Tocqueville, *Democracy in America,* ed. J. P. Mayer and Max Lerner (New York: Harper and Row, 1966), 267–77. See also Robert T. Handy, *A Christian America: Protestant Hopes and Historical Realities* (New York: Oxford University Press, 1971); Noll, *History of Christianity,* 163–90, 219–44; Timothy L. Smith, "Protestant Schooling and American Nationality, 1800–1850," *Journal of American History* 53 (March 1967): 679–95; and David Tyack, "The Kingdom of God and the Common School," *Harvard Educational Review* 36 (fall 1966): 447–69.

15. Baer and Carper, "'To the Advantage of Infidelity,'" 604–5; James C.

Carper and William J. Weston, "Conservative Protestants in the New School Wars," *History of Education Quarterly* 30 (spring 1990): 79–87; Francis X. Curran, *The Churches and the Schools: American Protestantism and Popular Elementary Education* (Chicago: Loyola University Press, 1954); L. Edward Hicks, "Republican Religion and Republican Institutions: Alexander Campbell and the Anti-Catholic Movement," *Fides et Historia* 22 (fall 1990): 42–52; and Sidney E. Mead, *The Lively Experiment: The Shaping of Christianity in America* (New York: Harper and Row, 1963).

16. William B. Kennedy, *The Shaping of Protestant Education* (New York: Association Press, 1966), 27.

17. James C. Carper, "History, Religion, and Schooling: A Context for Conversation," in *Curriculum, Religion, and Public Education,* 17.

18. Edward E. Gordon and Elaine H. Gordon, *Centuries of Tutoring: A History of Alternative Education in America and Western Europe* (Lanham, Md.: University Press of America, 1990).

19. James C. Carper, "Home Schooling, History, and Historians: The Past as Present," *The High School Journal* 75 (April/May 1992): 252; and Linda Dobson, *The Art of Education: Reclaiming Your Family, Community, and Self* (Tonasket, Wash.: Home Education Press, 1995), 236.

20. Randall, *Private Schools and Public Power,* 50–115; and William G. Ross, *Forging New Freedoms: Nativism, Education, and the Constitution, 1917–1927* (Lincoln, Neb.: University of Nebraska Press, 1994). At least one nineteenth-century reformer foresaw the threat that a state compulsory school attendance law might pose to nonpublic schools and their patrons. He contributed unique language to the Kentucky Constitution that states "nor shall any man be compelled to send his child to any school to which he may be conscientiously opposed." See James C. Carper, "William Morgan Beckner: The Horace Mann of Kentucky," *Register of the Kentucky Historical Society* 96 (winter 1998): 29–60.

21. James Davison Hunter, *Culture Wars: The Struggle to Define America* (New York: Basic Books, 1991), 37. See also A. James Reichley, *Religion in American Public Life* (Washington, D.C.: Brookings Institution, 1985).

22. Anson Phelps Stokes and Leo Pfeffer, *Church and State in the United States,* rev. ed. (New York: Harper and Row, 1964), 371.

23. Charles K. Shannon, "The Religious Content of Secondary School American History Textbooks" (Ph.D. diss., Pennsylvania State University, 1995).

24. James C. Carper, "The Christian Day School Movement," *Educational Forum* 47 (winter 1983): 135–49.

25. Carper, "History, Religion, and Schooling," 20.

26. James C. Carper and Jack Layman, "Independent Christian Day

Schools: Past, Present, and Prognosis," *Journal of Research on Christian Education* 4 (spring 1995): 7–19. See also James C. Carper and Jack Layman, "Black Flight Academies: The New Christian Day Schools," *Educational Forum* 61 (winter 1997): 114–21.

27. Patricia M. Lines, *Homeschoolers: Estimating Numbers and Growth* (Washington, D.C.: United States Department of Education, 1998); Brian D. Ray, *Home Schooling on the Threshold: A Survey of Research at the Dawn of the New Millennium* (Salem, Ore.: National Home Education Research Institute Publications, 1999); and Brian D. Ray, *Strengths of Their Own: Home Schoolers across America: Academic Achievement, Family Characteristics, and Longitudinal Traits* (Salem, Ore.: National Home Education Research Institute, 1997).

28. For example, see Gordon H. Clark, *A Christian Philosophy of Education,* 2d rev. ed. (Jefferson, Md.: Trinity Foundation, 1988); Perry Glanzer, "Religion in Public Schools: In Search of Fairness," *Phi Delta Kappan* 80 (November 1998): 219–222; Nord, *Religion and American Education;* Paul C. Vitz, *Religion and Traditional Values in Public School Textbooks: An Empirical Study* (Washington, D.C.: National Institute of Education, 1985).

29. Mary Douglas as quoted in Martin E. Marty and Edith L. Blumhofer, *Public Religion in America Today* (Chicago: Public Religion Project, 1997), 6.

30. Jane A. Van Galen, "Ideologues and Pedagogues: Parents Who Teach Their Children at Home," in *Home Schooling: Political, Historical, and Pedagogical Perspectives,* ed. Jane A. Van Galen and Mary A. Pitman (Norwood, N.J.: Ablex Publishing Corporation, 1991); Gayla C. Batterbee, "The Relationship of Parent-Child Interactive Systems to Cognitive Attributes in the Home Schooled Child" (Ph.D. diss., United States International University, 1992); Shirley Mae Breshears, "Characteristics of Home Schools and Home School Families in Idaho" (Ed.D. diss., University of Idaho, 1996); Norma Jean Freeman Linden, "An Investigation of Alternative Education: Home Schooling" (Ph.D. diss., East Texas State University, 1983).

31. Mary Anne Pitman, "Compulsory Education and Home Schooling: Truancy or Prophecy?" *Education and Urban Society* 19 (May 1987): 288; Maralee Mayberry, "Doing It Their Way: A Study of Oregon's Home Schoolers" (Ph.D. diss., University of Oregon, 1988); Maralee Mayberry, "Why Home Schooling? A Profile of Four Categories of Home Schoolers," *Home School Researcher* 4, no. 3 (1988): 7–14; Brian D. Ray, *Home Education in Indiana: Family Characteristics, Reasons for Home Schooling, and Academic Achievement* (Salem, Ore.: National Home Education Research Institute, 1997).

32. John A. Fegley, "Home Schooling in Connecticut," *Home School Researcher* 8, no. 4 (1992): 9–16; Sonia K. Gustafson, "A Study of Home Schooling: Parental Motivations and Goals" (senior thesis, Woodrow Wilson School

of Public and International Affairs, Princeton University, 1987); Sonia K. Gustafson, "A Study of Home Schooling: Parental Motivation and Goals," *Home School Researcher* 4, no. 2 (1988): 4–12; J. Gary Knowles, "Parents' Rationales and Teaching Methods for Home Schooling: The Role of Biography," *Education and Urban Society* 21 (November 1988): 69–84; John H. Litcher and Steven J. Schmidt, "Social Studies in the Home School," *Social Education* 55 (1991): 239–41, 248; Maralee Mayberry et al., *Home Schooling: Parents as Educators* (Newbury Park, Calif.: Corwin Press, 1995).

33. Terrence John Arthur Harding, "Why Australian Christian Academy Families in Queensland Choose to Home School: Implications for Policy Development" (master's thesis, Queensland University of Technology, Australia, 1997); Wendy Priesnitz and Heidi Priesnitz, *Home-based Education in Canada: An Investigation* (Unionville, Ontario, Canada: Alternative Press, 1990); Paula Rothermel, "A Nationwide Study of Home Education: Early Indications and Wider Implications," *Education Now* 24 (summer 1999): 9.

34. Tracy Romm, "Home Schooling and the Transmission of Civic Culture" (Ed.D. diss., Clark Atlanta University, 1993), 303, 351, 355, 350.

35. For example, see Ray, *Strengths of Their Own*. See also many home school sites on the World Wide Web.

36. Daniel Lapin, *America's Real War* (Sisters, Ore.: Multnomah Publishers, 1999); Christian Overman, *Different Windows* (Wheaton, Ill.: Tyndale Publishers, 1988): 29; see, for example, Clark, *Christian Philosophy of Education*, ch. 4; Christopher J. Klicka, *The Right Choice: Home Schooling*, rev. ed. (Gresham, Ore.: Noble Publishing Associates, 1993), ch. 3; and Richard Wheeler, *Public Schools Aren't for Christians* (Bulverde, Tex.: Mantle Ministries, 1998).

37. Michael Bauman, "The Falsity, Futility, and Folly of Separating Morality from Law," *Christian Research Journal* 21 (1999): 20–23, 36–41; Glanzer, "Religion in Public Schools"; Phillip E. Johnson, *Reason in the Balance: The Case against Naturalism in Science, Law, and Education* (Downers Grove, Ill.: InterVarsity Press, 1995); Nord, *Religion and American Education;* Vitz, *Religion and Traditional Values in Public School Textbooks;* Romm, "Home Schooling and the Transmission of Civic Culture," 303. Children are considered "arrows" in Psalm 127:3–5.

38. Mayberry et al., *Home Schooling*, 101, 102.

Contributors

Robert Benne is director of the Center for Religion and Society at Roanoke College, Salem, Virginia.

Edith L. Blumhofer is currently director of the Institute for the Study of American Evangelicals and professor of history at Wheaton College. She is the former associate director of the Public Religion Project.

Alison L. Boden is the dean of Rockefeller Memorial Chapel at the University of Chicago.

James C. Carper is professor of social foundations of education at the University of South Carolina, Columbia, South Carolina.

Mark U. Edwards Jr. is the former president of St. Olaf College, Northfield, Minnesota.

Edison O. Jackson is president of Medgar Evers College of the City University of New York.

Roger Lundin is the Clyde S. Kilby Professor of English at Wheaton College, Wheaton, Illinois.

Martin E. Marty is the Fairfax M. Cone Distinguished Service Professor Emeritus at the University of Chicago and former director of the Public Religion Project.

James C. Moyer is chair of the Religious Studies Department at Southwest Missouri State University, Springfield, Missouri.

Warren A. Nord is director of the Program in the Humanities and Human Values at the University of North Carolina, Chapel Hill.

Brian D. Ray is president of the National Home Education Research Institute and founding editor of the quarterly journal *Home School Research*.

Robert Sullivan is associate professor of history and senior associate director of the Erasmus Institute at the University of Notre Dame, South Bend, Indiana.

Charles Zech is a professor of economics at Villanova University, Villanova, Pennsylvania.

Index